The Civil Service in Poland

STUDIES IN POLITICS, SECURITY AND SOCIETY

Edited by Stanisław Sulowski
Institute of Political Science of the University of Warsaw

VOLUME 4

PETER LANG
EDITION

Jolanta Itrich-Drabarek

# The Civil Service in Poland

## Theory and Experience

PETER LANG
EDITION

**Bibliographic Information published by the Deutsche Nationalbibliothek**
The Deutsche Nationalbibliothek lists this publication in the Deutsche Nationalbibliografie; detailed bibliographic data is available in the internet at http://dnb.d-nb.de.

This publication was financially supported
by the Institute of Political Sciences of the University of Warsaw.

**Library of Congress Cataloging-in-Publication Data**
Itrich, Jolanta
The civil service in Poland : theory and experience / Jolanta Itrich-Drabarek.
pages cm
Includes bibliographical references.
ISBN 978-3-631-65743-0
1. Civil service–Poland. 2. Public administration–Poland. 3. Poland–Politics and government. I. Title.
JN6762.I87 2015
352.6'309438–dc23
2015029558

ISSN 2199-028X
ISBN 978-3-631-65743-0 (Print)
E-ISBN 978-3-653-05019-6 (E-Book)
DOI 10.3726/978-3-653-05019-6


Peter Lang Edition is an Imprint of Peter Lang GmbH.

Peter Lang – Frankfurt am Main · Bern · Bruxelles · New York · Oxford · Warszawa · Wien



This publication has been peer reviewed.

www.peterlang.com

# Contents

# Introduction

> 'Wealth does not centre in the person of the wealthy. Celebrity is not inherent in any personality. To be celebrated, to be wealthy, to have power requires access to major institutions, for the institutional positions men occupy determine in large part their chances to have and to hold these valued experiences.'
>
> Charles Wright Mills *The Power Elite* (1956)

It might be well to perceive the civil service as the creation of modern democracies, and, at the same time, democracy's defining feature. Depending on the function each state choses to play the role and duties of the civil service will vary accordingly. Tradition, political culture and the state's socio-economic development are responsible for this variety, as are state-specific arrangements and the political agenda of the government of the day.

The civil service is best understood as a body of people employed under public or private law for the purpose of fulfilling law-governed-tasks, guided by a system of norms, values and procedures for the purpose of serving society and maintaining the state's vital functions.

Central to the raison d'être of the civil service is the mission of the public service which is based on standards such as: adherence to the constitution and the state ruled by law, political neutrality, impartiality, loyalty to one's superiors, stability of employment, reliability, professionalism and equality of opportunities. Equal access and competitiveness in recruitment to public administration positions is seen as service to the citizens and the effective performance of state duties. The notion of 'service' is repeated in this statement not without reason – indeed, this very notion lies at the heart of public service. In the aftermath of WW I and the building of Polish statehood – there was a general belief that the civil service is not the place for those who want to make a fortune; it is for those who wish to serve the state as a philanthropist who sets up a foundation seeking to serve society; it is a certain type of civil heroism, as a soldier who stands the chance of becoming a hero in the battlefield. In the commercialised world we inhabit today – overrun by nihilism and cynicism – words like these seem illegible or ridiculous to some people, or simply meaningless to others. However, it is my strong belief that there are some for whom these views express a longing for a certain ideal, an attitude worthy of emulation, which could briefly be described as the 'mission of the public service'.

Analysing the intentions of contemporary law-makers and publicly expressed social expectations, we are led to assume that, both, civil service employees and civil servants would be required to fulfil various social needs in the dynamically changing reality effectively, rationally and efficiently. Therefore, from the point of view of state interests, this professional group should be treated as an important one.

The essence of the civil service, according to Professor Hubert Izdebski, is the further distribution of power in public or state administration, between the recruited management (political or at least politically supported – thus changeable, following the rules of democratic play) and the permanent, professional civil service. This is a peculiar division as it presumes cooperation and at the same time subordination – professional and partially personal – of the members of the civil service. The establishment of a professional civil service, independent of the political authority chosen in democratic elections, is necessary in as much as civil servants obey and enhance democratic principles. Taking advantage of the rights they are awarded they must act in line with the policy of the government which they serve and they should recognise that the ultimate power rests with those elected by the people. This is an important step in preventing the autonomization of the civil service in the decision-making process, especially in the context of the fact the civil service corps is not an elected body, and thus lacks democratic legitimization. On the other hand, it is equally important to counteract the high party penetration of the civil service as this causes internal destabilisation and suspicions of bias and political clientelism. The situation can only be remedied by clearly worded rules governing competitive recruitment, promotions, professional competencies of administrative employees (based on professionalism, honesty, impartiality and political neutrality) as well as a clear separation between administrative and political posts.

The troubled relationship with politicians is just one problem that the civil service has to contend with; others include non-existent guarantees of employment stability, relatively low pay and frequent changes to civil service law. More often than not, the civil service has been treated as a cumbersome duty and in the Third Polish Republic, depending on the political party in power, it was either abolished, limited or marginalised. Moreover, braking the rule of political neutrality of the Polish civil service has become an everyday practice. The prospects for promotion are based on candidates' ties with politicians, while personnel policy remains discretionary. It is a paradox of sorts that politicians point to the many achievements of the state, bragging about how effective and successful it is and at the same time complain about the disappointing performance of the administrative staff. Somehow, the link between a smoothly running state and the work carried out by employees of the service escapes their notice. Building a civil service corps in Poland and consolidating a sense of public service mission in the minds of civil servants is a painstaking process, and what is also important, one that is vulnerable to shifting theories and conceptions.

The rules under which the civil service currently operates in Poland are based on the 2 April 1997 Constitution. Article 153 of the Polish Constitution states that the civil service will be set up in the organs of government administration in order to ensure a professional, diligent, impartial and politically neutral discharge of the state's obligations. Article 7 provides that the organs of public authority must function on the basis of and within the limits of the law. The civil service operates as required by administrative law, that is on the basis of the norms which regulate the organisation and conduct of government administration, as part of the state apparatus, and physical persons in the scope not regulated by other laws. In the light of the values which serve as the foundation for the Polish Constitution, public administration has four distinctive features, namely, competence, efficiency, political neutrality (apoliticality) and a subservient nature.

Since 1918, the Polish civil service has been governed by five repeatedly amended acts and regulations. The current framework for the operation of the civil service was set out by the Civil Service Act of 21 November 2008 (Journal of Laws, No. 227, item 1505 as amended). Under the Third Polish Republic, in just barely 20 years, several drafts and four acts came into being providing the grounds for the organisation and operation of the civil service. These acts rested on different assumptions. One was patterned on French arrangements (the 5 July 1996 Civil Service Act), another followed the Japanese model (the 18 December 1998 Civil Service Act) and two acts dated 24 August 2006, the Civil Service Act, and the State Staffing Pool and High-ranking Positions Act were seen, alternatively, as the breakthrough or 'downfall' of the civil service. It thus transpires that the typical trait of the Polish civil service is the absence of legal-institutional continuity while the solutions adopted in the laws mentioned indicate the inconsistency with which lawmakers regard the civil service, suggesting also that the legal evolution of the civil service represents a strong dependence on the fluctuating political scene in Poland.

The civil service as a subject of research calls for an interdisciplinary approach because of the choice and methodology of sources. The manner of framing the questions, analysing civil service mechanisms, and at the same time, answering the question about the nature of the Polish civil service, require the methods of political inquiry.

The study of the civil service (circumstances, standards and change) has been undertaken for a number of reasons. To start with, the analysis of past developments and the evolution of the civil service allows for drawing interesting conclusions for the civil service in Poland – still in its infancy. Secondly, the functioning of the civil service is interesting from an axiological perspective since among the Polish people (including members of the civil service corps) the knowledge of their ethical identity still requires systematic enrichment. Thirdly, the ongoing discourse in European academia on the dilemmas facing the civil service is an encouraging environment in which to study issues such as reforms, statutory arrangements (especially politicians vs. administrators) and ethics management. Fourthly, the Polish civil service is in need of a SWOT analysis, so presenting the overall picture, the service's strengths and weaknesses could prove to be a valuable exercise. Fifthly, it is worthwhile to define the role of a democratic state in the organisation and management of the civil service. Sixthly, this analysis addresses the question of how ethical management affects the image of the public service sector in the eyes of the citizens/customers.

As well as a host of circumstances, amongst them historical, political and legal factors affecting the civil service, this volume aims to explore the standards which should be guiding the civil service in its quest to implement its most important mission – the mission of public service. The next stage of the research should explain the processes which map out the course of change. Thus the different tendencies present in the Polish civil service, the premises underlying the policies chosen and all available options would be studied. This is a thorough analysis and it draws upon the accepted European expertise.

This brings the following assumption: the civil service in Poland functions in an external and internal setting. The former involves the achievements of democratic states, economic processes, integration and globalisation. The internal setting includes legislation, historical heritage, a strong statist tradition, subjecting the civil service to political decisions and sweeping economic, social and cultural shifts which have affected Poland over the last 20 years.

A further assumption is that the influence of European and world achievements in the field of civil service on the establishment of quality standards in the civil service in Poland has been more important than the country's own experiences. It is also recognised that any disorders affecting the Polish civil service – apart from those which are common in other countries – are specific and typical of Poland. Finally, it is assumed that the reorganisation of the Polish civil service is linked to the process of social and political transformation, development of information technology and trends in European and world civil service.

The structure of this book flows from the systematic realisation of the whole project and consists of seven chapters.

Chapter 1 offers a thorough examination of the nature of the civil service and its value system. It traces the origins of the civil service, the role of democracies in organising and managing the civil service, and examines the unique features of the civil service as it operates in European Union institutions charting out the road-map of change in member states. Chapter 2 provides an overview of the historical and cultural setting of the Polish civil service, with its formal beginnings going back to the interwar years, pointing to the way tradition, historical models, social relationships, cultural and mental determinants influenced the shape of the civil service. Chapters 3 and 4 analyse the legal and institutional arrangements in Polish civil service and the way this setup impacts the consistency and effectiveness of its operation, and also how it modifies Polish civil service identity. Modern management methods employed in the civil service are discussed in Chapter 5. Following a portrayal of these methods, focusing on quality standards and political neutrality, the author discusses how these methods contribute to the fulfilment of the prime objective of the civil service – its public mission. Chapter 6 takes up the question of the way the civil service functions, exploring many of its aspects (those factors that inhibit and facilitate its development), including civil service interest, modernisation, and the language used by the administration. In Chapter 7 there is a discussion of the ills plaguing the civil service (such as incompetence, arrogance, mobbing and corruption) and the instruments put in place in order to remedy the situation. The author assesses the impact of these problems on the quality and effectiveness of civil service employees as well as the social, institutional and economic consequences they create. Despite their number and variety, the tools designed to counteract these problems like international conventions, national laws, ethical codes, inspection, citizens' access to information, methods of recourse and complaints and training courses often fail to bring the expected results.

The book is based on a comprehensive array of literature covering European and Polish civil service; primary sources include Polish and European legal acts, documents, inspection reports, Constitutional Court rulings, statistical data, public opinion polls and official web sites. Interpretations and analyses include books written in Polish, English and French. Foreign language literature, with its most impressive output and insight proved indispensable in exploring European civil service standards and their axiological underpinnings.

Only a handful of authors have written extensively about the Polish civil service. In this group are experts in the field, professors: Hubert Izdebski, Grzegorz

Rydlewski and Elżbieta Ura. Parts of papers written by the author of this book are used in this publication.

Notwithstanding the demagogue arguments and populist voices, the civil service is not the cause of an ill-functioning state, but rather the outcome of internal and external circumstances under which the service operates. It faces many challenges and threats: unstable legal and social status or the standardisation of administrative services in the form of the Citizens' Charter. Many questions remain unanswered, for instance, what methods should be used to make the civil service a vehicle for modernising the state? What conditions must be met in order to implement the idea of ethical management and introduce knowledge management methods, the tri-sector partnership, or the transparent relationship between politicians and civil servants?

In view of the considerations above it seems only natural to say that significant changes are on the horizon for the Polish civil service. Inasmuch as the status of the European civil service has become more diversified and new and more effective management methods are being sought, Polish civil service should take advantage of the time-tested workable solutions. The rigid, hierarchized system needs to become more flexible, and the changes should amount to new clear arrangements encouraging cooperation between politicians and civil servants taking account of their different status, nature and goals.

# Chapter 1: The Theoretical Model of the Civil Service

## The Origin and Development of the Civil Service

The belief that the civil service originated in China has gained many followers. It is, indeed, the Middle Kingdom which saw a new social group emerge consisting of officials subordinate solely to the emperor, thus, striking at the heart of the system of ancestral aristocracy. There was a growing demand for individuals prepared for state service: faithful, diligent and eager to represent the emperor's authority in the field. The 'world's men of unusual ambitions have been trapped in my bag!' boasted the Emperor Tai-tsung in the seventh century AD which explained the process of seeking for state service the most talented people from different walks of life.[1] In the selection of candidates, the examination committees were guided by a list of roughly 60 most-preferred traits of the future official, amongst them: moral conduct, literary upbringing, administrative talent and knowledge of military matters.[2] In China the system of civil service became a path leading to social advancement and the civil service itself the most honourable profession.[3]

A similar process of the separation of personal interests from those of the monarch began to take place in Europe in the Middle Ages. Recruitment to work in the King's service based on merit became common under King Philip IV, the Fair, who employed lawyers specialising in Roman law. This historical role played by his civil servants led to the future focus of the civil service on 'rules, procedures and rationality.'[4]

The 17th and 18th centuries brought changes in the status of persons working for monarchs in modern Europe, beginning in Sweden in 1634.[5] In Russia,

---

1 M. Walzer, Spheres of Justice: A Defense of Pluralism and Equality, New York: Basic Books, Inc., 1983, p. 140.

2 Ibid., 141.

3 I. Miyazaki, *China's Examination Hell: The Civil Service Examinations of Imperial China*, trans. by C. Schirokauer, NewYork: Weatherhill 1976.

4 Ch. Demmke and T. Moilanen, *Effectiveness of Good Governance and Ethics in Central Administration: Evaluating Reform Outcomes in the Context of the Financial Crisis*, EIPA, 2011.

5 *Central government and delegated employer responsibility – the Swedish Model*. <http://www.arbetsgivarverket.se/upload/Avtal-Skrifter/Skrifter/Central%20government%20090817.pdf> accessed 6 July 2012.

the reforms of Peter I represented a powerful influence over the evolution of the disparate status of those who served the ruler. In 1720 he issued the General Regulation for the new government apparatus, introducing a principle which obliged the new officials to keep regular hours of work while 'each matter was settled at joint meetings as they appeared on the office's agenda, with the stipulation of priority for matters of national importance'.[6] His Table of Ranks created a hierarchical system of official positions in the government and determined the obligations, competences and remuneration for each, thereby bringing into existence an elaborate and complex administration in Tsarist Russia. The final regulation of the civil service corps in Russia came in the form of a civil service law introduced on 10 (22) March 1859 which established the realisation of state tasks and state public functions as the basic duty of officials. It also set up a multi-grade structure in the service, hierarchical subordination, appointment to positions and the performance of tasks on behalf of the state and at its cost.[7] In 1832 the principle of the legalism of the state apparatus was introduced – a controversial move in that up until 1906 the Tsar was the only source of law.[8]

Towards the end of the reign of Marie Therese in Austria, civil servants started receiving permanent remuneration from the state coffer. This led directly to the ban in 1752 on accepting additional payments from customers, known as 'bribes', turning the functionary into a servant of the state.[9]

The establishment of the Higher Examination Committee in 1770 to help select personnel for the administration proved a considerable influence on the formation of the civil service in Prussia. Under the reign of King Frederic Wilhelm I and his son, Frederic II, Prussian officials achieved a high status within the state wielding considerable political clout. The 18th century saw the 'birth of group awareness of the bureaucracy and its corporative nature'. Although the Prussian king's officials were not paid very well the 'traits typical of Prussian officials such as loyalty, sense of responsibility, obedience, sense of honour and loyalty, frugality, simplicity and above all diligence and selflessness' began to develop at that time.[10]

---

6 J. Malec, 'Historyczne modele rozwoju biurokracji', in K. Zuby, (ed.), *Biurokracja. Fenomen władzy politycznej w strukturach administracyjnych,* Toruń 2007, pp. 20–21.

7 Ibid., p. 21.

8 See more in G. Smyk, *Korpus urzędnik ów cywilnych w guberniach Królestwa Polskiego w latach 1867–1915,* Lublin 2004.

9 Malec, p. 19.

10 Ibid., p. 20, quoting from S. Salmonowicz, *Fryderyk II,* Wrocław 1985.

In order to secure the operation of a strong and centralised absolute monarchy, 18th century France recruited to government service people who did not belong to the privileged classes. This swelled the ranks of the corps of administrators working for the king in accordance with the principle voiced by Luis XIV: 'I am the state'.

The French Revolution in 1789 was a contributing factor in the advancement and consolidation of the modern civil service system. In the Declaration of the Rights of Man and of the Citizen we can read the following: 'All citizens, being equal in the eyes of the law, are equally eligible to all dignities and to all public positions and occupations, according to their abilities, and without distinction except that of their virtues and talents.'[11] This provision created equal opportunities for candidates to work in public service and initiated a system of competitive exams. Article 12 stated: 'The security of the rights of man and of the citizen requires public military forces. These forces are, therefore, established for the good of all and not for the personal advantage of those to whom they shall be entrusted.' Article 15 stipulated that 'Society has the right to require of every public agent an account of his administration.' It is worth noting that the Declaration introduced equal access to official positions, thereby ending the predominance of the nobility in this area and prompted the professionalisation of this career group putting an end to the practice of selling government offices.[12]

Similarly, it is in France that we find the origins of the European civil service, specifically the praxis of the III French Republic which vowed by the principle 'governments and parliaments pass but the administration remains'.[13] At the turn of the 18th and 19th centuries, labour relations in the civil service resembled those existing in the private sector: employment was seen as a privilege and the employee was totally subordinate to his superiors. Thus, the government took over the role of the monarch and treated the civil service as a 'spoils system' since 'public office was perverted into private fiefdom as arrogance, greed and opportunism prevailed over honour, openness and prudence. Favouritism, cronyism, intimidation, corruption, waste, scandals and rampant dismissals were widespread in that squalid era. Rather than emphasising good government and

11 'The Declaration of the Rights of Man and of the Citizen', 26 August 1789, Art. VI, in A. Radziwił and W. Roszkowski, (eds.) *Historia 1789–1871*, Warszawa 1995.

12 J. Baszkiewicz, *Powszechna historia ustrojów państwowych*, Gdańsk 1998, p. 196.

13 H. Izdebski and M. Kulesza, *Administracja publiczna. Zagadnienia ogólne,* Warszawa 2000, p. 207.

policy, the system encouraged mediocre governance; its highest priority was to reward its friends, to grant favours for favours given.'[14]

A hierarchical, centralised and professional civil service owes its existence to the processes underway after 1789 in the administrations of various European states. These processes were significantly affected by the consequences of the Napoleonic Wars which, among other things, led to the propagation of the idea of the state. The development of the notion of a liberal democratic state was taking place in parallel with the development of the civil service, which throughout the 19th century showed similarities across all European countries and further afield. It is only in the 20th century that civil service models begin to diversify.

Outside Europe, the idea of the civil service developed, among other places, in the United States since there also the administration was criticised for treating the civil service like a 'spoils system', where the victorious political party rewarded its active supporters with public jobs. The spoils system, created by Andrew Jackson, reigned supreme in US politics until the 1880s. The administration was highly politicised, lacked continuity of action and saw federal employees hired and fired with each change of presidential administration. In order to remedy the situation a reform movement, headed by Woodrow Wilson, acted to adopt in 1883 the Civil Service Reform Act (the Pendleton Act) ushering in a separation of political and administrative positions. The criticism of political control over the administration led to the recognition of the need for a permanent, specialised and protected civil service.[15] In 1944, the Veterans Preference Act was passed – the first regulation entitling a civil service employee to appeal against the decisions of his/her superiors.

The origins of the modern civil service in Japan go back to the year 1948, when the National Personnel Authority was established by the 1947 National Public Service Law.[16] It was designed to achieve maximum efficiency in the performance of public duties in the service, improve human resources management, protect working conditions and the social status of government administration employees in Japan.

---

14 J.S. Bowman and J.P. West, 'Removing Employee Protections: A "See no Evil" Approach to Civil Service Reform' in Leo W. J. C. Huberts et al (eds), *Ethics and Integrity of Governance: Perspectives Across Frontiers (New Horizons in Public Policy)*, Cheltenham: Edward Elgar Publishing Ltd, 2008, p. 183.

15 F. Mosher, *Democracy and the Public Service*, New York, 1968, p. 8.

16 The Polish Civil Service Act of 18 December 1998 was patterned on Japanese arrangements.

## The Nature of the Civil Service and its System of Values

Public administration has been defined as the servant of the political system and law and as the executive apparatus of political power,[17] but modern democracies increasingly often perceive it primarily as a service provider for members of the public. The ability to reconcile all these functions together informs the thinking on modern civil service today.

A professional cadre of officials making up the civil service emerged through slow shifts in customs, traditions and law. The course of this evolution, in parallel with the development of democracy, was mapped by an effort to inspire the people, whose work it was to perform their duties in the interest of the state, to obey all socially approved principles.[18] The term itself, civil service, was used for the first time by the East India Company in 1793 when the British government developed a civil service code for the Indian territories – later on transferring this system to the British Isles.

In order to understand the nature of the civil service, several seminal issues must first be addressed and defined. English-language literature on the subject initially distinguished civil service from military service, and so appropriately civil servants were those non-political employees who worked in public administration excluding those employed by the army, police forces and the judiciary.[19]

The basis of a civil service always consists of employees of the executive (broadly understood), that is ministers, central offices, state inspection and territorial government administration. The notion of 'civil servant' should be understood very broadly if it is assumed that it encompasses all the people entitled to act on behalf of the state, in other words, individuals employed in the public administration or public sector, referred to as civil servants, officials, employees/functionaries of public or state services, etc.

In some countries the category 'civil servant' is restricted only to those who work for the government administration (United Kingdom, Lithuania, Poland, Turkey, Cyprus); in others it also covers local government employees (Denmark, Czech Republic); in still others – public sector employees (France, Germany, Slovenia). The status of civil servants, that is those who are subject to public law as opposed to the general labour law, is granted to employees in Belgium, France,

---

17 B.Guy Peters, *The Politics of Bureaucracy*, London: Routledge, 2001.

18 See more in M. Gintowt-Jankowicz, *Służba cywilna w wybranych państwach demokratycznych,* Warszawa 1995, p. 4.

19 R. Pyper, *The British Civil Service*, London: Prentice-Hall/Harvester Wheatsheaf, 1995, p. 1 et seq.

Greece, Ireland, the Netherlands, Portugal and Spain. In the United Kingdom, pursuant to constitutional principles, matters relating to civil servants are in the hands of the government, which is one of the reasons why there is no civil service law in that country. In Germany, Austria, Luxemburg, Italy and Denmark the status of civil servant is afforded to those permanent government administration employees who exercise and protect public authority. Non-civil servants are considered as performing a profession in the public sector.

The reasons why state employees should not be viewed as merely state workers have to do with the fact that the former have to fulfil the following goals: 'establish mechanisms of control and accountability in order to prevent abuse of public powers and mismanagement of public resources; give legitimacy to the public administration in the eyes of citizens and taxpayers in order to build up public confidence in the administration and in the end, in the state as a whole; [...] provide professional continuity in public administration and to foster a certain pattern of conduct in all parts of the administration; [...] attract the best available candidates in the country for the civil service and to retain them through a reasonable prospect of career development and personal self-fulfilment.'[20]

In several European countries (Spain, France and Portugal) the responsibility for the civil service lies in the hands of the ministry of public administration or public services which is charged with drafting laws in regard to the civil service; voicing its views on the budgetary draft regarding the civil service, the organisation, recruitment and coordination of the management system of human resources; negotiating with civil service unions on behalf of the government; running training courses and managing public administration schools or institutes. In Northern Ireland, Austria, Belgium, Germany and the Netherlands the civil service is managed by the Ministry of Finance and Ministry of Internal Affairs. While in Italy and Sweden special agencies are appointed for negotiating with civil service trade unions on behalf of the government, agencies and local authorities.

Despite the fact that work in the public administration should be continuous, civil servants have the right to strike in the majority of European Union countries. Provisions to this effect have been included in the legislation of Belgium, Luxemburg, Greece, Ireland, Sweden, France, Cyprus and Hungary. Although in practice the right to strike exists in the United Kingdom, it is not mentioned

---

20 *European Principles for Public Administration*, SIGMA Papers No. 27, SIGMA-OECD, <http://www.oecd.org/dataoecd/22/45/39560306.pdf> pp. 22–23 – accessed 6 July 2012.

in its statute books. The list of countries with laws that allow for strike action includes Malta (with certain exceptions in regard to senior posts in the civil service), Latvia, Portugal (with several exceptions), Lithuania (excluding a certain category of senior officials), the Czech Republic (although it is made difficult), the Netherlands (although there are restrictions in this respect for the military, police, train service personnel, senior officials), Romania (with some exclusions), Slovakia (excluding high-ranking officials) and Slovenia (apart from the military and police). In contrast, only a few countries, Estonia, Germany and Poland lack the right to strike; only symbolic protest action is allowed in Bulgaria.

Apart from the right to strike, in each country there are regulations in place requiring social dialogue between employees, employer representatives and the state. Although there are no laws governing striking in Austria, the constitution guarantees social dialogue on social matters concerning civil servants, such as remuneration, wage system reform, pensions and social guarantees. Civil servants belong to two main trade unions: Public Service Trade Union (GOD – 230, 000 members) and Municipal Workers Trade Union (150, 000 members), both of which comprise the Austrian Trade Union Federation (OGB).

In Luxemburg settlements are negotiated between the employer (represented by the Minster of the Civil Service and Administrative Reform) and trade union representatives. These settlements are binding for the government and must be taken into consideration in drafting new laws. The provisions negotiated remain in force for a three year period.

In Lithuania negotiations concerning collective agreements take place between government representatives, employers and trade organisations and unions in a Tripartite Council of the Lithuanian Republic and concern remuneration and work conditions. The signed agreements are legally binding. Just under 15% of civil servants belong to a trade union, compared to 40–55% in Belgium.

In Malta, the trade unions grouped in the Malta Confederation (CMTU) play a significant role in negotiating collective agreements, work conditions and the pay scale of those employed in the public sector and agencies.

The percentage of civil servants belonging to a trade union varies from under 15% in Estonia to about 40–55% in Germany and up to 80–90% in Finland.

In Poland the term 'civil servant', *urzędnik służby cywilnej,*[21] denotes a state official who has been nominated to civil servant rank under the existing law and is

21 In colloquial Polish, however, the term 'civil servant' is used broadly not only to signify a civil servant (nominated state official in the civil service), but also an employee who is a member of the civil service corps, an Embassy employee, post-office or bank employee, or contrary to normative rules – a self-government (local) employee, who

employed by the government administration in a professional capacity.[22] Public service, according to the view expressed by Maurycy Jaroszyński is not a separate profession but a specific legal relationship of employees of different professions.[23] What is crucial for distinguishing state officials as a group, he emphasised, are special legal relationships that exist between the officials, the state or other players exercising public functions. Zbigniew Leoński names ten traits which define an official, as specified by Stanisław Kasznica in 1946: public-legal nature of the profession; freedom to enter and exit the profession; in addition to the legal nature there is also the moral aspect of the profession (which includes the obligation of loyalty to the state); special expertise appropriate to the function; subordination to authority; special obligations and accountability; the capacity to speak on behalf of the state; and availability.[24]

Civil servants act in line with the rules of law and within the confines of the law, apply bureaucratic methods of acting, in other words, methods based on specifically determined organisational, managerial and supervisory activities. The activities of the organisation they work for are based on statutes and regulations which hierarchize the organisation internally and externally, as well as individual acts such as employment agreements, nominations and others. In spite of the numerous regulations, the official is given some leeway in terms of internal activities. There might be difficulties in defining the term – civil service – for the following reasons: changes introduced in individual countries, unique national traditions, diverse systems of promotion and training, dissimilar recruitment techniques, disparities in the legal and social status of civil servants and civil service employees. In the early 1990s, this growing diversity led many to think that perhaps we were seeing the end of the idea of the civil service.[25]

The civil service could be compared to a 'machine steered by the government, or [...] to a grand piano which remains the same irrespective of whoever plays it

under the 21 November 2008 Act on Self-government Employees, is not an official but a self-government employee.

22 In 2005 in an amendment to the Self-government Employees Act the terms 'officials' positions' and 'managerial officials' positions' were introduced for the first time.

23 M. Jaroszyński, M. Zimmermann and W. Brzeziński, *Polskie prawo administracyjne. Część ogólna*, Warszawa 1952, p. 296.

24 S. Kasznica, *Polskie prawo administracyjne*, Poznań 1946, pp. 88–89, from Z. Leoński, *Wyodrębnienie zawodu urzędniczego i swoistych jego cech. Biurokracja w polskich warunkach ustrojowych*, Krynica – Rzeszów 2006.

25 Compare R. A. Chapman, 'The end of the civil service?', *Teaching Public Administration* 1992, No. 2, pp. 1–5.

and which composition. After playing Beethoven there is no need to disassemble the instrument or remove any of its parts in order to play a piece by Bach or Chopin.'[26] And, as David Robertson said, the basic principle of the functioning of the civil service is the recognition, that the civil service alone does not make laws or politics, but only advises and fulfils, in the most impartial way, the instructions of political bosses.[27]

In the view of Barbara Kudrycka, civil servants are distinguished from other officials by the special legal status, regulated by public law (both constitutional and administrative), afforded to them. This generates specific employee obligations, political tasks and administrative duties. An important feature of the civil service is the manner in which public matters are 'managed': it is distinctly executive; it consists in a direct and practical implementation by the civil service corps of the policies pursued by the government and parliament.[28] A peculiar feature of the civil service is its group identity,[29] which translates into civil service officials being the inheritors of tradition and law, and at the same time enjoying a distinctly elevated position in society.

The civil service is a 'system of filling public positions and performing the duties of a public functionary based on the principles of professionalism, apoliticality, impartiality and legalism. In terms of the subject, it is a corps of officials which comes into being on the basis of the above-mentioned principles and which is assigned a special professional status within the state (stability of employment emanating from appointment – privileged salary and pension regulations). In functional terms, it signifies rules of employment and management of administration personnel, which guarantee their high qualifications and efficient discharge of public duties by the state irrespective of the changeability of the political command over the administration'.[30]

---

26 V. Turcey, 'Rola służby cywilnej w demokratycznym społeczeństwie – doświadczenia francuskie', in J. Jackl (ed.), *Służba cywilna a etyka w życiu publicznym*, Warszawa 1996, pp. 45–46. In the literature on the subject we find the civil service compared to a ship, the integral part of which are its passengers and crew; the passengers (politicians) must reach the designated port, but their fate depends on the skills of the crew (the civil service).

27 D. Robertson, *The Penguin Dictionary of Politics*, London: Penguin Books, 1986, p. 44.

28 B. Kudrycka, *Neutralność polityczna urzędników*, Warszawa 1998, p. 17.

29 Ibid., p. 11.

30 J. Gąciarz, 'Organizacja i zasady działania administracji publicznej w Polsce', in J. Hausner (ed.), *Administracja publiczna*, Warszawa 2005, p. 167.

The civil service is a system of 'arrangements institutional and functional [...] for the purpose of consolidating the guarantee to fulfil the tasks set before employees of administrative offices in an impartial and professional manner.'[31] The already non-existent Civil Service Office defined the civil service as a system of values, norms, procedures and institutions called upon to fulfil the state's tasks by the civil service corps acting within its structures, professionally, diligently, impartially and in a politically neutral manner.

It has to be emphasised that defining the civil service is not an easy task. Explaining the meaning of civil service in the axiological context through the nature of this phenomenon is imprecise but nevertheless should be attempted for the purpose of this volume. It can thus be assumed that *the civil service is a distinct body of people employed under public or private law for the purpose of discharging tasks defined by law, and guided by a definite system of norms, values and procedures, aimed at serving society and maintaining important functions of the state.*

An inseparable element of the civil service is the mission of the public service which rests upon standards[32] such as: allegiance to the constitution, apoliticality or political neutrality, impartiality, loyalty towards superiors, stability of employment, diligence and professionalism, equal opportunities criterion, equal access and competitiveness in recruitment to the service, management with the participation of those involved and in the interest of the citizens.[33] These precepts should answer the question of how the civil service corps is to serve society in order to satisfy numerous different social needs in the dynamically changing reality?

Even if a different set of civil service traits is quoted in some countries[34, 35], the one mentioned above lies at the heart of them all.

---

31 G. Rydlewski, *Służba cywilna w Polsce. Przegląd rozwiązań na tle doświadczeń innych państw i podstawowe akty prawne,* Warszawa 2001, p. 12.

32 A discussion of the principles follows in the ensuing Chapters.

33 Barbara Kudrycka, for instance, names the following requirements: political neutrality, impartiality, honesty and loyal service to the government of the day, in B. Kudrycka, *Neutralność polityczna urzędników*, Warszawa 1998.

34 For example, in the UK the following traits are quoted: stability of employment, honesty, impartiality, political neutrality, ban on using position for personal gains, special hiring and promoting procedures, administering the spending of public funds, the political accountability of ministers to the parliament, in R. Butler, 'The Evolution of the Civil Service – A Progress Report', *Public Administration Review* 1993, vol. 71, No. 3, pp. 395–406.

35 Germany points to civil servants' uniform legal status and remuneration system, both regulated by law; statutory restriction of some of civil servants' public rights such as

The intrinsic nature of the civil service is the 'further division of power within public or at least state administration, between those who are recruited on a political basis, or at least politically supported – hence, change according to the rules of democratic play, and a permanent, professional civil service'.[36] This is a rather peculiar division as in addition to cooperation it also assumes the subordination (entirely professional and to some degree personal as well) of the members of the professional civil service.

## Civil Service Models

Democracies have seen three principal systems of the civil service emerge over the period from the first half of the 19th century to the first decade of the 21st century:

- Career-based system, also called promotional or closed;
- Position-based or managerial system;
- Mixed, hybrid system.[37]

*The career system* is marked by several peculiar features. Under this model the basic criterion opening the door to the civil service is an exam which tests the candidate's general predisposition to work in public administration rather than his/her suitability for a given post. The exams, which are quite demanding, take place at least twice: at the entry-level to the service and following the preparatory stage.

The system envisages a gradual career in the service – starting with the initial positions up to the top posts in the official hierarchy. Nominations are made only in the initial positions. Promotions are determined solely on the grounds of seniority in the public service. Essentially, office is held for life, meaning that if civil servants obey the rules they can work until they reach retirement age. This is a highly hierarchical model: one cannot be promoted forgoing a given career rung,

their passive electoral rights and right to strike; guarantees of special retirement and disability pensions; obligation of involvement in activities to the benefit of the country, allegiance to the constitution; political neutrality; merit-based recruitment and promotion criteria, in H. U. Derlien, 'Historical Legacy and Recent Developments in the German Higher Civil Service', *International Review of Administrative Sciences*, London 1992, No. 57, p. 387.

36 H. Izdebski, *Fundamenty współczesnych państw*, Warszawa 2007, pp. 225–226.

37 D. Długosz, 'Służba cywilna – jaki system dla Polski', *Res Publica Nowa*, June 1998, p. 32 et seq.; H. Izdebski and M. Kulesza, *Administracja publiczna, Zagadnienia ogólne*, Warszawa 2000, pp. 208–209.

or start working from a middle-ranking position or top one, for that matter. The civil servant's status is defined by public law, in other words, he/she is employed by the state rather than a specific office/institution. Education requirements for the job under this system are specified in detail by law, so the focus is on the candidate's certificates and diplomas. In some countries (Germany), it is the statute that determines the graduates of which higher education institutions will be considered for recruitment into the civil service. What counts in this model is formal education. The work process itself is more command-style than it is end-driven. A separate system of remuneration and pensions for civil servants is defined in statute by the authorities, which are not bound to work out agreements in this matter with the trade unions. In the work carried out by the civil servants emphasis is placed on diligence, honesty and obeying the law, as well as special disciplinary regulations.

While allowing for national differences, the career system was adopted by countries such as: Austria, Belgium, France, Greece, Spain, Northern Ireland, Luxemburg, Germany, Portugal, Slovenia Romania, Cyprus, Slovakia, Bulgaria and Turkey.[38] However, calling it the 'Mandarin' or the 'closed fortress' system, the system's detractors point to its numerous faults: hierarchical nature, low motivation on the part of the employees to generate new ideas and attain maximum levels of efficiency and quality. To this list of drawbacks they add its ritualism, rigid behaviour, lack of flexibility, inability to cope in extraordinary non-standard situations, routine involvement in job being performed, and the employees' resistance towards change and reform. The system is also accused of being responsible for raising internal barriers to personnel mobility in the civil service (mobility between the public and private sector and between individual careers and within one career).[39]

The other charges levelled against the career system involve the side-effects of standardisation occurring on the level of the group, whereby civil servants shut themselves away from the public leading to a gulf between officials and citizens. By specialising the goals to be attained, which encourages the division of the roles played by employees, officials become more independent from politics and from citizens – this increases the alienation of the administration from the public. It undermines the ties between the service and society and makes all information on the work of public administration inaccessible to the wider public.

38 Since the career system was adopted by founding states of the European Communities this was the dominant model in the institutions of the European Union up to 2000.

39 D. Bossaert and Ch. Demmke, *Civil Services in the Accession States: New Trends and the Impact of the Integration Process*, 2003 EIPA Publications.

Rent-seeking as a phenomenon, that is the effective use of civil servants' privileged position in representing their own interests vis-à-vis the authorities, the state or its citizens is yet another flaw in the way the career system functions.[40] Another typical trait of this system is the ageing of the staff and the low level of representativeness, especially at the top end of the civil service corps.

A further drawback related to the career model involves upping the costs of services performed by the bureaucrats and performing with diligence only those tasks the effects of which can be easily evaluated by supervisory bodies. This logic leads to the bureaucratisation of the service and inability to solve problems which are important from the perspective of the state and society.

Career system enthusiasts point to many of its advantages, such as stability of employment, work continuity, and, consequently, less political influence on the administration (since it becomes near impossible to employ one's cronies), eliminating discretionary promotions and excessive political pressure.

Those who voice their support for this system, point to the opportunities it affords for gaining experience by civil servants in the long years of service and creating 'institutional memory' which is absent when officials are employed on contracts. The memory of how the office functions, its procedures, precedencies, potential and methods of solving problems enables the administration to function more efficiently, without undue delay and, furthermore, contributes to alleviate the costs related to fluctuating personnel.

The typical traits of the career system include loyalty towards the office and a mature professional ethos both of which make for a better identification of the tasks at hand with the public interest.

Accordingly, those who support this model argue that from the perspective of the development of democratic states, egalitarianism is a crucial principle, understood as the chance to apply for a job with the civil service by everyone – irrespective of their social status. This is made possible thanks to the system's objectivity and application of the competence-criterion in the recruitment process.[41]

---

40 P. Tłaczała, 'Podstawy ekonomicznej teorii biurokracji', in J. Wilkin (ed.), *Teoria wyboru politycznego. Wstęp do ekonomicznej analizy polityki i funkcjonowania sfery publicznej*, Warszawa 2005, p. 156.

41 This is not an entirely true argument, as higher positions in the career system adopted in the French civil service are as a rule filled by graduates of the elitist ENA (École National d'Administration).

Finally, through its system of promotions the career model encourages officials to self-improve, motivating them to professionalise and increase their qualifications, and points to the urgency of cultivating ethical values.

*The position, or open, system* is typical for states which have avoided major political conflicts in the past.[42] In this case, candidates are recruited to the service for concrete positions, so in the recruitment procedure the candidate's qualifications and skills for performing tasks in a given position are examined, rather than the number of certificates and diplomas or his/her seniority in public administration. Recruitment methods are based on those which operate in the private sector. Work experience gained in the private sector carries the same weight as in the public sector, sometimes it is even seen as an advantage. Again, when it comes to promotions, experience outside the public sector turns out to be helpful. It is not a model which guarantees lifelong employment as employees enter into fixed term contracts and are not automatically considered for promotions to the next rungs of the official hierarchy. They are, on the other hand, evaluated in terms of the manner in which they discharge their duties and the effects of their work. As a rule, in many countries where the position system exists, there are no separate regulations governing the civil service, especially those which involve disciplinary conduct. Regulations governing employee issues (such as work conditions, remuneration and retirement gratuity) are usually set out in collective agreements negotiated between the government and trade unions.[43]

Remuneration is determined on the basis of the perceived difficulty and responsibility related to a given position and, at the same time, labour market conditions are also taken into account. The terms of the contract are flexible and adjusted to suit employers' needs. Since this model allows for opening initial and middle positions to all eligible European Union citizens, work experience gained in another country is accepted.

---

42 G. Rydlewski, *System administracji publicznej w państwach członkowskich Unii Europejskiej*, Warszawa 2007, p. 47.

43 M. Mróz, *Służba cywilna w państwach Unii Europejskiej (system awansowy i pozycyjny w badaniach Europejskiego Instytutu Administracji Publicznej*, Biuro Studiów i Ekspertyz, Kancelaria Sejmu, Information No. 746, Warszawa, November 2000, p. 4.

The position model can be found in Denmark, Netherlands, Finland, Sweden, Bulgaria[44], United Kingdom, Estonia[45], Norway and in non-European countries such as the USA or New Zeeland.

This model is also described as 'managerial' as it relies on 'market recruitment'. This is where, according to its adherents, its advantages come into play: flexibility, motivation, individualised performance-related system of remuneration, decentralised recruitment system – without favouring former civil servants in the recruitment process; informal ties between lower and higher ranking officials imparting a special quality to these relations (they are unconstrained, voluntary and natural); higher performance; open to communicate with members of the public; improved communication between the individual units of the civil service and the political sphere.

Recruitment facilitates the administration's ambition to quickly adapt to changing needs, while the performance-related remuneration system promotes higher effectiveness and quality of employees' work.[46] In this model seniority plays a minor role. There is ample place for, both, people with considerable professional experience and the young. The relative ease of moving between the various public administration organisations (provided the employee wins the competition) is another advantage emphasised by the model's supporters.

In contrast to the career model, the lack of professional stability, seen as the flaw of the position system, translates into a relatively weak sense of public mission. The considerable rotation of personnel is linked to the loss of institutional memory which, in turn, leads to the cyclical learning of procedures and mechanisms binding in a given organisation by the new recruits and this adversely effects the quality, effectiveness and costs of labour. Another fault comes to the fore when towards the end of their fixed term contracts, the officials' motivation and performance falls because they no longer wish to renew their contracts.

---

44 Bulgaria is in the process of building the position system in its civil service but its final features are still being debated.

45 Although listed among states which have adopted the position model (D. Bossaert and Ch. Demmke, *Civil Services in the Accession States: New Trends and the Impact of the Integration Process*, EIPA Publications, 2003), in its latest 2008 Report, Estonia describes its civil service system as belonging to the career category, compare *Administration and the civil service in the 27 Member States*, Ministère du Budget, des Comptes Publics et de la Fonction Publique, France 2008.

46 G. Rydlewski, *Polityka i administracja w rządach państw członkowskich Unii Europejskiej*, Warszawa 2006, p. 171.

What is more, the position system may give rise to a conflict of interest when personnel moves between the public and private sectors.[47]

It seems, however, that in their pure form, the two systems have become less clear to the average person. In many advanced states across the globe, attempts are made to combine classical features of the model of bureaucracy described by Max Weber with a modern, competent and creative organisation, which places strong emphasis on the economic costs involved.

In modern democracies *a third, hybrid, system* has gained prominence – one which combines features of the career and position models, with or without the predominance of either one of them. The evolution of the civil service, as recorded in the second half of the 20th century in many countries, indicates that there is a slow departure from the career system in favour of the position system. Thus, even in countries such as Germany and Northern Ireland – staunch supporters of the career system – reforms were introduced with the intent of strengthening civil servants' motivation for work. A similar trend became apparent in the institutions of the European Union after 2000.

Poland[48], Hungary, Malta, Lithuania, the Czech Republic, Latvia, Switzerland and Italy have all adopted the mixed model.

Italy is the closest it gets to the mixed system. Despite the fact that it is included among states guided primarily by the position model, classical elements of the career model occur in its civil service, such as: formalised recruitment procedures, an established promotion system and remuneration unrelated to performance.[49]

It is also possible to study the models of civil service in terms of the division into 'old' and 'new' states of the European Union. Artificial as its seems, this classification does suggest considerable differences between the two groups of countries, and allows for emphasising certain features of the civil service typical of a given group of states for research purposes.

The current tendency in the 'old fifteen' is to unify regulations in the public sector with those in the private sector. This mainly involves the introduction of market economy features into the public administration, especially regarding remuneration, pension systems, performance-related management, evaluation of

47 Compare Rydlewski, *Systemy administracji*, p. 47.

48 Up to 2006 the Polish civil service system was defined by the European Institute of Public Administration as representing the mixed model although the debate is still ongoing about its true nature with even Polish lawmakers switching sides.

49 D. Długosz, 'Kadry w administracji publicznej', in J. Hausner (ed.), *Administracja publiczna*, Warszawa 2005, p. 243.

positions, standardising assessment principles in regard to employees, promotion models, as well as participatory and deregulatory reforms.[50]

By contrast, most of the states which have joined the EU after 2004, sought to construct a civil service where the terms of employment differ considerably from those in the private sector.

Despite the several negative features of the two models, both of them have a place in advanced societies in civil service practice. The civil service is the fulcrum of the democratic system, a system that allows for an exchange of governing elites but assumes the continuity of its structures.

The arrangements advocated within each model are designed to serve the purposes of a specific concept of the state, its objectives and its mission. What is of paramount importance from the perspective of state governance, is the placing of individuals in top positions in the civil service. For this reason, some countries have adopted separate solutions to cover this area. Defining the notion of the senior civil service in Europe does not seem particularly difficult. In the United Kingdom the expression 'Senior Civil Service' is used; in the Netherlands it is 'Senior Public Service'; in Estonia the expression 'Top Public Service' is applied. On the other hand, in France and Romania individuals occupying senior positions in the civil service are described as 'high-ranking civil servants' or 'state service functionaries'.

Following the definition coined by the OECD, the Senior Civil Service 'is a structured and recognised system of personnel for the higher non-political positions in government. It is a career civil service providing people to be competitively appointed to functions that cover policy advice, operational delivery or corporate service delivery. The service is centrally managed through appropriate institutions and procedures, in order to provide stability and professionalism of the core group of senior civil servants, but also allowing the necessary flexibility to match changes in the composition of Government by using appropriate due processes'.[51]

---

50 For more see Chapter 3.

51 OECD, (GOV/PGC/PEM (2008) 2), 'The Senior Civil Service in National Governments of OECD Countries', Paris, 31 January 2008, pp. 17–18 in H. Kuperus and A.Rode, *Top Public Managers in Europe. Management and Working Conditions of the Senior Civil Servants in European Union Member States,* EIPA, Maastricht 2008, p. 3.

## The Civil Service in European Union Member States: Charting New Courses

The path of reforms in public administration, including the civil service, has been determined by various social, economic and political developments which have taken place over the last two decades of the 20th century and in the first decade of the current one.

The first decade of the 21st century dampened the excessive zeal of the reformers to compare public administration to a shop wherefrom the customer/citizen emerges with a top quality product/service. It transpires that public administration personnel have lost sight of the basic goal for the purpose of which they had been appointed. Their primary aim, after all, was not economic profit but the mission of public service, including serving social needs and ensuring social satisfaction by delivering high quality services. The need for a discussion on the role and tasks of the civil service in modern countries across the globe has been reaffirmed by the challenges facing public administration: economic recession, the increasingly complex European integration process and terrorism.

Regarding public administration in EU member states, the following trends have come to the fore in the 1980s and 1990s according to the European Institute of Public Administration:

- Applying a more flexible and decentralised system of remuneration, one which takes account of officials' real achievements;
- Modernising recruitment systems in order to stay competitive vis-à-vis the private sector;
- Linking employee evaluation systems with performance criteria;
- Improving number and quality of training courses regarding European and international issues;
- Decentralising personnel management;
- Employing evaluative methods concentrating on motivation and individual results;
- Increasing importance of collective agreements and social dialogue in establishing remuneration;
- Increasing labour flexibility;
- Introducing a more effective pension system,
- Reducing number of employees in the public sector (not in all member states);

- Abandoning regulation through public law in favour of private law in civil service;
- Introducing equality between women and men.[52]

Guy Peters is of the view that there are three basic types of public administration reform in democracies and this has a profound effect on the functioning of the civil service in these countries, a view also shared by the author of this volume. The reforms in question include market oriented, participatory and deregulatory reforms.[53]

Market-related reforms introduced in advanced democracies involve the following features:

- The introduction of an agency model. An arrangement of this sort was used for the first time in the Netherlands in 1984 but the most radical and at once typical form was adopted in the United Kingdom four years later. It involved the elimination of many positions and reduction of the number of departments in favour of setting up specific private agencies acting in the name of and on behalf of the state;
- Marketisation, in other words enabling public buyers with substantial funds at hand to seek the best suppliers in terms of cost and quality of service. Reforms of this type were initiated by New Zeeland in 1987;
- A remuneration system for civil servants based on an evaluation of the effects of their work. In practice this means that salaries are individualised and diversified depending on the officials' involvement and performance. This is the sort of change introduced by the USA towards the end of the 1970s. Most reforms concerning civil servants' salaries (especially those in high-ranking positions) were made after the year 2000;
- The introduction of the 'one-stop' system, whereby at a given organisational level the citizen can access in one location the numerous services offered by the office, while the office itself provides the appropriate services through its own internal circulation. This system allows for coordinating programs introduced for the purpose of avoiding, for instance, conflicts of competence. These reforms were seen in Denmark and Japan in the late 1980s for the first time;
- The fall in number of officials employed in the civil service, for instance the number of officials in Austria went down from 300, 000 in 1985 to 133, 000 in

52 D. Bossaert et al., *Civil Services in the Europe of Fifteen: Trends and New Developments*, European Institute of Public Administration, Maastricht 2001, pp. 250–251.

53 B. Guy Peters, 'Policy Transfers Between Governments: The Case of Administrative Reform', *West European Politics*, 1997, vol. 20 (4), p. 73.

2009, whereas in Finland by the year 2011 the number of officials was reduced by 9,645;

- A partial privatisation of services by outsourcing to private companies, as practiced in Austria;
- Accountable and efficient governments focused on effects (for instance in Belgium[54], Greece, Estonia[55] and Luxemburg[56]);
- The projection of the government's image as an innovative, dynamic and attractive employer (Belgium, the Netherlands);
- The creation of conditions contributing to the development of the idea of public-private partnership (UK and Bulgaria);
- Treating the citizens as customers of the office (procedure in place in every European Union state after 2000);
- Abolishing ministries and departments – in Hungary[57] and Portugal where the year 2006 saw the abolishment of 69 public offices and institutions, 1,037 departments and 1,468 management-related positions;
- The introduction of m-government, that is administrative services for citizens accessible via mobile telephones (Malta). This way citizens may obtain exam results, summons to appear in court, a renewal of a driving licence and the like.

Participatory reforms, in turn, involve assuming responsibility for the decision-making process by officials and customers alike. One such measure is decentralisation, that is moving responsibility for certain programmes or decisions from the central to the local level. Others include the introduction of citizens' cards

54 The first stage of reforms in Belgium was accomplished in February 2008: the remuneration system was reorganised and a 'new-old civil service' created.

55 On 21 June 2007 Estonia adopted as one of its priorities the introduction of the 'management through results' system into its administration and the promotion of regional development.

56 In 2006 the next stage of quality management was implemented in Luxemburg. As part of this system the central coordination of management-related initiatives has taken place, as well as the enforcement of subsequent changes and the charting of the best-practice map.

57 A reform of public institutions and public finance was launched in 2006. In the main it was designed to cut the number of institutions in public administration with similar competences; develop agencies which performed service roles; reduce the number of decision-making bodies in public administration; modernise public administration management techniques; and develop services for citizens. The reform aimed at reducing the number of officials by redefining the mission of each department and scope of duties of individual officials. The reorganisation resulted in increased transparency of public administration operation and the enhanced effectiveness of operation control.

(United Kingdom) or Cards for Variety (France), which guarantee that the services provided by officials and public agendas comply with citizens' expectations and are highly professional.[58]

Deregulation, among other things, consists in the public administration's withdrawal from many areas of social and economic life and forsaking out-dated laws and legal regulations. Goals are attained by means of different methods, zero budgets, review committees or the 'twilight' law (USA)[59].

Deregulation also implies growing numbers of officials employed on short-term contracts (Slovakia and the Netherlands[60]) or the emergence of a new category of part-time employees. In Germany law-makers ruled against the discrimination of part-time workers and encouraged employers to hire them, thereby activating this group of employees, such as child carers or pre-retirement age employees, who find it difficult to get a full-time job. Working in short-term employment is treated as a means of counteracting unemployment by job-sharing. One of the opportunities of working short-term are mini-jobs, which require working less hours with weaker social protection. This model is attractive for both employers, who are thereby exempt from paying a part of social security as well as employees who are partially exempt from income tax. These regulations made mini-jobs appealing to growing numbers of people, in 2006 for instance 22% of all employed worked under this scheme.[61]

Flexible work arrangements allowing for combining work with personal life have become popular (UK). They provide for flexitime, compressed working hours, annualised hours and time accounts. In 2007 European institutions adopted the policy of flexicurity in order to increase the flexibility of working time and

---

58 R. Herbut, 'Administracja publiczna – modele, funkcja, struktura', in A. Ferens and I. Macek (eds.) *Administracja i polityka. Wprowadzenie*, Wrocław 1999, p. 52.

59 D. Osborne and T. Gaebler, *Reinventing Government. How the Entrepreneurial Spirit is Transforming the Public Sector*, New York: Plume, 1992.

60 The working time of a civil servant in the Netherlands is 36 hours per week, and the official may agree with the employer a weekly work system whereby the 36-hour working week is spread over four days of nine hours each, or any other combination. From 1 April 2002 it is possible to increase the number of hours worked up to 40 hours a week provided that the number of hours does not go against the interest of the employee and does not violate his/her fundamental rights.

61 M. Rycak, 'Polityka w zakresie czasu pracy oraz zasady jego prawnej regulacji w Holandii, Niemczech i Danii', in L. Florek, *Czas pracy*, Warszawa 2011, pp. 315–316; K. Stefański, *Regulacja czasu pracy w Kodeksie pracy. Ocena i propozycje zmian*, Łódź, 20 December 2011. <http://cml.kpp.org.pl/upload/binaries/act/3635/Ekspertyza.pdf> pp. 18–19 – accessed 6 July 2012.

improve the security of the labour market. This program encompasses the following items: flexible and predictable terms of contracts (from the perspective of the employee and employer, and those without permanent employment) thanks to modern labour law, collective contracts and work organisation; complex lifelong learning strategies which increase employees' ability to continuously adapt to labour market needs, especially the most underprivileged groups on the labour market; an effective labour market policy which helps people cope with rapid change, shortens unemployment periods and facilitates changing jobs; modern system of social security which provides appropriate income support, facilitates employment and enables labour market mobility.[62] Many countries have adopted legislation which provides for the easier removal of civil servants from office.[63]

Reforms designed to divorce the civil service from the classical Weberian bureaucracy model in favour of decentralisation have many supporters among UE member states. Decentralisation, no doubt, brought positive results in the form of transferring competences, means and tasks to lower ranking bodies which has contributed to increasing their effectiveness and performance. Regarding human resources management, however, it is thought that decentralisation leads to the decline of professionalism, the weakening of civil service ethics, and the fragmentation of policies – as seen from the strategic point of view.[64] Reacting to the 2008 financial crisis, European Union states hastened their human resources management reforms in order to be able to employ for fixed term contracts. The side effect of this process is a situation whereby different terms of employment are offered to the same professions and the same employees working in the same sector.

There seems no doubt that excessive decentralisation without laying down its scope and strategic objectives can trigger conflicts between public agencies and institutions; it can also lead to organisational chaos, overlapping competencies and a lack of exchange of information and expertise available in a given organisation.

62 Communication from the Commission to the European Parliament, the Council, the European Economic and Social Committee and the Committee of the Regions of 27 June 2007, entitled 'Towards Common Principles of Flexicurity: More and better jobs through flexibility and security', COM(2007) 359, Brussels 2007, p. 6.

63 For more see J. Itrich-Drabarek, *Uwarunkowania, standardy i kierunki zmian służby cywilnej w Polsce na tle europejskim,* Warszawa 2010.

64 Ch. Demmke and T. Moilanen *Effectiveness of Good Governance and Ethics in Central Administration: Evaluating Reform Outcomes in the Context of the Financial Crisis,* EIPA, December 2011, p. 73.

# Chapter 2: The Polish Civil Service: Tradition and Experience

## The Civil Service in the Second Republic of Poland (1918–1939)

On 17 February 1922 the Polish parliament passed an act providing for the comprehensive regulation of the legal and social status of civil servants in the Second Republic of Poland.[65] It included the terms and conditions for entering the service, establishing and changing the employment relationship, disciplinary responsibility as well as the rights and duties of state administration employees. The State Civil Service Act was one of the first pieces of legislation to be applied across the whole country, three years after independence.

The Act took effect on 1 April 1922 and for fifty-two years formally remained on the statute book up to 31 December 1974 when the Labour Code of 26 June 1974 came into effect.[66] By the year 1939 the 1922 Civil Service Act was amended fourteen times. In addition, all matters concerning the civil service were regulated by numerous regulations and circulars issued by the Prime Minister, the Minister of Internal Affairs and by the Penal Code of 11 July 1932. Complementing the State Civil Service Act in a significant way were the provisions inherent in the Prime Minister's regulation of 19 December 1922 establishing a grading system of positions in the top echelons of government, offices, state facilities and organisations. In the same category were other executive orders regulating the following issues: preparatory service, exams to positions in various employment categories, state functionaries' pay and official allowances, qualifying commissions and disciplinary procedures.[67]

---

65 Ustawa z 17 lutego 1922 r. o państwowej służbie cywilnej [Act of 17 February 1922 on State Civil Service], Dz.U. R.P. (Journal of Laws of the Republic of Poland, hereinafter abbreviated Dz.U.) No. 21, item164 as amended.

66 *Kodeks Pracy z dnia 26 czerwca 1974r.* [Labour Code of 26 June 1974], Dz.U. No. 24, item 141 as amended.

67 Rozporządzenie Rady Ministrów z dnia 19 grudnia 1933 o ustanowieniu tabeli stanowisk, we władzach, urzędach i instytycjach państwowych [Regulation of Council of Ministers of 19 December 1933 on Establishing a Table of Positions in Authorities, Offices, State Facilities and Institutions] Dz. U., 1933, 102, item 780 and others.

Finally, in 1932 a thorough modernisation of civil service legislation took place including a reform of state functionaries' pay.[68] Twelve official grades in three categories were established (Art. 17). Each official had to undergo a qualifying evaluation carried out by two individuals and was awarded one of the following marks: good, satisfactory or unsatisfactory (Art. 20). If three years in a row an official received an 'unsatisfactory' mark twice he/she was dismissed from the service but with his/her acquired right to a pension intact (Art. 65b). Despite an ongoing debate on the complex relations between politicians and civil servants the legislation stopped short of dividing officials' positions into 'political' and 'non-political' ones.

The basic premise behind this Act was to give the civil service a public-legal nature to signify that the employment relationship of civil service members is regulated by public law. This resulted in excluding public service functionaries from universally binding provisions of the labour law. It was a different story with local government employees: in compliance with the decision of the Supreme Court, their labour relationships were regulated by private law.

The provisions of the State Civil Service Act covered government administration employees, Parliament and Senate Chancellery officials and those working for the Civil Chancellery of the President. The scope of the Act also covered Ministers unless the Constitution or other detailed acts stipulated otherwise.[69] The law did not apply to Supreme Audit Office (NIK) officials, judges and prosecutors, state and public school teachers, university professors, railway and post-office employees and employees of state enterprises and monopolies.[70] This law no longer applied to functionaries of the police, prison guards and state monopolies, who were originally covered by its provisions.

The 1922 State Civil Service Act included a provision establishing two categories of state functionaries: civil servants and lower-ranking state functionaries. This provision was later scrapped. Initially, the Act did not specify the terminology in regard to those employed in the state civil service, calling them either 'state officials' or 'state functionaries' – introducing the concept of 'state employees' only in the Act's amendment.

---

68 Based on the Rozporządzenie Prezydenta RP z dnia 7 października 1932 r. *w sprawie zmiany niektórych postanowień ustawy z dnia 17 lutego 1922 r. o państwowej służbie cywilnej* [Regulation of the President of the Republic of Poland of 7 October 1932 on amending several provisions of the Act of 17 February 1922 on the State Civil Service], Dz. U. R.P, No. 21, item 737.

69 1922 State Civil Service Act, Art. 2.

70 Ibid., Art. 118.

A census conducted in 1923 revealed that the Polish administration employed 120,000 officials, of which 13% had higher education, 40% had secondary education, 30% had completed 4–6 grades of grammar school, and 17% had elementary or home education. Only 15% had previous experience in the administration of one of the three partitioning powers, and those hailed mainly from the region of Galicia. They were mostly criticized by the opposition from the *Obóz Narodowy* (National Camp), for allegedly personifying the flaws of the Austrian system of bureaucracy known for its 'formalism, slow-paced work, lack of independence and excessive number of posts', but at the same time, they were widely appreciated for not taking sides and providing equal treatment to all citizens.[71] Poles constituted the vast majority of state administration officials (92.2%), and within this group there were mostly men. Of the 29,000 officials working in the capacity of office assistants, 10,000 were women; out of the 18,500 senior officials only 630 were women, which is only 3.4%.

The structure of the interwar civil service was hierarchical. It was determined by education which defined three categories of officials:

- First category – requiring tertiary education;
- Second category – requiring secondary education;
- Third category – requiring elementary education.

In view of the theoretical and practical training received, state employees were divided into two groups, that is special services employees and general service employees.

Non-managerial staff could be employed on the basis of work-contracts. In line with the State Civil Service Act they were called state contract service employees, working under individual contracts as opposed to civil servants employed under the terms of the Act.[72] It must be noted however that the education requirement was not strictly adhered to. In special cases the Council of Ministers was afforded the right to appoint individuals to senior positions without the necessary education.[73] What is more, as of 1932 those appointed to positions of professional officers were not even obliged to have secondary education.

71 G. Radomski, 'Wzór urzędnika administracji publicznej w myśli obozu narodowego 1918–1939', in B. Sprengiel and A. Strzelecki (eds.), *Urzędnik w administracji publicznej*, Włocławek 2005, p. 9.

72 1922 State Civil Service Act, Art. 14.

73 J.Kopczyński (ed.), *Przepisy normujące stosunek państwowej służby cywilnej*, Zarząd Główny Stowarzyszenia Urzędników Państwowych, Warszawa 1925, p. 15.

In the Second Republic of Poland, candidates for the civil service had to meet the following requirements:

- Polish citizenship;
- Impeccable past;
- Fluency in the Polish language in speech and in writing;
- Physical and mental capability to fulfill official duties.

Generally, the civil service recruited candidates in the 18–40 age bracket. Candidates for posts of civil service functionaries were required to have a sufficient command of the Polish language, while candidates for the post of civil servant had to be fluent in the language. The condition of language fluency stemmed from Polish historical experiences and was part of the effort to accomplish the fastest possible harmonisation of all territories belonging to Poland. The language criterion also seemed significant in that there were many large national minorities in Poland. That said, in the early days of Polish statehood the condition of fluency in the Polish language was not meticulously observed.

In the Second Polish Republic recruitment into the civil service took place on the basis of nomination.[74] Employment was either permanent or temporary (until dismissal). Under temporary nominations staff were employed for a maximum period of five years, unless the appointee expressed his/her consent to an extension and on the understanding that the extension of employment would not spearhead demands for a permanent job.[75] As a rule, a one-year long preparatory period (internship) preceded the nomination, which was a unilateral official administrative document whereby an employment relationship was established. In some nominations the consent of the appropriate superior authority was needed, as in the case of individuals younger than 18 years of age, candidates above 40 years old with no previous experience of work in the civil service and those dismissed from the service or given court sentences. An official could be appointed to one of the twelve official ranks, with the first rank being the most senior of them all. Nominations to the first four ranks were made exclusively by the President of the Republic. This system was abolished in 1933 by the introduction of 12 basic pay groups.

A nomination to a permanent position provided the civil servant with a certain degree of professional stability. Without the functionary's request there was no way his/her employment relationship could be terminated, although there

74 1922 State Civil Service Act, Art. 4.

75 Ibid., Arts. 21 and 25.

were some exceptions to this rule. The functionary could be dismissed from service by a disciplinary commission, or by moving him/her into inactive employment status due to restructuring if it resulted in the lack of suitable post. By failing to provide an appointment to active service within six months, the civil servant was removed from state service while allowing him/her to keep their pension entitlements. From 1932 a discharge from service could also be caused by an unsatisfactory grade received twice over a period of three years. A civil servant could obtain leave from performing his duties, with his salary withheld for the duration of his parliamentary or senate mandate. The official was transferred into retirement automatically on reaching 65 years of age, or 55 – on his/her own request.

By virtue of the 1922 Act it was possible to assign a member of the state civil service to work in a different town or to a different post without his/her consent in the same administrative department maintaining the same pay group – but it was impossible to dismiss him/her without his consent. In practice, however, and after 1926 in particular, thanks to the provisions of the Act concerning the possibility of changing the labour relationship of public functionaries, personnel changes were made, mainly among senior staff.

Judging by the scope of duties listed in the Act, one can surmise that individuals choosing a civil service career were fully aware that by doing so they were limiting their civil liberties and employment rights and of their own accord subjecting themselves to many restrictions.

For breaching their professional duties civil servants rendered themselves open to professional, civil and criminal liability.[76] Those who in the course of discharging their official duties received material gains for themselves or for other parties were liable to imprisonment for up to five years; for breaching the law with the intent of achieving material gains they were liable to a sentence of ten years in prison. The whole of Chapter 5 of the 1922 Act was devoted to officials' legal liability. Officials who did not respect the provisions of the Act apart from criminal and civil liability (if that was indeed the case) could also have disciplinary measures meted out to them. In the light of Art. 68 of the 1922 State Civil Service Act, a civil servant could incur disciplinary liability for gross professional misconduct, and could be issued a warning for a minor offence. Serious professional misconduct was tantamount to the breach of official duty, becoming an offence against public interest or the jeopardising of the public weal.[77]

76 Ibid., Art. 21.
77 Ibid., Art. 69.

In addition to the State Civil Service Act the legal standing of the service was also regulated by the Penal Code of 1932.[78] Chapter XLI on official misconduct was concerned with the abuse of power, which involved either exceeding one's authority or the failure to act. For falsely certifying an untrue statement the penalty prescribed was up to five years in prison, and ten years behind bars for attempting to derive personal gain.

If through a civil servant's negligence a person was imprisoned, the official could be sentenced to three years in jail. Harsh sentences were prescribed for divulging state secrets: they were punishable by a prison sentence of up to five years, or ten years if this act was carried out with the aim of deriving material gain. If it was proven that the official did not act on purpose, the act was punishable by a prison sentence of six months. Gross professional misconduct and misconduct were not subject to the statute of limitations (Art. 87). The smallest penalties included a warning and a refusal to grant leave.

The Government Regulation on Preparatory Service and Exams for Candidates to Second Group Positions in the State Administrative Service was issued on 16 January 1925.[79] In line with the provisions of the State Civil Service Act passed on17 February 1922 the first paragraph of the Regulation indicates the mandatory nature of preparatory service. The ensuing paragraphs provide in detail the procedure related to this preparatory service, pinpointing eligibility requirements, for instance, dignified conduct, initiative and diligence at work. The preparatory service lasted one year and was followed by a practical exam. It was a prerequisite for being nominated into the service unless the candidate was exempted from this obligation by the head organ.[80] Appropriate head authorities were also entitled to prolong or shorten the one-year long preparatory period. In practice, this provision enabled decision makers to nominate the candidates they designated for the job irrespective of their qualifications for the position in question not because they wanted to manipulate the recruitment process but to alleviate the shortage of human resources, itself a consequence of the partitions

---

78 Rozporządzenie Prezydenta Rzeczypospolitej *wprowadzające Kodeks Karny i Prawo o wykroczeniach* [Regulation of the President of the Republic Introducing the Penal Code and Misdemeanour Act of 11 July 1932], Dz.U. R.P. No. 60, item 571 as amended.

79 Rozporządzenie Rady Ministrów *o służbie przygotowawczej i egzaminie kandydatów na stanowiska II kategorii w państwowej służbie administracyjnej z dnia 16 stycznia 1925 r.* [Regulation of the Council of Ministers on Preparatory Service and Exams for Candidates to Second Group Positions in the State Administrative Service of 16 January 1925] Dz. U. R. P., No. 16, item 103.

80 1922 State Civil Service Act, Art. 11.

Poland had endured. On completing the preparatory service candidates were evaluated. If the result was positive the candidate was allowed to take the two-part exam, written and oral,[81] and with these exam results the candidate's fate was sealed.

The professionalism of civil service employees was monitored as part of the annual evaluations system conducted by qualifying commissions attached to the top authorities or to the ones directly below.[82] The appraisals (a choice between: good, satisfactory and unsatisfactory) were given by two persons recruited to perform the official supervision. Upon receiving an unsatisfactory mark twice in a row the employee was dismissed with a three months' notice period.[83]

During his/her employment in the public service the civil servant enjoyed special legal protection. The job offered several privileges: a relatively high salary, an allowance for work in adverse conditions (the Eastern borderlands, Śląsk, Gdynia and Gdańsk), a high pension (better than for other employees), free medical care, children education allowance, discounts for train tickets as well as tied accommodation.

In spite of this, however, the Great Depression did not leave this professional group unscathed: in 1931 its salaries were cut by 15% in accordance with the law. But even then civil servants in the Second Polish Republic enjoyed a privileged financial position. For one thing, they were entitled to various executive bonuses related to their post which were introduced on 28 October 1933 by the Regulation of the President of the Republic on State Functionaries' Remuneration.[84] Pursuant to Article 8 of the said Act, the remuneration, rewards and benefits were exempt from income tax and pension charge. Functionaries were divided into 12 groups and awarded appropriate remuneration from the highest 3,000 złoty to the lowest – 100 złoty. Pay increased not only with promotions to the next rungs but also with the length of service. In 1933 salary grades were replaced by groups of basic salaries, which comprised of groups of civil servants, lower ranking functionaries, professors and assistant research workers of state

---

81 Regulation of Council of Ministers of 16 January 1925 on Preparatory Service.

82 Rozporządzenie Rady Ministrów z dnia 23 lipca 1923 r. *o komisjach kwalifikacyjnych* [Regulation of Council of Ministers on Qualifying Commissions of 23 July 1923], Dz. U. R. P., No. 82, item. 638.

83 1922 State Civil Service Act, Art. 20.

84 Rozporządzenie Prezydenta Rzeczypospolitej z 28 października 1933 r. *o uposażeniu funkcjonariuszy państwowych* [Regulation of the President of the Republic of Poland of 28 October 1933 on State Functionaries' Remuneration] Dz. U. R. P., No. 86, item 663.

universities, teachers of all levels and functionaries of the prison service. In addition to the actual salary, officials received financial benefits (when there was a family to support) and a 'local benefit'(initially only if an official's work was located in Warsaw or the Eastern borderlands).

Over the years 1933/1934 the system of benefits was extended to include a local benefit for those working in Warsaw, Gdynia, Hel, Gdańsk and in major cities of the Silesian voivodship; a management allowance for those holding managerial positions; and a special allowance for those in a particular kind of service but not legible for the management allowance.

In addition to their salaries, the material condition and social standing of public functionaries was affected by their occupational stability and social security related to being entitled to a pension as well as a social security scheme for widows and orphans. This is something that was appreciated especially at the time of the worldwide economic crisis which took longer to recede in Poland than in other countries across the globe and which wreaked more havoc than in other parts of the world.

Functionaries of the state civil service acquired their pension rights after 10 years of service; the length of service increased to 15 years for, both, civil and military service after 1934. In case of a permanent disability or illness incurred after entering the service with no fault on the part of the functionary he/she was entitled to a pension after five years of service.

When the permanent incapacity for service was due to an ill-fated accident during service or due to an infection from a contagious disease when on official duty, the time requirement for acquiring pension rights was no longer binding. These regulations concerned the police, post-office and railway workers, professors and teachers. The pension was determined by the length of service: after 10 years of service it amounted to 40% of the final salary before retirement and increased annually by 2.4–3%, up to a 100%.

During the war and German occupation, the authorities of the Polish Underground State attached considerable importance to defining the status of civil servants. Acting on the President's Decree they introduced certain temporary changes into the State Civil Service Act (for the duration of the war).[85] Persons appointed to positions in the state service after 30 September 1939 could be dismissed without adherence to the provisions of Articles 54–56 of the Act of

85 Dekret Prezydenta Rzeczypospolitej z dnia 12 lipca 1940 r. *o tymczasowej zmianie przepisów ustawy o państwowej służbie cywilnej*,[Decree of the President of the Republic of Poland of 12 July 1940 on the Temporary Revision of the State Civil Service Act] Dz. U., No. 11 item 29.

17 February 1922. This meant that civil servants had to forsake their privileged status for the time of war (they did not receive their full salary, they did not become inactive) and could be dismissed, in which case they received a dismissal wage equal to three months' worth of their last salary. The month in which the dismissal took place was not included in the 'three months'.[86]

## State Administration Employees Under the Polish People's Republic (1945–1989)

The Polish People's Republic rejected the notions underpinning the idea of the civil service and undermined the image of the civil servant developed in the Second Republic. Despite its declarations to the opposite, the new authorities did not require devotion to the service and administrative employees did not serve their customers with respect although the 1922 State Civil Service Act continued to serve as the foundation of the status of state administration employees. The amendments that were to follow sought to equalise the legal and social status of administration employees with that of other professional groups. The first amendments were introduced by decree already in 1944, the next in 1946, 1948 and later.

Decrees issued by the Polish Committee of National Liberation (PKWN) on 27 December 1944 and its Decree of 14 May 1946 allowed the new authorities to replace the politically inconvenient cadre of officials by dismissing state functionaries with a three months' notice.[87] These decrees were responsible for weakening the principle of professional stability of state administration employees. The next Decree of 25 October 1948[88] unified the entitlements of contract and nominated employees and introduced a new remuneration system making their pay equal with that of other employee groups. The decree introduced a uniform

---

86 Ibid., Art. 1. 2.

87 Dekret PKWN z dnia 27 grudnia 1944 r. *o tymczasowym unormowaniu stosunków służbowego i zaszeregowaniu funkcjonariuszy państwowych,* [Decree of PKWN on the Provisional Normalisation of the Employment Relationship and Classification of State Functionaries] Dz. U., No. 16, item 89; Dekret z dnia 14 maja 1946 r. *o tymczasowym unormowaniu stosunku służbowego funkcjonariuszy państwowych*, [Decree on the Provisional Normalisation of State Functionaries' Employment Relationship] Dz. U., No. 22, item 139.

88 Dekret z dnia 25 października 1948 r. *o zmianie ustawy z dnia 17 lutego 1922 r. o państwowej służbie cywilnej* [Decree on the Amendment of the Act of 17 February 1922 on the State Civil Service] Dz. U., No. 50, item 381.

term – 'administrative employee' replacing the previously binding terms: 'functionary' and 'civil servant'.

Subsequent amendments to the Civil Service Act of 1922 indicated that the course of changes initiated in 1944 aimed at equating the legal status of employees performing tasks for the state with that of other groups of employees in terms of their salaries, security schemes or job stability.[89] This trend was expressed in curtailing the scope of nominations as a form of establishing employment relations[90] and expanding disciplinary liability of contract employees, sanctioned by the 1950 Act on Safeguarding the Socialist Discipline of Work.[91] The final stage of the standardisation was the enactment of the Labour Code (on 31 December 1974) which provided a complete unification of the legal status of state administration employees with other professional groups.

In the literature on the subject in the times of People's Poland the term 'civil servant' was seldom used; if at all – it occurred in a pejorative sense, the term used in its place was 'state administration employee'. One of the legacies of People's Poland is the image of the official as a 'thick', spiteful, contrarian who prevents the citizens from successfully settling their matters in the office and, on top of this, is blindly loyal to his superiors from the Polish United Workers' Party rather than to the constitution or the law. Despite – or was it perhaps due to – the political transition, the post-1989 public administration was still perceived as an ossified structure: inept, with excessive bureaucracy and corrupt officials. This image is slowly beginning to alter, but the pace of change is sluggish and arduous – adversely affecting the way the public perceives the state, undermining the state itself and causing delays in the reform process.

More and more frequently, however, the specific nature of administrative work would come to the attention of decision-makers and, notably, the fact that it was not founded on a coherent system. Accordingly, steps were taken to systematise and regulate the status of employees working for state organisations. The correlation between the efficient implementation of state goals and the attitude, quality, efficiency and responsibility of administrative cadres was finally recognised in the 1970s. Solutions were found in improving the education system, refining the organisation and operation of the administrative apparatus, streamlining jobs,

89 M. Jełowicki, *Instytucje prawa urzędniczego,* Warszawa 1986, p. 24.

90 Wytyczne Prezesa Rady Ministrów z 31 stycznia 1949 r. *w sprawie polityki kadrowej*, [Prime Minister's guidelines concerning personnel policy] Dz. U. Min. Admin. Publ., No. 21, item 57.

91 Ustawa z 19 kwietnia 1950 r. *o zapewnieniu socjalistycznej dyscypliny pracy*, [Act on Safeguarding Socialist Discipline of Work of 19 April 1950] Dz. U., No. 20, item 168.

applying predictive methods and long-term planning, improving management styles, constructing government IT systems and harmonising work. Emphasis was placed on increasing the administration's work effectiveness by introducing a host of measures: new regulations, separation of competences, authorities and responsibilities, building healthy relationships between workers, providing organisational and technical instruments and defining work performance.[92] The administrative cadre was assigned modern goals. Firstly, it was to inspire and participate actively in the life of society. Secondly, through its contacts with members of the public they were to help in learning about the individual and collective needs of society. Thirdly, the social interaction was to serve in part as a vehicle of control over the administration.

The publication of the Labour Code on 20 December 1974 coincided with the adoption of the Regulation of the Council of Ministers on the Rights and Obligations of Employees of State Authorities, encompassing employees of the head, central and local bodies of state administration and offices subordinate to them, as well as employees of the *Sejm*, the Council of the State and the Supreme Audit Office.[93] In the light of the Regulation, the requirements for becoming a state employee included the ability to guarantee the due discharge of the tasks undertaken by the office in terms of one's ideological and moral attitude (§2), Polish citizenship, a minimum of 18 years of age, full civil rights and the appropriate professional qualifications for the civil service (§2 and §3). State employees were required to take an oath whereby they declared to spare no effort in contributing to the prosperous socialist development of the Polish People's Republic, adhere to the principles of the 'popular rule of law' and support the 'public interest and principles of socialist development'(§6).[94]

State employees were required to assert the authority of People's Poland and seek to increase the citizens' trust in the country's rulers and its institutions. They were also expected to work with insight, speed and impartiality; readily supply the necessary information; make sure that the citizens suffer no damage as a result of their lack of legal knowledge, thus offer the necessary explanation of rules and regulations; upgrade their professional skills and improve their abilities to

---

92 B. Ostapczuk, 'Odpowiedzialność jako środek usprawnienia administracji', in *Odpowiedzialność*, pp. 230–233.

93 Rozporządzenie Rady Ministrów z dnia 20 grudnia 1974 r. *w sprawie praw i obowiązków urzędników państwowych* [Regulation of the Council of Ministers on the Rights and Obligations of State Employees of 29 December 1974] Dz.U. No. 40, item 300.

94 Ibid.

perform the tasks assigned.[95] The Regulation contained a provision which said that if the state employee was convinced that the official order from his/her boss was erroneous, contravened the law or was detrimental to social interest, the employee was obliged to report his/her doubts to his superior. In case the order was confirmed in writing, the employee was obliged to execute it and immediately inform the manager or a superior organ in the office about his/her reservations.[96]

In the socialist state it was thought that state administration employees were not there to 'blindly execute official orders but rather co-create the tasks of the administration', while personnel policy was designed to transfer extensive competences to the employees in connection with their, broadly understood, political responsibility and to make them more independent.

The 1970s brought criticism of the legal regulations in place, as the need to provide separate regulations regarding the scope of employment relations of state employees became increasingly apparent. Concerns were raised that the administration was not keeping up with social and economic changes. It was also pointed out that the methods and arrangements that bring the most effective functioning of the public administration do not consist in the number of penalties imposed on it but in providing it with appropriate tasks to accomplish.[97]

On the basis of delegated legislation introduced in Art. 298 of the Labour Code executive provisions were issued in the form of orders separately regulating the rights and responsibilities of state office employees, conditions for entering the service, special requirements in respect of personal and occupational qualifications and rules for appointing candidates to managerial positions in central and local administration.[98] On the basis of this delegated legislation, several detailed pragmatics regulating the legal status of the secret service were issued at a later stage.[99]

The following criteria were to define the role and position of state administration officials in the socialist state administration: obligation to provide continuous expert professional advice to their superiors; creativity in regard to serious social projects; competence and activity underpinned by responsibility – as everything the officials would undertake was attributed to the state.

95 Ibid.

96 Ibid.

97 J. Łętowski, 'Niektóre problemy służby państwowej w świetle aktualnych rozwiązań prawnych', *Państwo i Prawo*, 1975, Nos. 8–9, pp. 49–50.

98 Rozporządzenie Rady Ministrów z dnia 20 grudnia 1974 r. *w sprawie praw i obowiązków*.

99 Jełowicki, p. 27.

The legal status of state employees evolved in a process of several stages:

- Making the legal status of nominated employees level with that of contract employees;
- Limiting the number of nominations as means of entry into the service;
- Unifying the legal status of administration employees in state organisational units at various levels;
- Covering all employees, including administration employees, with common labour law.[100]

The 1980s usher in new conditions for the Polish administration. The centre of power continues to reside with the Political Bureau of the Polish United Workers' Party – the external headquarters and political control centre – but on the other hand, the early 1980s also see the advance of new social relations, including new relations between the citizens and the public administration, and the emergence and growth of the 'Solidarity' movement – signalling the future radical shifts. It must be borne in mind that underpinning the operation, organisation and structure of public administration in Poland of that time was the Constitution of 1952, which despite the new political and economic developments in a clear way still imposed the 'old' manner of proceeding. The statutory changes involving the administration introduced in the years leading up to the transition of 1989 seem at times only superficial, thus they are very often ignored or glossed over with short references in the accounts of many analysts, although some of them definitely merit closer inspection and careful study.

The legal standing of state administration employees was harmonised by the Act of 16 September 1982 on State Office Employees which came into effect on 1 January 1983 and was later amended on numerous occasions. The scope of the Act covered employment relations: the establishment, changes and termination of the employment relationship, duties and rights of office employees, liability for maintenance of order, disciplinary liability and terms of investigating labour relations claims.

Until its 2 December 1994 amendment, the Act distinguished two types of nominated officials: firstly, those employed in managerial and independent posts, and secondly, contract employees employed on the basis of a labour contract in all the other positions, or in exceptional cases, for a fixed term, preceding appointment to managerial and independent posts. In the light of this Act state office employees could be recruited from amongst those who met the following

100 Ibid., p. 28.

criteria: Polish citizenship, 18 years of age, full legal capacity, holder of civil rights, impeccable character, appropriate education, apprenticeship in the administration and the individual's health allowing for employment in a given position.[101]

Article 17 of the 1982 Act defined the responsibilities resting with the employees, such as: obeying the constitution and other regulations, guarding the authority of the Republic of Poland; seeking to increase citizens' trust in organs of the state (sensible management of public funds; diligence; impartial, efficient and timely discharge of duties); keeping official secrets; expanding their professional knowledge; dignified conduct at work; fulfilling professional duties set by their superiors; asking for the manager's consent before taking up additional outside employment; refraining from manifesting their political views; guarding state interests; observing the law; and advancing the legitimate interests of the citizens. The Act imposed the obligation to: upgrade professional qualifications, participate in various forms of training, take exams and participate in competitions. Officials were also required to stand for periodic performance evaluations.[102]

The Act introduced four categories of officials depending on their education level, professional training, skills and personality traits.[103] It specified the rules of recruitment for the service and the scope of qualifying procedures. The detailed scope of the qualifying procedure was not regulated until 1997, when the Qualifying Committee for the Civil Service passed the appropriate resolution.

After the Civil Service Act of 5 July 1996 came into effect, the Act of 1982 remained binding only in regard to employees of government administration offices holding non-civil service positions.

The 1982 Act failed to provide a definition of a civil servant, although Article 2 obliged the Council of Ministers to define, by way of a government regulation, positions staffed by employees in the rank of civil servant. Such a regulation was issued on 8 November 1982 and embraced nearly all positions in the office, from the office manager to the typist, with the exclusion of maintenance workers, who were called 'other employees of the office' who are not civil servants.[104]

---

101 Ibid. Art. 3.

102 K. Sitkowska, *Służba cywilna w nowym ustawodawstwie*, Toruń 1998, p. 9.

103 Ustawa z dnia 16 września 1982 r. *o pracownikach urzędów państwowych,* [State Offices Employees Act of 16 September 1982] Dz.U. No. 31, item 214 as modified in 1994, Dz.U. 1994, No. 136, item 704] Art. 28.

104 Rozporządzenie Rady Ministrów z dnia 8 listopada 1982 r. *w sprawie określenia stanowisk urzędniczych oraz zasad nawiązywania z urzędnikami państwowymi stosunku pracy na podstawie mianowania*[ Regulation of the Council of Ministers on the Definition of Officials' Positions and Rules of Establishing Employment Relationships

Nomination as means of establishing employment relations with civil servants was cancelled after 1994 thus closing this path to increasing the ranks of public officials nominated according to the old procedures. The intention was to create a civil service corps under new terms. Nevertheless, nominations were still allowed in offices – set up under the Council of Ministers' Regulation – in regard to employees of state offices other than those mentioned in the Act.

From 27 January 1995 officials employed in offices listed in the Act could be employed solely on the basis of labour contracts. Only if a nominated official was moved to work in another office, on the basis of Article 10.2 of the 1982 Act, or promoted to a higher post by virtue of Article 2.3, he/she could be employed in the new position on the basis of nomination. Employment by virtue of nomination also took place when a nominated civil servant returned to work on the basis of previously applied terms after the office unlawfully terminated his/her employment relationship.

## The Civil Service Act of 5 July 1996: the Process of Civil Service Development in the Third Republic of Poland

The first stage of the process of laying the legal groundwork for the civil service in Poland began in 1993 – although the creation of the National School of Public Administration in June 1992 was a harbinger of the changes to come – and ended with the introduction of the Civil Service Act in 1996, which came into effect on 1 January 1997.[105] This law was introduced by the SdRP/PSL coalition government with the intent of establishing a milestone in the functioning of state administration in the Third Republic. The scope of the Act of 5 July 1996 in terms of the subject matter, dealt with nominated civil servants only. The Act divided all public administration employees into two groups:[106] the first embraced nominated civil servants employed in government administration offices, while the second consisted of those who were employed in government administration offices on the basis of appointment and did not belong to the civil service.[107]

---

with Officials Through Nominations of 8 November 1982] Dz. U., No. 39, item 257 as amended.

105 Ustawa z dnia 5 lipca 1996 r. *o służbie cywilnej,* [Civil Service Act of 5 July 1996] Dz. U., No. 89, item 402; of 1997 No. 106, item 679; of 1998 No. 58, item 366 and No. 162, item 1126.

106 Ibid, Art. 3.

107 Ibid, Art. 1. 1.

The scope of the Act, in terms of the subject, was limited to officials employed on the basis of a nomination in the highest, central and local organs of government administration. The nomination took place in the name of the Republic of Poland, so as under the 1922 Civil Service Act, the hiring was made under public law. It could take place for a fixed term or for an indefinite period. In the case of the former the maximum period was two years. This only involved employees who had been employed in the public administration for less than two years. Nominations for fixed terms could be shortened if the official received a positive evaluation on completing his first year of employment. If the official received a negative rating, the procedure was repeated six months later. The Act safeguarded the officials' professional stability on the premise that officials performed tasks set by the state and for the state. The fact of adopting such an interpretation boosted the prestige and importance of nominated officials and the civil service itself, but on the other hand, attracted criticism for devising arrangements which were giving way to chaos by differentiating the legal status of persons employed in the government administration.

The subject scope of the Act did not cover administration employees hired on the basis of labour contracts, who were still subject to the 16 September 1982 Act concerning employees of state offices. Similarly, the civil service corps did not include those nominated officials whose employment relationships were established in government administration offices before the Civil Service Act came into effect, that is before 1 January 1997.[108] Under the 1996 law, employment relationships were to exist up to 31 December 2007 at the latest, after which date they were to expire by virtue of the statute. Not many officials were appointed on the basis of the 5 July 1996 Act: 109 altogether, 85 of whom belonged to category A and 24 to category B. This group of officials included the Deputy Head of Civil Service, nine directors-general of ministries and central offices and 15 directors-general of voivodship offices. Officials nominated on the back of the 5 July 1996 Act kept their nomination under the new Civil Service Act of 18 December 1998, but irrespective of their official category or position, they were awarded the lowest possible rank and provided with no guarantee of keeping their pay at the same level.

Among the drawbacks of the Act of 5 July 1996 were the following: insufficient judicial control (entry into the civil service and disciplinary measures were determined by intra-administrative bodies), lack of clearly depicted career paths and rules for promotion and, finally, the weak position awarded to the officials

108 Ibid, Art. 95.

(employment contract could be terminated in the event of a negative assessment occurring twice in succession). Also noted was the slow implementation of the Act.

The introduction of a civil service system into Polish government administration was designed to alter the style of work and management of human resources in the administration, and equip this institution for, firstly, its integration with the European Union and, secondly, to meet the challenges brought by cultural and economic globalisation. In the same way, it was believed that the Polish ad ministration would thus be better prepared to fulfil the growing requirements and high expectations held by a better-educated society.

## The Operation of the Civil Service Under the 18 December 1998 Act

When compared to its predecessor in terms of the legal status of civil servants, the 18 December 1998 Act sought to cover all government administration officials with uniform legislation. This marked a radical departure from the previous situation whereby two different laws applied to government employees: the 1982 State Offices Employees Act and the 1996 Civil Service Act. Introduced by the ruling conservative-liberal AWS/UW coalition, the new legislation saw identical and consistent principles apply to all government administration employees in the area of recruitment and selection, official privileges, terms of promotion and cyclical assessment of employees, rules governing the discharge of official duties and professional ethics requirements.

Since 1998 the civil service corps has included government administration employees, distinguishing those who were civil service employees hired on the basis of labour contracts and civil servants who were employed on the basis of a nomination. The 1998 Act introduced a different recruitment system into the civil service, one that was based on the principles of openness and competitiveness as well as legal measures guaranteeing both. A further change was associated with the procedures for filling senior positions. On the strength of the 1998 Act only persons recruited from amongst the winners of competitions organised by the Head of Civil Service could fill these posts. What is more, compared to the previous Act, the constitutional position of the Prime Minister as the Head of the Civil Service corps was weakened (Article 158.2 and Article 148(7)) and his tasks reduced. In this regard, also, the competences of the Minister of Internal Affairs and Administration were taken away from him. The new organisation of the civil service was based on the principle of centralisation and all matters relating to the civil service were from now on concentrated in the hands of the Head of

Civil Service, as the supreme organ of government administration. Law-makers strengthened his position by designating a relatively long term of office. In 2005 for a short spell a competition was instituted for the post of Head of Civil Service and his Deputy.[109]

The 1998 Act introduced obligatory preparatory service for anyone selected in the recruitment process and employed in the civil service for the first time on the basis of a fixed term labour contract. The programme for the preparatory service was developed by the Head of Civil Service with the approval of the National School of Public Administration (KSAP). KSAP graduates were exempted from preparatory service. A director-general of office was responsible for organising the preparatory service.

The preparatory service was to last six months and conclude not later than 18 months from the date the employee was hired by the office. It was aimed at passing on theoretical knowledge and practical skills to the employees to help them meet their professional responsibilities and to ensure an equal start for everybody. The director-general could expand the programme of the preparatory service by including training focused on the work of a given office. It was also seen as another testing ground for determining whether the participants were predisposed to work in the office.

The theoretical part of the programme embraced the basics of knowledge regarding the government and law, including the functioning of public administration (administrative procedures, the constitutional system of the sources of law, national economy, system of public finance, psychology and sociology); the European Union; and rules governing the organisation and operation of the parent office (strategy and legal basis of office, etc.). In the practical part the employee was supposed to grasp the structure and operation of the office, its individual units, the structure of the subordinate units, especially those which had direct contacts with the citizens. Employees were required to produce a written work appropriate to the position they held.

Employees attending the prep service were assigned a tutor by the director-general. Tutors could have up to three employees under their guard at any one time. Only a civil service corps member with high qualifications, an independent position and at least five years of work in public administration could become a tutor.

109 Ustawa z dnia 17 czerwca 2005 r. *o zmianie ustawy o służbie cywilnej oraz niektórych innych ustaw*, [Act of 17 June 2005 on Amending the Civil Service Act and Several Other Acts] Dz.U. No. 132, item 1110, Art. 2.

Tutors were charged with the task of making sure that employees carried out the practical part of the preparatory service. On its completion the tutor had to write an assessment of his gourd for the examining committee set up by the director-general. The preparatory service ended with the examining committee's evaluation of the employees' knowledge. A positive verdict resulted in the signing of an open-ended employment contract between the employee and the director general, while a negative one led to the termination of employment.

The 1998 Act provided exemptions from the preparatory service as well as arrangements for shortening its duration. In any event, the decision was taken by the director-general in regard to employees who displayed the required theoretical knowledge, had the qualifications to use it in practice and at the same time were knowledgeable about how the office was organised and how it functioned. The Act, however, failed to define the manner in which the employees were to demonstrate their knowledge of the operation of the office, thus giving the director-general a generous margin of discretion.

The Act of 18 December 1998 established competitions for senior positions but at the same time the scheme of hiring 'acting officials' made it possible to bypass this requirement. Furthermore, a 2001 amendment in the form of Article 144a introduced the possibility of employing individuals from outside the civil service corps for positions in offices and state institutions, which under the terms of valid legislation should be staffed with individuals selected in competition from amongst those who had professional experience.[110] Amendment 144a was referred to the Constitutional Tribunal by the Ombudsman in the belief that it violated the essence of Article 153 of the Constitution which said that the civil service corps was created 'in order to ensure a professional, diligent, impartial and politically neutral discharge of the State's obligations.' The Constitutional Tribunal ruled on 12 December 2002 that a provision which allows for employing persons from outside the civil service corps to senior state positions indeed violates the Constitution. According to the Tribunal, Article 144a of the 18 December 1998 Civil Service Act was inconsistent with Article 153.1 of the

110 Ustawa z dnia 21 grudnia 2001 r *o zmianie ustawy o organizacji i trybie pracy Rady Ministrów oraz o zakresie działania ministrów, ustawy o działach administracji rządowej oraz o zmianie niektórych ustaw*, [The Act of 21 December 2001 Amending the Act on the Organization and Operation of the Council of Ministers and the Scope of Activities of Ministers, and the Act on Government Administration Departments and on Amendments to Certain Acts] Dz.U. No. 54, item 1800.

Constitution.[111] The Tribunal found that this regulation struck at the impartiality, political neutrality and professionalism with which civil service members go about discharging their tasks. It transpired, however, that the significance of the judgement was only symbolic as it did not lead to the dismissal of those who had already been employed because the sentence lacked retroactive effect. Furthermore, new officials were not hired since the regulation allowed new recruitments to be made only up to the end of 2002. This gave rise to a situation whereby from amongst 1,400 senior officials in the civil service, by the year 2006 around 800 worked as 'acting officials'.

The 1998 Act also allowed for nominations to be made preceded by qualifying procedures. The procedures were carried out by the Head of Civil Service in order to test the knowledge, qualifications and predispositions required for work in the civil service. To be accepted for qualification the candidate had to meet the following criteria:

1. Employment in the civil service for at least two years;
2. Completed preparatory service or exempted from it;
3. MA degree or equivalent;
4. Command of a foreign language;
5. The status of a reserve soldier or not being subject to military service.

Failure to meet any one of the above requirements disqualified the contestants from applying for the nomination.

The command of a foreign language had to be attested by a certificate such as a diploma confirming the completion of foreign language and literature studies, a foreign language teachers' college, studies abroad or the National School of Public Administration. Also accepted were certificates confirming successful passage of ministerial exams at the Ministry of Foreign Affairs, Ministry of Economy and the Ministry of Defence, as well as certificates given by KSAP, the Ministerial Foreign Language Examining Committee of the Civil Service Office and other entitled institutions.

The qualifying procedure was in writing and consisted of three parts:

- testing overall abilities;
- testing the individual's knowledge in the form of an optional choice test;
- written work.

---

111 Wyrok Trybunału Konstytucyjnego z dnia 12 grudnia 2002 [Judgement of Constitutional Tribunal] File ref.no: K.9/02, Dz.U., No. 238, item 2025.

Candidates seeking a nomination and endowed with additional skills were eligible to receive additional credits (20 altogether), awarded for instance for a positive written opinion from the director-general of office (three credits); command of another foreign language different from the one entered for the qualifying procedure (three credits); knowledge of two foreign languages other than those the candidate entered for the qualifying procedure (six points). The full list of the documents and certificates confirming the candidates' knowledge of foreign languages, was catalogued in Annex 2 to the Prime Minister's Regulation.

A participant could be excluded from the qualifying procedure by a member of the examining team for using materials other than those provided by the Civil Service Office, communicating with each other or disrupting the exam. All parts of the exam were coded – decoding took place after all the answers were checked. Each stage of the qualifying procedure was monitored by representatives of the Civil Service Council. Thus, the overall setup indicates that consolidating the value of civil service professionalism was a priority for Polish lawmakers.

In the course of the qualifying procedure a candidate could gain a maximum of 200 credits. The results were listed in a descending order and made public. Those who did not make the mark were not mentioned on the list. The 1998 Civil Service Act clearly stated in Article 37.1 that the list could include only persons who exceeded the minimum 120 credits. In other words, in order to receive a nomination one had to receive more credits than the required minimum of 120 or complete the National School of Public Administration and, at the same time, fall within the limit of nominations for a given year.

The Head of Civil Service was obliged to make a public statement indicating the ceiling of nominations for a given budgetary year within 14 days from the date of the budget act announcement. Apart from the limit of nominations, the budget act also defined the financial means earmarked for the remuneration and training of civil service corps members. The Council of Ministers is obligated to construct annually a three-year plan defining the limit of nominations to the civil service and present it to the *Sejm* together with the budget act.

## The Year 2006: A Change for the Better or the Decline of the Polish Civil Service?

Two Acts signalled the far-reaching changes to come: one was concerned with the civil service itself and the other dealt with the State Staffing Pool and senior state positions, both were adopted on 24 August 2006. The former removed senior positions from the ambit of the civil service, thereby limiting the civil service corps to mid-level employees; Article 2.3 provided that officials' positions could also be held by 'persons seconded or transferred on the basis of separate regulations to perform tasks outside the employing agency if the transfer serves the vital interest of the civil service'.[112]

In order to become a civil servant the applicant had to be a civil service employee with at least two years of job experience in the civil service, have completed preparatory service or been exempted from it, hold an MA degree or an equivalent title, have demonstrated the command of at least one foreign language and have the status of a reserve soldier or be exempt from military service.[113]

Pursuant to the 2006 Act, nine official civil service grades were listed determining official pay levels. Civil servants were promoted to a higher grade provided they were rated positively in the evaluation they were subjected to at least once every two years. The motion for promoting officials to a higher grade was raised by their immediate superior.

Under the terms of this Act, the civil service could employ only those applicants who had Polish citizenship and enjoyed full public rights. In line with the suggested 2008 amendment, some positions in the Polish civil service by virtue of European Union law were to be opened up to EU citizens.

Directors-general were obliged to publicise information on vacancies in the offices under their guard. Thus, advertisements were placed in easily accessible spots in the seat of the office and published in the Civil Service Bulletin. The requirements for a given post were to be specified in a clear and legible manner. Candidates to the civil service were to be recruited on the basis of competition and the selected candidate was given a job proposal.

However, in the wake of the 2006 Civil Service Act recruitment to the civil service started declining, registering, both, a drop in the numbers of applicants for work in government administration and an outflow of employees from the service after the first couple of years of work.

Employment relations with a civil service employee were established on the basis of:

- Fixed term contracts of up to three years;
- Open-ended work contracts.

---

112 Ustawa z dnia 10 marca 2006 r. *o zmianie ustawy o pracownikach samorządowych, ustawy o Najwyższej Izbie Kontroli oraz ustawy o służbie cywilnej*, [Act of 10 March 2006 on Amending the Act on Self-government Employees, the Act on the Supreme Audit Office and the Act on the Civil Service] Dz. U., No. 79, item 549.

113 Ustawa z dnia 24 sierpnia 2006 r. *o służbie cywilnej*, [Civil Service Act of 24 August 2006] Dz. U., No. 49, item 483, Art. 28.

Nominations still remained the alternative form of establishing employment relations. The 24 August 2006 Act diminished the significance of the preparatory service, scaling it down to three months and mandating it only in case the director-general deemed it at all necessary. This undermined the professional nature of the civil service emphasised in Article 153 of the Constitution.

The scope of the 24 August 2006 Act on the State Staffing Pool and High-ranking State Positions[114] covered senior state positions transferred from the civil service. The law was subsequently amended on 11 May 2007, and came into force on 24 July 2007[115], providing the grounds for including all persons with a PhD to be included in the State Staffing Pool. Also, the job experience required for sitting the exam which entitled a candidate to seek access to the State Staffing Pool was cut from five to three years, while the duration of State Staffing Pool membership was lengthened from five to ten years. These changes unequivocally indicate that access to senior state positions was made easier for individuals with not-that-long-experience in public administration and, at the same time, those who had connections to the government of the day.

It seems that the 24 August 2006 Act on the Civil Service came into being mainly for political reasons reflecting the will to politicise the legal underpinnings of personnel policy to suit the needs of the new government (a coalition of PiS, LPR and *Samoobrona*).

The changes introduced on the back of the 2006 Act limited the scope of the civil service by excluding from its ambit senior positions, such as the director-general of office, internal audit chief inspector, the director or deputy director and managers in central and voivodship offices. This, of course, went against the pronouncement of the Constitutional Tribunal made in 2001 to the effect that senior positions in the civil service constituted an integral part of the civil service. By excluding senior positions from the civil service the latter now consisted of medium ranking employees, thus diminishing the status of the civil service. Harking back to rules set down in the 1996 Civil Service Act, a division was once again introduced into the cadres of the government administration into civil service members (less significant this time) and into political positions – the more important ones (hailing from the State Staffing Pool).

---

114 Ustawa z dnia 11 maja 2007r., *o zmianie ustawy o państwowym zasobie kadrowym i wysokich stanowiskach państwowych oraz o zmianie niektórych innych ustaw*, [Act of 11 May 2007 on Amending the Act on the State Staffing Pool and High-ranking State Positions and Amending Several Other Acts] Dz.U. No. 123, item 847.

115 Ibid.

Thus, it was made possible for state office employees, local government employees and employees of the Supreme Audit Office to take officials' positions in the civil service by 'transfer' rather than by competition. This constituted a blatant violation of the principle of equal opportunities, equal access and competition which all lie at the heart of a democratic civil service and Article 60 of the Polish Constitution.

The status of the civil service was lowered by abolishing the institution of Head of Civil Service as the central organ of government administration and replacing it with the post of director-general of the State Staffing Pool and by abolishing competitions for senior positions – introducing instead discretionary appointments.

The Act of 2006 violated the principle of political neutrality as the creation of the State Staffing Pool was its contradiction. In 2002 the Constitutional Tribunal stated that political neutrality guarantees the proper execution of state tasks with the help of a stable cadre of officials.

The Office of Civil Service was abolished as well as the, already mentioned, Head of Civil Service, while the new Department of Civil Service was brought under the control of the Head of the Prime Minister's Chancellery – itself a purely political organ. The new arrangements did little to guarantee that the directors-general, incorporated into the State Staffing Pool – a political organ, would maintain political neutrality despite the fact that they still continued in the role of the employers of civil service employees and civil servants – both belonging to the politically neutral civil service corps.

# Chapter 3: Employment Relationships as Provided for in the Civil Service Act of 21 November 2008

## Recruitment Principles

It is an established rule in the European system of public administration that in order to 'ensure high-quality of its cadres, future members of the corps have to undergo a qualification procedure that will select the best – professionals, experts in their fields, those with a predisposition to work in the administration, loyal to the state and friendly to the citizen. The civil service is expected to build a positive image of a public administration official. The qualification procedure is to enable the selection of candidates displaying specific traits, knowledge and skills that improve the efficiency and effectiveness of the civil service corps'.[116]

It is also widely accepted that 'the right recruitment mechanisms are a key element to the proper human resources management in the civil service'.[117]

The civil service corps in Poland comprises civil service employees and civil servants (by nomination) working in government administration: the Chancellery of the Prime Minister, the offices of ministers and chairpersons of committees within the Council of Ministers as well as the offices of central government administration bodies, voivodship and other offices that together form the apparatus that provides assistance to the territorial organs of government administration subordinate to particular ministers or central organs of government administration, headquarters, inspectorates and other organizational units forming the supporting apparatus to heads of the unified voivodship services, inspections and guards as well as heads of poviat services, inspections and guards, unless otherwise provided by relevant law, the Forest Reproductive Material Office, state budget units managing state appropriated specific-purpose funds at the disposal of government administration bodies.

The civil service corps also comprise poviat and border veterinary surgeons and their deputies. Office positions can also be held by persons delegated under separate provisions to perform tasks outside the organisational unit that employs them.[118]

---

116 Prime Minister's Chancellery, <http://dsc.kprm.gov.pl/system-sluzby-cywilnej>.

117 Ibid.

118 Civil Service Act of 21 November 2008, Art. 2.

Recruitment for the civil service is based on the principle of openness and competitiveness. The requirement of merit-based recruitment to the civil service 'is aimed, *inter alia*, at enhancing the legitimacy of the public employment system as a whole'.[119] The Polish legislator therefore provided that every person who fulfilled the formal requirements would be given the opportunity of entering the civil service. The recruitment system in Poland is thus founded on the principle of open access to employment in government administration of every Polish citizen and every citizen of the European Union Member States (as well as other countries that Poland has concluded agreements with in that respect).[120]

As for civil service candidates, all consecutive acts on the civil service (except for the Act of 24 August 2006) guaranteed the application of the accessibility, openness and competitiveness criteria. Recruitment for the Polish civil service is formally independent of such factors as the candidate's political affiliation, social background, material status, sex, religion or race. This also means that any criteria applied in the selection of employees for specific positions should be merit-based, i.e. take into account the candidate's relevant education, qualifications and skills.

Anyone wishing to join the civil service is required to meet certain standardised conditions that are general knowledge. Recruitment should be open in nature, in other words follow the principles of openness, equality and transparency, and information about vacant posts available to all without discrimination. Open recruitment may also entail the duty to provide access to documents and information as well as to allow representatives of relevant institutions to personally participate in the recruitment procedure. The general binding principle is that of equal opportunities for all those wishing to enter public service.

Competitive recruitment means the requirement of organising qualification procedures in such a way as to enable the selection from among the applicants one that best meets the requirements specified for the post in question. The proper implementation of the competitive recruitment principle means ensuring uniform rules, methods, instruments, evaluation criteria and conditions to all candidates for self-presentation, and the guaranty that the requirements in the recruitment announcements remain unchanged throughout all stages of the recruitment process.

---

119 OECD (1999), 'European Principles for Public Administration', *SIGMA Papers*, No. 27, OECD Publishing. p. 22.

120 In accordance with the 1982 ruling of the European Court of Justice (currently the Court of Justice) every EU citizen has the right to seek employment with the administration of every EU Member State.

Pursuant to the Act of 21 November 2008, to be eligible for employment in the civil service, one must be a Polish citizen (subject to provisions under Article 5), enjoy full civil rights, have no convictions by a final judgement for a deliberate fiscal offence, have the qualifications required for a given post and enjoy an impeccable reputation.

The impeccable reputation requirement returns as the topic of discussion with the latest act on the civil service. None of the acts to date have set the basis for determining the criteria for the interpretation of the concept of 'impeccable reputation'. The impeccable reputation requirement is not verified; there are no institutions that issue a 'certificate' to that effect or verify the candidate's claim of having it. It is an underdefined requirement, blurred, necessitating moral and ethical evaluation, difficult to interpret and apply in practice, as concrete principles of determining whether a candidate is in fact enjoying impeccable reputation have not been worked out.

The concept of 'impeccable reputation' therefore expresses how the candidate is perceived by other people. Undoubtedly, a person is identified as enjoying an impeccable reputation if he represents such traits as honesty, integrity, responsibility, loyalty, the ability of putting public interest before private interest, the skill of working with other people. These criteria however are not very precise.[121]

It is the director-general who organises the recruitment of candidates for the civil service corps (including the recruitment of graduates of the National School of Public Administration) and has the duty to make information on existing vacancies in the civil service available by announcing it in the ministry's Public Information Bulletin and the Bulletin of Public Information of the Chancellery of the Prime Minister as well as indicating, with the consent of the Head of the Civil Service, the vacant posts that are available not only to Polish but also other EU

---

121 For recruitment purposes in the case of senior civil service posts in the Mazowsze Voivodship Office in Warszawa, the fact of a candidate, selected through the recruitment procedure, having impeccable reputation is determined following the opinion of the office's top management. It is worth mentioning here that the decision of employing the best qualified candidate is taken each time by the director-general of that office, while the task of the recruitment committee is to assess – in accordance with Art. 56.4 of the 2008 Civil Service Act – the candidate's professional experience, knowledge required to perform the duties in the specific post and managerial competence. The document confirming the candidate having impeccable reputation are the minutes of recruitment approved by the director-general of the office. K. Mroczka, Head of Human Resources Management Branch, Personnel and Organisation Bureau at the Mazowsze Voivodship Office in Warsaw, statement made on 15 May 2012.

citizens as well as citizens of other countries, provided that they have the right to take up employment in the territory of the Republic of Poland pursuant to international agreements or Community law. Non-nationals can be employed in posts that do not involve direct participation in the exercise of public authority or in any activity aimed at protecting the general functions of the state, provided that they have a certificate confirming their command of Polish.[122]

In 2010 the Head of the Civil Service received 91 applications from non-nationals for approval to seek employment in the civil service and issued 77 approvals (85% of total submitted). In 2011 there were 138 such applications submitted, of which 118 were positively approved. In 2011 there were 129 vacancy announcements open to non-nationals published – however, no one was employed.

Applications were turned down for posts involving, for example, tax proceedings, issuing decisions, conducting inspections (in public administration as well as in private businesses) and imposing fines.[123]

The deadline for submitting documents, specified in the recruitment announcement, cannot be less than 10 days from the date of the recruitment announcement and in the case of an offer for replacement of an absent corps member – 5 days (Article 28.3). First and last names of the candidates as well as the recruitment results constitute public information (Article 29).

In the recruitment of candidates for the civil service to posts related to national defence, priority is given to persons discharged from professional military service.

If the employment quota for disabled persons, as defined under provisions of regulations concerning occupational and social rehabilitation and employment of disabled persons, is below 6% in the month preceding the date of the recruitment announcement in that office, priority of employment is given to a disabled person, provided the candidate is among the five[124] best qualified candidates or

---

122 Rozporządzenie Prezesa Rady Ministrów z dnia 23 kwietnia 2009 r. *w sprawie rodzajów dokumentów potwierdzających znajomość języka polskiego przez osoby nieposiadające obywatelstwa polskiego, ubiegające sie o zatrudnienie w służbie cywilnej*, [Regulation of the Prime Minister dated 23 April 2009 on the Type of Documents Certifying Command of the Polish Language by Persons not Carrying Polish Citizenship Applying for Employment in the Civil Service], Dz.U. No. 64, item 539.

123 D. Suprun, 'Cudzoziemcy a służba cywilna. Doświadczenia związane ze stosowaniem Art. 5 ustawy o służbie cywilnej, przewidującego możliwość zatrudniania w korpusie cudzoziemców', *Przegląd Służby Cywilnej*, 2012, No. 1 (16), p. 10.

124 Civil Service Act of 21 November 2008, Art. 29a.

among two[125] in the case of senior positions in the civil service. Employment of disabled persons in the Polish civil service in 2011 was at a level of merely 2.8% compared to the targeted minimum employment index specified in the Act on Occupational and Social Rehabilitation and Employment of the Disabled. In 2011, as a result of recruitment to posts in the civil service other than the senior ones, 67 disabled persons were employed, which is 1% of the total employed in 2011. There were no applications for senior positions from disabled persons.[126]

Among the most often cited problems concerning the adaptation of disabled persons in the offices are: 'the office (as a whole) not being adapted to the needs of disabled persons, the specificity of a number of jobs that limits or prevents the discharge of duties by disabled persons or workplaces not being adapted to the needs of disabled persons'.[127]

Recruitment to posts for border veterinary surgeons and their deputies is organised by the chief veterinary surgeon. The voivodship veterinarian organizes recruitment for the posts of poviat veterinary surgeons and their deputies. The recruitment procedure for the civil service applies in all these cases.

Once recruitment is completed, the director-general immediately makes its results available in a publicly accessible place in the office premises, in the office bulletin and the bulletin of the Chancellery. The information contains: the name and address of the office, the specification of the post, name and surname of the selected candidate and his place of residence, as stipulated by the Civil Code provisions (i.e. town – the full address is not given). The full names of candidates who meet formal requirements and the recruitment results constitute public information to the extent covered by the requirements specified in the recruitment announcement.

Should there be a need to assign the same position again within 3 months from establishing an employment relationship with the person selected in the recruitment process, the director-general of the office can employ in that position the next person from among the best qualified candidates listed in the minutes of that recruitment procedure.

The selection of candidates for employment in the Polish civil service is but one of the stages of the recruitment procedure during which candidates who do not meet formal requirements are eliminated. Formal requirements include

125 Ibid, Art. 57.

126 'Sprawozdanie Szefa Służby Cywilnej o stanie służby cywilnej i realizacji zadań tej służby w 2011 roku', 2012 Head of CS report for 2011, Warszawa, March 2012, pp. 24–25.

127 Ibid, p. 26.

relevant education, professional experience, seniority, prompt delivery of all required documents, working experience in public administration, relevant expertise, computer skills and knowledge of computer programmes, ability to operate office equipment, suitable professional qualifications and certificates, command of foreign languages, completed courses and training (including continuous education).

Pursuant to the Ordinance of the Head of Civil Service of 30 May 2012[128] the director-general of office had the duty to define, or adapt to the new standards, internal recruitment procedures for the civil service in that office within 6 months of the Ordinance coming into effect. The procedures should ensure that recruitment methods and techniques as well as assessment criteria are clearly defined before the recruitment is announced in order to ensure fair and objective evaluation. They should specify clearly the criteria for participation in successive stages of the recruitment procedure; indicate the threshold required to pass the competence tests; maintain the same recruitment principles for all participants; assure conformity of the recruitment announcement with the job description; ensure selection of candidates in accordance with requirements specified in the recruitment announcement; inform candidates of equal opportunity principles, of being qualified to the next round of the recruitment procedure and so on. The ordinance is intended to guarantee the upholding of the principles of openness and competitiveness in the recruitment for employment in the civil service and ensuring the employment of those with the best qualifications for work in the corps.

The number of those interested in employment in the Polish civil service varies each year. It would seem that employment in the civil service would reflect the situation on the labour market; that a growing economy would reduce interest in work in the civil service and the opposite in times of recession. However, for each work place in government administration, there were 34 applicants in 2004, 26 in 2005, down to merely 12 in 2007 and 14 in 2008. In 2009, 39% of government administration offices reported having difficulty in recruiting suitable persons for employment in the civil service. Increased interest was noted in 2010; for each job in positions other than senior civil service posts, there were 27 candidates on average, and their number rose to 35 in 2011.

---

128 Załącznik do Zarządzenia Nr 3 Szefa Służby Cywilnej z 30 maja 2012 r. *w sprawie standardów zarządzania zasobami ludzkimi w służbie cywilnej, III. Nabór i wprowadzenie do pracy,* [Attachment to Ordinance No. 3 of the Head of Civil Service dated 30 May 2012 on Standards of Human Resources Management in the Civil Service, Chapter III. Recruitment and Introduction to the Job.]

The Chancellery of the Prime Minister describes recruitment for the civil service as based on the institution of 'good practice' that means 'the principle of equal treatment, the principle of constancy of the requirements and evaluation criteria, the principle of impartiality and independence, the principle of professionalism, the principle of controlled subjectivity, and the principle of transparency'.[129] The novelty is the 'principle of controlled subjectivity' which has not been applied until now. It is understood to mean a recruitment process conducted by a team which by 'reaching a consensus reduces the degree of subjectivity in the assessment. The decision is made jointly after consideration of all options and the discussion enables the rejection of the most extreme valuations'.

The principle of 'controlled subjectivity' should come under criticism for the discretionary element in the team's decision-making process when selecting the best qualified candidate, as it can result in the employment of a candidate who had not achieved the highest scores. This principle raises justified controversy not only among the rejected candidates who were not employed despite achieving the highest scores but also, in the opinion of this author, as it raises the suspicion of partiality and competition 'fixing' to employ a particular candidate.

The principle of 'controlled subjectivity' was restricted in 2012 by the amendment of the Civil Service Act[130], by ordering the commission to employ a candidate who is a disabled person should he/she be among the five best qualified candidates, and in the case of recruitment for senior positions – among the two of the best qualified candidates.

The recruitment process in the Polish civil service is formalised and laborious and 'does not provide guarantees that the future civil servant selected through this process will have the necessary qualifications and skills to execute the duties of a civil servant professionally'.[131]

Among the most cited problems connected with the recruitment process are those related to the functioning of the labour market, the recruitment itself, its preparation and execution, the financial situation of the office, government

---

129 Prime Minister's Chancellery, <www.kprm.gov.pl>, accessed 10 May 2012.

130 Ustawa z dnia 19 sierpnia 2011 r. *o zmianie ustawy o służbie cywilnej oraz niektórych innych ustaw*, [Act of 19 August 2011 Amending the Civil Service Act and Certain Other Acts], Dz.U. No. 201, item 1183, Art. 29a.

131 NIK audit report, 'Funkcjonowanie służby cywilnej w ramach obowiązujących regulacji prawnych, Informacja o wynikach kontroli', Najwyższa Izba Kontroli, Warszawa, March 2012, p. 32.

policy and mistrust towards non-nationals.[132] It should also be noted that the civil service law does not foresee many options to appeal decisions for those who passed the recruitment process, qualified for the qualification interview but nevertheless were not employed. They can appeal to the Head of the Civil Service or a labour court.

Another problem is the long waiting period for results of recruitment to posts of director-general, in some cases as long as one year. What is more, one of the arguments for changes in the 1998 Civil Service Act was the very need to eliminate the long process of filling these positions so important from the view of civil service administration. The recruitment procedure for director-general posts itself also raises serious objections; candidates for this post take competency tests consisting of a hundred questions. This is a rather archaic form in that it is a one-sided test that does not allow the verification of genuine competency of a candidate for a managerial position responsible for the administration of an office. It is also difficult to explain why there is no posted list of candidates who meet the formal requirements. Considering that the legislator assumed the recruitment to be open and competitive, the lack of information about the candidates for director-general contradicts this principle.

It also seems that the problem with recruitment lies not only in the lack of interest in employment with the civil service by the so-called experts (specialists) but in the lack of stability in the legal status of civil service corps members; the result of the frequent changes in regulations due to which work in the civil service is treated as a springboard to future professional careers in private businesses.

## Employment Relationships

The employment relationship of a civil servant is established on the basis of an employment contract for a fixed or permanent term. In the case of a first-time employment in the civil service, the contract is made for a fixed-term – 12 months – that can be terminated at two weeks' notice. The director-general of the office decides on a permanent term employment contract with the employee on the basis of a positive assessment of his/her work. A permanent term employment contract can be established with persons who completed their preparatory service period and received a positive first assessment in the civil service;

132 In 2009 an Italian citizen staying in Poland was seeking employment in the civil service and was rejected on the grounds of not holding Polish citizenship. By order of the district court in Warsaw he was allowed to take part in the competition.

with those who had been employed in the civil service earlier or on the basis of the Employees of State Offices Act of 16 September 1982; or persons who had a fixed-term employment contract and had been discharged from professional military service with the Ministry of National Defence or local administration units reporting to that ministry.

It seems quite interesting that among countries covered by an OECD study the highest proportion of women employed in central administration has been noted in Poland – 69%, next in Portugal and Iceland – 61%, New Zealand and Greece – 59%. Their proportion is the lowest in Turkey – 12%, Japan – 20% and Germany – 22%.[133] The high share of women employed in the Polish civil service could be explained by greater work stability for that group of workers which, although offering lower wages, is particularly attractive to women with families, especially those with children, yet unappealing to men seeking better-paid jobs.

Employment by age in the Polish civil service indicates that the 30 to 50 age group is the largest, accounting for more than 50% of the total employed, while the smallest is that of the under 30s – around 15%.[134]

In the opinion of the civil servants themselves, the most attractive aspects of work in the civil service are remuneration, work stability, working climate and satisfaction from work accomplished. Professional prestige is at the bottom of the list.[135]

## Qualifying Procedures in the Civil Service – Nomination

Another form of employment in government administration offices that impacts the development of professionalism is nomination. A nomination is an individual act of administration that confirms the civil servant satisfies a set of specific requirements. It is a specific form of expression of the will of the state to employ a person. 'Appointment, otherwise known as a nomination, is the basis of entering an administrative employment relationship. An administrative (official) employment relationship differs from a labour (obligatory) employment relationship in that the parties thereto – the employee, called in some of these relations an official, and the employer – are not equal. The specific nature of work, referred to in Article 76 of the Labour Code, may require from the employee (official) greater flexibility and availability as the employer and situation require. In other words, the employer is entitled to temporarily change the relevant terms and conditions

133 Prime Minister's Chancellery, <www.kprm.gov.pl>, accessed 10 May 2012.
134 'Sprawozdanie Szefa Służby Cywilnej', 2012, op.cit., Table No. 8.
135 NIK audit report, March 2012, op.cit., p. 54.

of employment of the nominated employee whose duty is to do as instructed. Such an employee, a civil servant, can be temporarily reassigned to another office in the same or another town/city, to a similar or a different post to that for which he/she was originally nominated. Civil servants have the duty to obey the orders of their superiors. They undergo systematic qualifications assessments. They cannot take up additional employment without previous approval from the head of the office. For violation of duties they are subject to regulations concerning disciplinary responsibility. Greater subordination and availability of those employed on the basis of administrative employment relationships are compensated with greater stability of employment'.[136]

The act of nomination is performed by the Head of the Civil Service in the name of the Republic of Poland. The act is drawn in written form and contains the first and last name of the civil servant and the date of the nomination. The nomination does not mean entering into a new employment relationship but only the conversion of the existing employment relationship into one on the basis of nomination.[137] A nomination means, on the one hand, a higher degree of availability on the part of the employee but, on the other hand, a high level of security of a steady employment relationship.[138] Despite this, the draft of the so-called Act[139] on Optimisation prepared by the government did not exempt civil servants from dismissal as it did in the case of work-safety inspectors. The

---

136 Compare A. M. Świątkowski, *Kodeks pracy. Komentarz*, Warszawa, 2010.

137 Civil Service Act of 18 December 1998, Art. 37.4.

138 W. Drobny, M. Mazuryk and P. Zuzankiewicz, *Ustawa o służbie cywilnej. Komentarz*, Warszawa, 2010, p. 248.

139 On 27 October 2010 the Council of Ministers approved a draft bill on optimising employment levels in state budget entities and in certain other entities of the public finance sector in the years 2011–2013. The draft predicted the introduction of regulations that were to curtail employment in public administration, improve the effectiveness and performance of tasks through the introduction of changes in the employment structure, and lower the operating costs of public administration. The draft predicted a 10% decrease in employment in the public administration sector compared to employment levels for the end of the second quarter of 2010. On 7 January 2011 President Komorowski applied to the Constitutional Tribunal to verify the consistency of certain provisions of the bill with the Constitution. In its judgement of 14 June 2011, the Tribunal adjudicated that Art. 2 in conjunction with Art. 7.1 of the Act of 16 December 2010 on Optimising Employment Levels in State Budget Entities and in Certain Other Entities of the Public Finance Sector in the Years 2011–2013, insofar as it regards civil servants, was inconsistent with Art. 2 and Art. 153.1 of the Constitution. Judgment of the Constitutional Tribunal dated 14 June 2011. File ref.: Kp 1/11.

question whether this suggests the depreciation of the position of civil servants seems rhetorical.[140]

There is a qualification procedure that serves to verify the candidate's knowledge and skills indispensable in performing the duties of a civil servant. Scores are allotted for each part of the test. The number of nominations is limited in accordance with their limit set down in the Budget Act. As a result, apart from a positive completion of the qualification procedure, the applicant needs to achieve results sufficient for appointment within the set limit.

The employment relationship of those employed on the basis of nomination pursuant to the Employees of State Offices Act of 16 September 1982 was converted as of 1 January 2004 to an employment relationship on the basis of a permanent-term employment contract. In August 2003 the Constitutional Tribunal determined that this conversion was consistent with the Constitution. The changes in the regulation were made in such a way, however, that employment relationships on the basis of nomination in government administration offices pursuant to the 1982 Act continued to function beyond the set date, i.e. until 31 December 2010. In the meantime, in accordance with the Civil Service Act of 24 August 2006 employment relationships on the basis of nomination were altogether scrapped as of 1 January 2007.

Civil servants nominated in compliance with the Act of 5 July 1996 kept their status under the new Civil Service Act of 18 December 1998, but regardless of their civil service category and position, they were awarded the lowest official rank without guarantee of keeping their previous remuneration.

Nomination preceded by a qualification procedure was also decreed under the 1998 Act.

Since 2006 the qualification procedure for civil servants applying for nomination is conducted by the National School of Public Administration (KSAP). Pursuant to the Act of 24 August 2006 applicants for nomination in the civil service have to be civil service employees with a minimum years of employment with the service of three years (the duration of employment in a state government office was not taken into consideration before 1 July 1999) or have the consent of the office director-general to take the qualification tests before the end of that period but not earlier than after two years of employment with the civil service; hold an MA degree or its equivalent; command at least one foreign language from the group of working languages of the European Union; be a reservist soldier or exempt from general defence duty.

140 More in Chapter 6. The Politicisation of the Polish Civil Service.

Pursuant to the Act of 21 November 2008, to become a civil servant one has to apply through KSAP. Applicants for nomination in the civil service have to be civil service employees with a minimum of three years employment with the service or the consent of the office director-general to take the qualification tests before the end of that period but not earlier than after two years of employment with the civil service; hold an MA degree or its equivalent; command at least one foreign language from the group of working languages of the European Union or one of the following foreign languages: Arab, Belorussian, Chinese, Icelandic, Japanese, Norwegian, Russian, Ukrainian; be a reservist soldier or exempt from general defence duty. The fact that one meets those conditions requires confirmation from the director-general of the relevant office on the basis of documents held by that office or documents submitted by the applicant. The director-general also confirms whether the applicant has Polish citizenship, enjoys full civil rights and has not been convicted by a final judgement for a deliberate fiscal or other indictable offence.

The person wishing to enter the qualification procedure applies to the Head of the Civil Service by submitting his/her application directly to KSAP or by sending it by post addressed to KSAP with an annotation: 'application to enter the qualification procedure'. Proof of payment of the participation fee into the KSAP bank account is required with the application. In 2012 the fee was PLN 525. Graduates of the National School of Public Administration submit their applications for civil service nomination to the Head of the Civil Service.

Both, the application to enter the qualification procedure and the application for civil service nomination by KSAP graduates, need to be submitted in the period from 1 January to 31 May. The director-general of the relevant office confirms that the applicant meets the requirement of Polish citizenship, has a clean criminal record, sufficient number of years of service, the relevant education and knowledge of foreign languages.

The qualification procedure verifies the knowledge and skills necessary for the execution of civil service duties.[141] The results of the qualification tests are scored in points. Each part of the test is scored separately. To achieve a positive result one must obtain in each part of the test at least 1/3 of the maximum points attributed to that part and a total of at least 3/5 of the maximum points possible for

141 Rozporządzenie Prezesa Rady Ministrów z dnia 16 grudnia 2009 r. *w sprawie sposobu przeprowadzania postępowania kwalifikacyjnego w służbie cywilnej,* [Regulation of the Prime Minister dated 16 December 2009 on How to Conduct the Qualification Procedure in the Civil Service ], Dz. U. No. 218, item 1695.

the whole test. The summed up scores are published in the Chancellery Bulletin beginning with the highest total scores down to the lowest.

The requirements that have to be met by civil service employees seeking nomination have changed over time. A contentious point has been the issue of foreign language knowledge. In accordance with the Act of 5 July 1998, candidates were simply required to know a foreign language without specifying which language it should be. Pursuant to the Act of 18 December 1998 (by Regulation of the Council of Ministers), certificates confirming knowledge of specific foreign languages were introduced for candidates seeking nomination. The Act of 24 August 2006 indicated that a candidate should know at least one foreign language from the group of working languages of the European Union (thus excluding persons with knowledge of Russian, for example). The Act of 21 November 2008 is more precise and states that the precondition to taking the qualification procedure is knowledge of at least one foreign language from the group of working languages of the European Union or one of the following foreign languages: Arab, Belorussian, Chinese, Icelandic, Japanese, Norwegian, Russian, Ukrainian. The adopted solution is the effect of consensus and twelve years of experience of the civil service.

In 2009, with the aim of encouraging office employees to raise their qualifications, the Council of Ministers provided civil servants with 12 additional days of paid leave. After being nominated to civil servant, he/ she is awarded their first service rank. The civil servant can be advanced to the next service rank after receiving a positive periodical assessment if it contains a motivated request of the direct superior to advance the civil servant to the next service rank.[142] A civil servant who from his/her last advancement in rank received two successive positive periodical evaluations at one of the two highest levels of the score scale advances to the next service rank within a 30 day period from the date he/she receives the results of the periodical assessment.[143]

In 2000 the limit for nominations was 2800, the initial limit for 2001 was set at 2200 and for 2002–2500 nominations. After adjustments, it was determined that a realistic limit for the years 2001–2003 would be 500 for each of those years, but in 2004 the limit rose to 600 and to 1500 in 2005. In 2006 – the limit was set at 2000 nominations, in 2007–3000, in 2008–1000, in 2009–1500, in 2010–2000 and in 2011–2500. Due to the recession however the limit for the years 2008–2010 was lowered to 1000 nominations and for 2011 – to 500.

142 Civil Service Act of 21 November 2008, Art. 89.1.

143 Ibid, Art. 89.2.

The number of nominations actually kept falling below the set limits until 2009 when this tendency was reversed. In 2007, when the limit was 3000, only 718 applicants sat for the exams. In 2008, with the limit set at 1000, there were 887 candidates with only 598 achieving their goal of becoming civil servants. The year 2009 saw 1059 candidates sitting for the exams, of which 530 were successful. 1760 candidates took the exam in 2011. Of those, 1348 (76.59%) passed it with positive results, but only 32.05% of them (or 24.54% of the total that took the exam) managed to win nomination due to the limit set in the Budget Act for 2011 (the limit was 500 nominations and included graduates of KSAP who applied to the Head of the Civil Service for nomination to the civil service that year). Among those who passed the exam successfully, women were a majority – representing 72.33% of the total candidates. This was several percentage points higher than in 2009 and 2010 when women accounted for 68.49% and 67.88%, respectively.[144] The youngest candidate to enter the qualification procedure was 23 years old, and the eldest was 69 years old.

Despite much interest in the qualification procedure, the formation of a civil service based on nominated civil servants is still barely in its initial stage. The goal was for civil servants to account for 15%, at the very least, of the civil service corps and be selected through internal competitive recruitment to fill senior posts in the civil service. That the Polish civil service is in its infancy is clearly illustrated by the fact that in 2000 civil servants accounted for 1% of the civil service corps and as on 1 January 2012–4.4%. For the years 2013–2015 the Head of the Civil Service proposes a limit of 600 nominations a year.

Unfortunately, yet again the legislator displayed lack of consequence. It was originally assumed, as mentioned earlier, that the objective was for civil servants to account for 15% of the civil service corps, yet in the *Strategy for human resources management in the civil service* it was assumed that it would reach 10% in the years 2011–2020. Despite this, the limit of nominations in succeeding years is being systematically lowered. According to NIK, the Supreme Audit Office, this may impede the achievement of the *Strategy* nomination targets. NIK points out that '"optimisation" of expenses connected with the nomination of civil servants cannot rely exclusively on limiting their numbers'.[145]

144 'Postępowanie kwalifikacyjne w służbie cywilnej w 2011 r. Analiza danych statystycznych dotyczących osób, które w 2011 r. zakończyły sprawdzian w toku postępowania kwalifikacyjnego służbie cywilnej z wynikiem pozytywnym', in P. Marczewski (ed.), *Przegląd Służby Cywilnej,* 2011, No. 5 (14), p. 10.

145 NIK audit report, March 2012, op. cit., p. 13.

Civil servants enjoy a high degree of stability of employment. The majority of them occupy responsible posts in accordance with their qualifications. However, despite receiving high notes in their periodical assessments, the majority await promotion up the service hierarchy for years, receiving instead only an upgrading to the successive service ranks. Almost 2/3 of respondents, in a study conducted by NIK inspectors among civil servants, were convinced that principles of hierarchal promotion in their offices were not defined, or they were unaware of their implementation. The hierarchal promotion system was considered by 40% of respondents as unjust and by nearly half of them as lacking transparency. Many believed having friends in the right places greatly improved chances for promotion.[146]

## Preparatory Service

Preparatory service is undoubtedly conductive to professional development among the civil service.[147] It was introduced in the Polish civil service under the Act of 18 December 1998 and became the requirement for newly recruited personnel, employed for the first time in the civil service on the basis of a fixed-term employment contract.

In turn, the Act of 24 August 2006 minimised the importance of preparatory service limiting it to three months and requiring its application only in cases considered necessary by the director-general.[148]

The Civil Service Act of 21 November 2008 determined that the aim of preparatory service is to provide theoretical and practical knowledge to first-time employees in the civil service to prepare them for the proper execution of the tasks awaiting them.[149] The preparatory period lasts four months and needs to be completed, ending with a test, not later than the end of eight months from the civil servant's date of employment. By law, graduates of the National School of Public Administration are exempt from preparatory service. The Act allows a civil service corps member also to be exempt from preparatory service by the director-general. This however does not exempt the corps member from the requirement of passing the preparatory service test.

There is no doubt that the preparatory service serves the enhancement of professionalism among civil servants, however, even in this case the legislator seems

146 Ibid, p. 41.

147 Civil Service Act of 18 December 1998, Art. 25.

148 Civil Service Act of 24 August 2006, Art. 17.

149 Civil Service Act of 21 November 2008, Art. 36.2.

unable to agree as to its scope and duration. In effect, it seems that the calculation of preparatory service duration is not based on authentic needs or experience but the need to stress by another political decision-maker the distinction of newly introduced solutions concerning the civil service.

By 30 June 2011 practically all persons employed in the civil service under the provisions of the Act of 21 November 2008 had undergone their preparatory service that gave the newly employed persons the opportunity of becoming acquainted with the practical tasks the office deals with.[150]

## The First and Successive Periodical Assessments of Employees

Employee performance evaluations represent another factor in the professionalisation of the civil service cadres. The periodic evaluation of civil service corps members provides an important instrument in human resources management that serves the improvement of work effectiveness of civil service corps members.

A periodical performance assessment of civil service corps members has three main objectives and serves to:

- motivate employees,
- correct their conduct,
- develop their competency.

The periodical performance evaluation of civil service corps members is carried out by the direct superior of the employee under assessment (or other person, as designated in Article 81.2(1, 2, 4) of the Civil Service Act) on the basis of criteria relevant to the position of the employee undergoing evaluation.

The person performing the assessment should select the appropriate criteria after discussing with the person being evaluated the scope of his/her duties, his/her own expectations as to the level of meeting the criteria during the period under evaluation as well as discussing targets set out for the employee and methods of achieving them.[151]

The performance assessment fulfils an important role in the case of civil service corps members as long as it realises – as in the case of the private sector – several functions: evaluative, motivational, decision-making, developmental and educational. It develops the attitudes and conduct of civil service corps members.

---

150 NIK audit report, March 2012, op.cit., p. 27.

151 B. Stolarczyk, *Praktyczne aspekty zarządzania zasobami ludzkimi w służbie cywilnej. Poradnik,* J. Itrich-Drabarek et al. (eds.), Warszawa, 2012, pp. 37–45.

Subjected to the assessment, pursuant to the successive Acts, were either civil service corps members or only the civil servants. It seems obvious that if performance assessment is applied to all of the civil service corps its influence on the improvement of professionalism in the corps is greater.

The periodic assessment involves the evaluation of the performance of duties by a civil service corps member as specified in his/her job description. It is made in writing and duly presented to the person it concerns. The assessments are carried out every 24 months and contain conclusions as to the individual professional development programme of each corps member. They are also made when there a corps member is transferred to another position that involves a significant change in the scope of his/her duties if the period from the last evaluation exceeds six months. A person employed for the first time in the civil service undergoes the first evaluation if the period under evaluation is longer than six months. In the civil service a person substituting for an absent civil service corps member may also undergo a first evaluation. Exempt from the first evaluation are graduates of KSAP who applied for nomination to the civil service.

The first performance assessment takes into consideration the person's attitude, commitment, progress at work, relations with colleagues, timely execution of tasks, results of the preparatory service test and the report drawn up by the evaluated employee on the tasks he/she performed during the time of employment.

In 2011 there were nearly five thousand first-time performance assessments made, of which 97% were positive. In the opinion of the Head of the Civil Service, this high proportion may be the result of the successfulness of the recruitment process as well as the effectiveness and integration of the first performance assessment system in the civil service.[152]

Following the evaluation, the head of the organisational unit applies to the director-general of office for conclusion of a permanent-term employment contract in the case of a positively assessed result and for non-conclusion of such or termination of a fixed-term employment contract in the case of a negative result.

In cases of justified absence from work exceeding one month of the person to be evaluated the date of assessment is deferred accordingly. The assessing person can reschedule the date of assessment whenever: there was a change in the position of the assessing person during the evaluation period of the person to be assessed; absence of the person to be assessed is expected, longer and justified that can make the evaluation difficult or altogether impossible; the person being assessed applies

152 'Sprawozdanie Szefa Służby Cywilnej', 2012, p. 26.

for a change in the date of the assessment and the period from his/her last assessment exceeds six months; and, in the case of persons assessed for the first time, if the period subject to evaluation exceeds six months. Should the evaluation be negative, the civil service corps member will have to undergo the assessment process in six months time from the date of receiving the assessment results.

The assessed civil servant has the right to appeal against the assessment results within 7 days from receiving them. The appeal has to be considered within 14 days from the date of its submission. Should the appeal be considered justified, the periodical evaluation is changed or repeated. The assessed person is entitled to an identical appeal against a second assessment. Should the appeal not be considered in the prescribed time limit or be rejected, the civil service corps member has the right, within 14 days from receiving the decision or when the 14 day limit for the decision has passed, to appeal to the labour court.

In 2011 periodical assessments were made of 86 718 persons, of which 398 were negative (of which 17 concerned civil servants), or 0.4% of total assessments.[153]

## Liability and Penalties in the Civil Service

In the case of disciplinary liability of civil service corps members the key words are:

- explanatory proceedings,
- the course of disciplinary proceedings,
- disciplinary penalties,
- warnings,
- disciplinary commissions (their make-up, rulings procedure),
- disciplinary ombudsman,
- erasure of disciplinary penalties.

Disciplinary liability applies to both civil servants and civil service employees. All civil service corps members are disciplinarily responsible for breach of duty. Disciplinary proceedings cannot be initiated after the lapse of three months from acknowledgment by the director-general of office of information of the breach of duty by a civil servant or after two years from the time of the act's occurrence. Should the civil servant be unable to present his/her explanation due to his/her absence from work, the course of the three-month period does not commence or, if already commenced, is postponed until the civil servant reports back for work.

153 Ibid, p. 31.

Should the act of the civil servant bear elements of a criminal offence, the period of limitation cannot be shorter than that ruled by the provisions of the Penal Code.

Disciplinary penalties are various in nature. Disciplinary penalties applied to civil service employees are the following:

- warning,
- reprimand,
- decrease in the basic salary, but by no more than 25% for a period not longer than six months,
- expulsion from work.

Disciplinary penalties applied to civil servants are, on the other hand, the following:

- warning,
- reprimand,
- deprivation of the chance of promotion to higher service rank for a period of two years,
- decrease in the basic salary, but by no more than 25% for a period not longer than six months,
- downgrading to a lower rank in the civil service,
- expulsion from the civil service (the penalty carries a ban on employment in the civil service corps for a period of five years).

In cases of minor breaches of duty, the director-general of office may punish the civil servant with a written warning. The penalty may be preceded with explanatory proceedings to clarify the circumstances of the case. The civil servant is entitled to appeal the penalty to the director-general of office within seven days of its imposition. Should this happen, the director-general of the office should pass the appeal to the disciplinary ombudsman without delay. This done, the explanatory proceedings are initiated.[154]

Disciplinary cases involving civil service corps members are examined by disciplinary commissions:

- of first instance – the disciplinary commission,
- of second instance – the High Disciplinary Civil Service Commission.

154 In 2011 saw the initiation of 591 explanatory proceedings. In 288 cases, there was no need to adjudicate while in 277 cases disciplinary procedures were initiated. 158 disciplinary penalties were declared legally binding, including one that concerned expulsion from work, ibid, p. 37.

Disciplinary cases involving senior staff at director-general of office level are examined by the High Disciplinary Civil Service Commission, both in the first and in the second instance. Disciplinary cases involving persons holding positions of voivodship veterinary surgeons and their deputies are examined in the first instance by disciplinary commissions working in the offices of the chief veterinary surgeon.

Members of the disciplinary commission of the office are appointed by the director-general of office from among civil service corps members employed in that office. Directors-general of offices may, by mutual agreement, appoint a joint disciplinary commission for their respective offices. The Head of the Civil Service is immediately notified of the appointment of a disciplinary commission. A disciplinary commission comprising at least 10 members is appointed for a 4 year term. The commission selects from among its members the commission's chairperson and two deputies. The commission's working procedures are governed by rules of procedure adopted by the commission and approved by the director-general of office. Members of the commission are independent in their disciplinary rulings and are not bound by the decisions of other law enforcing bodies, with the exception of legally binding decisions of courts.

The High Disciplinary Civil Service Commission is appointed by the Prime Minister. The Commission comprises 15 members appointed for a 6 year term, including 12 who are appointed upon the request of the Head of the Civil Service from among civil servants and 3 upon the request of the director-general of foreign services from among members of the diplomatic and consular staff. These Commission Members perform their functions until the appointment of their successors. Members of the Commission select from among themselves the commission chairperson and his/her deputies. The Chancellery of the Prime Minister provides backup support to the High Disciplinary Commission. The High Disciplinary Commission examines appeals against the decisions of disciplinary commissions.[155]

The disciplinary commissions adjudicate composed of:

- in first instance, when the disciplinary ombudsman requests the application of the penalty of expulsion from the civil service or from work in the

155 Civil Service Act of 21 November 2008, Art. 113. In 2011 the Commission examined 57 appeals against the decisions of disciplinary commissions of particular offices, of which in 15 cases upheld in force the decisions of the disciplinary commissions in the first instance, ibid, p. 39.

office – five members, including the chairperson with a degree in law, and in other cases – three members,[156]

- in second instance – five members, of which at least two with law degrees when examining cases where the penalty adjudicated was expulsion from the civil service or from work in the office.

The chairperson of a disciplinary commission appoints the panel determining the case and the date of the hearing. In examinations of disciplinary cases of directors-general, the panel determining the case in second instance is composed of commission members who have not been involved in the examination of those cases in first instance.

The disciplinary ombudsman initiates explanatory proceedings on the order accordingly, as applicable, of: the director-general, Head of the Civil Service or chief veterinary surgeon, and informs them of the findings of such proceedings. The ombudsman informs the person concerned of the initiation of proceedings against him/her. The ombudsman decides whether to request the disciplinary commission to initiate disciplinary proceedings or, with the consent of those who first ordered it (the director-general, Head of the Civil Service or chief veterinary surgeon), of no need to proceed with the explanatory proceedings. The course of proceedings is as follows: the disciplinary commission initiates disciplinary proceedings on the day it receives the application from the disciplinary ombudsman to initiate proceedings; the defendant is entitled to assistance of defence counsel appointed by him/herself, subject to statutory law regulations concerning secrecy.

In cases when the disciplinary ombudsman applies for the penalty of expulsion from the civil service or from work in the office and the defendant has no defence counsel of his choosing, the panel's chairperson appoints the defence counsel from among civil service corps members.[157]

The disciplinary commission issues its decision at the end of proceedings after having heard the disciplinary ombudsman and the defendant and his defence counsel, if any, and after examination of all other evidence pertaining to the case.

---

156 By the end of 2011 there were disciplinary commissions appointed in over 84% of offices, ibid.

157 The disciplinary ombudsman of an office, and in justified cases his deputy, is appointed by the director-general from among civil service corps members under his authority. In 2011 there were 912 disciplinary ombudsmen and 694 deputy disciplinary ombudsmen working in government administration offices. The director-general is also entitled to appoint a joint disciplinary ombudsman for several offices. Such a joint ombudsman worked in 392 offices in 2011, ibid, p. 38.

An unjustified absence of the defendant or his defence counsel has no effect on the continuance of proceedings. The hearing is open, yet in certain justified cases the disciplinary panel may decide to continue in camera, but the decision is always pronounced in open session. The judgment along with the statement of reasons is delivered to the interested parties within seven days from the time of its pronouncement. The parties have the right to appeal against the judgment of the disciplinary commission via the disciplinary commission of first instance to the High Disciplinary Commission within 14 days from the date of its delivery. The disciplinary commission of first instance refers the appeal along with the case files to the High Disciplinary Commission within 14 days from the date the appeal was submitted. The above provisions apply respectively to hearings before the High Disciplinary Commission.

The judgments of the High Disciplinary Commission can be appealed against by the interested parties and the Head of the Civil Service to the appellation court – labour and social insurance court with jurisdiction over the place of residence of the defendant. The appeal is lodged via the High Disciplinary Commission. The appeal is adjudicated upon in accordance with the provisions of the Civil Procedures Code in the part concerning appeals. Cassation cannot be applied in the case of decisions of courts of appeal. A copy of the official decision of the disciplinary commission on the application of the penalty is appended to the personal files of the civil service corps member.

The penalty of a warning, reprimand, deprivation of the chance of promotion to higher service rank for a period of two years and decrease in the basic salary become spent and the copy of judgment in the personal file of the punished person destroyed after three years from the date the official judgment on the application of the penalty was delivered. At the request of the punished person, the conviction can be effectively ignored or erased after a period of two years.

Should the civil service corps member receive another disciplinary penalty before the previous penalty becomes spent, the three-year period mentioned above applies starting from the date of the delivery of the official decision on the application of the new penalty. In the case of the penalty of expulsion from the civil service or work in the office, the penalty becomes spent and the copy of judgment destroyed three years after the lapse of the period the person punished was barred from applying for employment in the civil service corps.

The greater part of initiated explanatory proceedings in 2011 referred to the principle of responsibility for actions or failure to act responsibly and to the principle of integrity – around 21% of proceedings each, and to the principle of dignified conduct – 19%. As for final and binding disciplinary penalties, they concerned, first of all, matters of integrity – over 27% of penalties, and the principle of responsibility for actions or the failure to act – over 23% of penalties.[158]

Civil servants and civil servant employees are subject to the Act of 20 January 2011 on the Financial Liability of Public Officials which sets down procedural regulations and principles in dealing with such liability and imposes the obligation of taking responsibility for damage caused in the course of exercising public authority, for actions or negligence that lead to flagrant breaches of law.[159]

Civil service corps members are financially liable when all the following conditions are met jointly: when pursuant to a court order or settlement, compensation was borne by the responsible entity for damage done in the course of exercising public authority with flagrant breach of law; the flagrant breach of law was due to a wrongful act or negligence and its specific conditions fall under Article 6 of the Act of 20 January 2011. Compensation cannot exceed the sum of twelve monthly salaries to which a public official is entitled. Should more than one public official commit a wrongful act or omission, each individually is liable for up to the total of twelve monthly salaries.[160]

## Change and Termination of Employment Relationships in the Civil Service

The Civil Service Act determines the circumstances in which an employment relationship in the civil service is changed[161], including a change that covers the possibility of reassigning the civil servant to another position within the same office or within the civil service corps. If such is the need of the office, the director-general may at any time transfer the civil servant to another position in the same office in the same town, taking into account his/her professional qualifications,

158 Ibid.

159 Ustawa z dnia 20 stycznia 2011 r. *o odpowiedzialności majątkowej funkcjonariuszy publicznych za rażące naruszenia prawa*, [The Act of 20 January 2011 on the Financial Liability of Public Officials for Gross Breach of Law], Dz. U., No. 34, item 173.

160 Ibid, Art. 9.

161 The staff turnover rate (i.e. the ratio between the number of leaves to the average number of employed in the period under study) remains at a safe and stable level in the civil service – in 2011 it was 7.3% (in 2010–7.1%), in M. Dąbrowski, 'Zatrudnienia i wynagrodzenia w korpusie służby cywilnej w 2011 r.', *Przegląd Służby Cywilnej* 2012, No. 3 (18), p. 13. The highest staff fluctuation rate in 2012 was observed in ministries – 11.9% and diplomatic missions – 15.5%, the lowest in tax inspection offices (3.6%) and treasury offices (6.3%), 'Sprawozdanie Szefa Służby Cywilnej', 2012, op. cit., Table No. 15.

or to another office in another town. If this is required in the interest of the civil service, the Head of the Civil Service may transfer the civil servant to another office in the same town. If particular interests of the civil service require it, the Head of the Civil Service may transfer the civil servant to another office in another town for a period of up to 2 years. This type of reassignment is not permitted more than twice during a civil servant's employment relationship.

It is inadmissible for a civil servant, a pregnant woman or the sole carer of a child under 15 years of age, to be transferred to another town without his/her consent. Such transfers are also not allowable when particularly important personal or family matters of the civil servant speak against them.

Reassignment of a civil service corps member to another office or to another location, at his/her request or by his/her consent, can be effected at any time. The transfer is made by the director-general of office to which the corps member is to be reassigned, in consultation with the director-general of office of his/her current employment. The transfer of a civil service corps member outside the civil service corps is made under separate provisions.

The transferred civil service corps member retains the right to his/her current remuneration, if it is higher than the one in the new position, for a period of three months starting from the end of the month when the transfer took place. The civil service supplement or bonus remains unchanged in the case of civil servants.

Should the office where the civil servant is employed be liquidated or reorganized in a way that makes further employment of that civil servant at that office impossible, the Head of the Civil Service transfers him/her to another office in the same or another town and instructs the director-general of that office to assign him/her a position in accordance with his/her professional qualifications.

The employment relationship of a civil service corps member held in temporary custody is suspended by virtue of law. During the suspension the civil service corps member receives half of the remuneration he/she were entitled to before detention. Should the proceedings be discontinued or there is an acquittal, the civil service corps member is entitled to the remaining part of his/her monthly pay. This does not apply in the case of a conditional discontinuance of proceedings. The period when the employment relationship was temporarily suspended due to detention is included in the period of employment which is the basis of employee rights in the civil service.

The director-general of office has the right to suspend members of the civil service corps in their duties if disciplinary or penal proceedings have been initiated against them. The suspension remains in force till the end of disciplinary or penal proceedings yet for not longer than three months. During the suspension period, the civil service corps member is entitled to remuneration and other rights and benefits in the civil service. The period of temporary suspension is included in the period of employment which is the basis of employee rights in the civil service.

The employee relationship with a civil servant is terminated when he/she:

- refuses to take the oath,
- loses citizenship of any EU Member State or other country whose citizens, under international agreements or provisions of EU laws, are free to take up employment in the territory of the Republic of Poland,
- receives a final and binding adjudication of the disciplinary penalty of expulsion from the civil service,
- receives a final and binding conviction of intentional fiscal or other indictable offence,
- receives a final and binding adjudication of loss of civil rights or interdiction of employment in the civil service,
- is absent from work for over three months due to having been placed in detention,
- refuses to comply with the decision of transfer to another post or fails to take up work in the office to which he/she was transferred.[162]

Termination of the employment relationship with a civil servant takes place, with a three-months' notice, in the case of:

- two successive negative periodical assessments,
- assertion by a certifying physician of the Social Insurance Institution of permanent disability that prevents further performance of duties,
- loss of impeccable reputation,
- liquidation of the office – if transfer is not possible,
- on reaching retirement age – if duration of employment meets the eligibility criteria for a retirement pension,
- refusal to undergo a medical examination by the certifying physician of the Social Insurance Institution.

Termination of the employment relationship with a civil servant without notice may take place due to his/her absence from work because of illness for a period of over one year. Termination of the employment relationship with a civil servant

162 Civil Service Act of 21 November 2008, Chapter 5.

may also take place by mutual agreement or at three-months' notice from the civil servant resigning from work in the civil service.

Termination of the employment relationship with a civil servant without notice by fault of the civil servant takes place in the case of:

- gross breach by the civil servant of basic duties of a civil service corps member – provided his/her fault is undeniable,
- a criminal offence committed by the civil servant in the period of employment, thus preventing his/her further employment – provided the offence is undeniable or has been confirmed by a final and binding verdict,
- loss by his/her own fault of licenses required for the performance of duties in the position held – if it is not possible to assign him/her another position which takes into account his/her professional qualifications.[163]

Termination of the employment relationship with a civil servant without notice by fault of the civil servant cannot take place over a month after the date of receiving information about circumstances that could give grounds for the termination of the employment relationship. During the notice period, a member of the civil service corps may be exempted from duties yet keeps the right to remuneration for that period.

163 Ibid.

# Chapter 4: The Organisation of the Civil Service in Poland Under the Civil Service Act of 21 November 2008

## The Civil Service Council

The Civil Service Council acts within the office of the Prime Minister. It is an opinion-giving and advisory body to the Prime Minister that issues opinions on matters concerning the civil service (asked for by the Prime Minister, the Head of the Civil Service or on its own initiative), such as the draft strategy for human resources management in the civil service, the draft of the Budget Act in the part concerning the civil service and on the annual budget execution in this respect as well as the proposed rate of remuneration increase in the state budget sector, the central training programme for the civil service, civil service corps professional ethics, the appointment and dismissal of the Head of the Civil Service, draft regulations governing the proceedings of the High Disciplinary Civil Service Commission and the reports of the Head of the Civil Service.[164]

The Civil Service Council also evaluates the course of the qualification procedures in the civil service. Its representative may participate as an observer in the recruitment process for the post of the head of an organisational unit, which is subordinate or supervised by the Prime Minister or the relevant minister, for which open and competitive recruitment is held pursuant to separate regulations. The Council can request the opinion of the Head of the Civil Service on matters determined by the Council with regard to the application of civil service rules. Should the Council spot any irregularities in the recruitment, it can ask the Head of the Civil Service to have the recruitment initiated anew. The Council's representative may participate as an observer of the recruitment process for a senior position in the civil service and in the qualification procedure. Should the Council spot any irregularities in the qualification procedure, it can ask the Head of the Civil Service to have the qualification procedure initiated anew.[165]

164 The Civil Service Act of 21 November 2008, Art. 19.

165 Ibid, Art. 19.

Civil Service Council members are entitled to remuneration in accordance with the regulation of the Prime Minister of 9 April 2009[166] that determines the flat-rate monthly remuneration for the Council members calculated using the minimum wage multiplication factor, as defined by the regulations on minimum wages. The multiplication factor for the Council President is – 1.5, for the Council Vice President – 1.4, for other Council members – 1.3. Remuneration is due all members of the Council, including experts and MPs who are representatives of parliamentary clubs.[167] The provision of remuneration for Council members gives it the character of a professional body.

The Council comprises fifteen members. Eight members of the Council, whose knowledge, experience and authority provide a guarantee of competent execution of the Council's tasks, are appointed for a 6 year term with half the members changing mid-term. The term in office of seven Council members, appointed from among MPs, senators and non-parliamentarians who represent all the parliamentary clubs, lasts the length of the *Sejm* (lower house of the Polish parliament) term. All Council members perform their functions until the appointment of their successors.[168]

Council membership expires with the death of the member or when the member ceases to be a Polish citizen, no longer enjoys full civil rights or has received a final and binding conviction of intentional fiscal or other indictable offence. The Prime Minister recalls a Council member at the request of the Council when the Council member fails to perform his/her duties or is unable to perform them due to chronic illness confirmed by a medical certificate. The Prime Minister can also dismiss a member of the Council who has ceased to meet the requirement of impeccable character after the approval of a minimum of 2/3 of the Council members. The Prime Minister also recalls a Council member should he/she submit their resignation.[169]

---

166 Rozporządzenie Prezesa Rady Ministrów z dnia 9 kwietnia 2009 r. *w sprawie wynagrodzenia członków Rady Służby Cywilnej*, [Regulation of the Prime Minister of 9 April 2009 on the Remuneration of Civil Service Council Members], Dz. U. No. 60, item 491.

167 This solution was first introduced in 2008 legislation. Earlier remuneration did not include parliamentary club representatives. Currently it does, as representatives of parliamentary clubs in the Council are not necessarily parliamentarians.

168 The Civil Service Act of 21 November 2008, Art. 20.

169 Ibid, Art. 22.

Should membership in the Council be terminated or its member dismissed before end of term, the Prime Minister appoints a new member of the Council for the remaining period of that term.

On 21 April 2009 the Council adopted its rules of procedure,[170] in which it specified some of the principles of the Council's organisation of work and its functioning – schedule of meetings, validity of meetings (one half of the Council's composition), election of its president and his role, convening and conducting the meetings.

## The Head of the Civil Service

The Head of the Civil Service is the central organ of government administration, competent in matters of the civil service. The Head of the Civil Service is appointed by the Prime Minister from among civil servants after consultation with the Civil Service Council. The Head of the Civil Service reports directly to the Prime Minister.

The Head of the Civil Service must be a Polish citizen, enjoy full civil rights, have never been convicted of intentional fiscal or other indictable offence, hold an MA degree or its equivalent, have command of at least one foreign language from among the working languages of the European Union, enjoy an impeccable reputation and have never been punished with the penalty of interdiction of holding managerial positions in the offices of public authorities, have a minimum five-year experience in managerial positions in government administration or a minimum seven-year experience in managerial positions in institutions of the public finance sector. And finally, the Head of the Civil Service is not and has not been a member of a political party in the 5 years before his/her appointment.[171]

The Head of the Civil Service is recalled from his/her post by the Prime Minister following his/her resignation, failure to meet any of the conditions set out in Article 11.1(1–4, 7 or 9) of the Civil Service Act or the inability to perform his/her duties due to chronic illness confirmed by a medical certificate.

The Prime Minister can recall the Head of the Civil Service after consultation with the Civil Service Council should the Head's annual report on the state of the civil service and the accomplishment of its tasks for the previous year be rejected, he/she betray their oath or no longer enjoy an impeccable reputation.

170 Regulamin Rady Służby Cywilnej z dnia 21 kwietnia 2009 r. Uchwała nr 1, < http://www.dsc.kprm.gov.pl >, accessed 8 August 2011.

171 Civil Service Act of 21 November 2008, Art. 11.

In the written request to the Civil Service Council for their opinion, the Prime Minister specifies the grounds for dismissal of the Head of the Civil Service.[172]

The duties of the Head of the Civil Service include: overseeing the observance of civil service principles, administering the process of human resources management in the civil service, gathering information regarding the civil service corps, planning, organisation and supervision of central training courses in the civil service, monitoring and supervision of appropriation of funds for the remuneration and training of civil service corps members, drafting of normative acts regarding the civil service, dissemination of information about the civil service, ensuring conditions for the dissemination of information about available vacant posts in the civil service, international cooperation in matters concerning the civil service.[173]

The Head of the Civil Service executes his duties with the assistance of directors-general and the support of the Civil Service Department of the Chancellery of the Prime Minister. The position of the Head of the Civil Service is presently weaker than that provided under the 1998 Civil Service Act. This is due to a more flexible concept of subordination of the civil service to policy-makers, while at the same time assuming protection of the integrity of the civil service of which the Head of the Civil Service is a guarantor.

## Senior Positions in the Civil Service

The Civil Service Act of 21 November 2009 came into force on 24 March 2009 and reintroduced senior positions in government administration into the civil service.

Senior positions in the civil service can be held by persons who:

- hold an MA degree or its equivalent,
- have never been punished with the penalty of interdiction of holding managerial positions in the offices of public authorities or of performing functions connected with the disposition of public funds,
- have managerial skills,
- have at least six years work experience, of which a minimum of three years of managerial experience in public finance sector institutions – if applying for the position of director-general,

172 Ibid, Art. 12–13.

173 Ibid, Art. 15.

- have three years work experience, of which a minimum of one year of experience in a managerial position or two years in work in an independent capacity in public finance sector institutions – if applying for the position referred to in Article 52.2–4.

Under the provisions of the Act, senior positions in the civil service are filled through competitive recruitment of candidates applying for that particular position. The most suitable candidates have to meet additional minimum requirements.

The Act also introduces the duty to organise recruitment without delay following the occurrence of circumstances justifying the need to fill a post and sets down rules of its organisation, such as the duty to appoint the recruitment team members and publication of information concerning the recruitment methods and techniques. The aim should be the selection of the best qualified candidate for the senior position in the civil service. Unfortunately, the organisation of competitions for positions of director-general of office is rather slow – the procedure takes six months to a year.

The legislator allowed two possibilities of staffing particular senior posts without the need of open and competitive recruitment: by the transfer or delegation of a civil service corps member, provided the person meets the formal requirements for that position and in his/her last periodical assessment, conducted within the last 24 months before the transfer, received scores that placed him/her at the two highest levels on the marks scale. This provision refers only to deputy directors and is termed a promotion. Such opportunities provide motivation to civil servants to work more effectively and outline their promotion path.

The guarantor that the recruitment is conducted properly is the Head of the Civil Service, as indicated in Article 15.1 of the Act, while a representative of the Civil Service Council and a representative of the Head of the Civil Service are empowered by the legislator to monitor the correctness of the recruitment procedures. The Act stipulates taking prompt action, which in practice means the elimination of a state of temporariness in the functioning of the office. This principle means that acting or ad interim appointments in the case of senior positions in the civil service are forbidden.

The provisions lack delegation to issue an executive act regulating this matter nor do they establish a comprehensive procedure, which in effect allows much freedom in choosing how to conduct the recruitment. In June 2009 the Head of the Civil Service established standards of the recruitment procedure for senior positions in the civil service. Three elements listed in the Act of 21 November 2008 – professional experience, knowledge and managerial skills – provide the starting point for working out the methods and selection of appropriate techniques to ensure the selection of the best qualified candidates. The methods and techniques are required to be clearly defined in order to eliminate discretionary and subjective evaluations. A complementary instrument is the qualification interview aimed at the verification of those traits of the candidate that cannot be effectively assessed otherwise. The qualification interview is conducted by a team or a person appointed by the team but not of the team.

The Head of the Civil Service may request the director-general of office to provide him/her with the documentation from the conducted recruitment to senior positions in the civil service. Should any irregularities in the recruitment process be spotted, the Head of the Civil Service promptly orders their immediate correction or repetition of the recruitment process. The Head of the Civil Service may apply to the Prime Minister to have the conducted recruitment process to a senior position in the civil service checked, as it is the Head of the Civil Service who is entrusted by law with the administration of the process of human resources management in the civil service. The Civil Service Council that also monitors recruitment to all positions in the civil service may, in the case of detecting any irregularities in the recruitment process for senior positions in the civil service, apply to the Head of the Civil Service to instruct repetition of the recruitment process. Unfortunately, there is real concern that despite the recommendations of the Head of the Civil Service the recruitment to senior positions will be discretionary, the more so that both the Head of the Civil Service and Civil Service Council members, including its President, are political appointees and, what is more, the political leadership of the relevant ministry does influence the appointments.

Senior positions cannot be filled with acting or ad interim appointments.[174] Pursuant to the Act, staffing of senior positions in the civil service is no longer by way of competition but open and competitive recruitment.[175] The most likely candidates have to meet additional minimum requirements.[176] There is no provision for a separate position of deputy director-general. The practice is for the director-general to designate a person to deputise for him/her from among the heads of departments or divisions. In government administration institutions in

174 Ibid., Art. 54.6. Currently there is a possibility of 'acting or ad interim' appointments.

175 Ibid., Art. 54.1.

176 Ibid., Art. 53.

2011, there were 64 positions of director-general of office,[177] of which 53 were filled (20 by women and 33 by men).[178]

One may conclude on the basis of observation of competitions for senior positions in the Polish civil service that the procedure rules require constant modification and adjustment in order to eliminate the favouring of persons appointed earlier to acting or ad interim managerial positions – a practice that discourages other potential candidates.[179] About 80 positions were filled by those in 'acting or ad interim' positions pursuant to Article 144a of the 1998 Civil Service Act (which came into force as of 2002 due to an amendment passed by the Sejm). Until March 2006, 757 of the 1700 senior positions in the civil service were staffed by way of competitions. There were also cases of ignoring candidates indicated by the competition commissions.

In 2011 there were 124 recruitments conducted for senior positions in the civil service, of which 82 ended with the selection of a candidate (there were 6 applications for each competition, on average). A lower number of candidates for senior positions than for non-managerial ones may have been due to remuneration being non-competitive to that achieved in the private sector.[180]

## The Rights of Civil Servants and Civil Service Employees

Civil service corps members have many entitlements pursuant to the Act of 21 November 2008, including:

- The right to legal protection provided by the employer. In connection with the performance of official duties a civil servant can be vulnerable to unwarranted attack. Civil service corps members are entitled to protection due public officials.[181]

  This protection is provided under the Polish Penal Code and concerns the protection of public servants against breach of personal inviolability, active assault, violence or unlawful threat intended to compel a public servant to

177 In 2010 there were 62 positions of director-general of office, but in 2011 the Ministry for the Administration and Digitisation, the Ministry of the Interior, and the Ministry of Transport, Construction and Maritime Economy were established.

178 'Sprawozdanie Szefa Służby Cywilnej o stanie służby cywilnej i realizacji zadań tej służby w 2011 roku', 2012 Head of CS report for 2011, Warszawa March 2012, p. 42.

179 J. Czaputowicz, 'Służba cywilna w Polsce – między polityzacją a profesjonalizacją', *Służba Cywilna*, No. 9, Warszawa, 2004/2005, p. 46.

180 'Sprawozdanie Szefa Służby Cywilnej', 2012, pp. 21–22.

181 The Civil Service Act of 21 November 2008, Art. 104.

undertake or abandon lawful official action and against insult. Public servants were also provided protection under civil law until 17 May 2012, which meant that the State Treasury was liable for damages caused by the actions of civil servants in the course of their duties.[182]

- The right to professional development. The professional career of a civil servant depends on his/her qualifications, capabilities and achievements. The director-general of office establishes an individual professional development programme, separately for each civil servant in his office, which becomes the basis for referring the civil servant for training. Participation in the training programme is compulsory.[183] Civil service corps members have various forms and instruments available to them for the development of their professional qualifications that include training courses, self-coaching, participation in internships and task teams, preparation of analyses and expert opinions, extra tasks, learning under instruction from others, mentoring, coaching, consultations, study visits.[184]
- The right to periodical assessment. An important element in the management of administration cadres is their official evaluation that forms the basis for referral of the civil servant for promotion to the next service rank or (if twice negative) the basis of dismissal. Previously, periodical assessment results were directly connected with the remuneration system and its amount. Today the assessment serves to evaluate and raise the level of effectiveness of employee performance and increase motivation and commitment among employees as well as to assist in shaping the future course of their development. Employee assessment can also be an instrument of the de-recruitment process.[185]
  Civil servants should undergo assessment at least once every two years. The director-general is assessed by the Head of the Civil Service in consultation with the relevant minister, head of the office or voivod. The Head of the Civil

182 More on the subject in Chapter 3.

183 In the opinion of those employed in the civil service, the greatest opportunities for career development are open in central institutions, the least in tax offices. See NIK audit report, March 2012, op.cit., p. 61.

184 Załącznik do Zarządzenia Nr 3 Szefa Służby Cywilnej z 30 maja 2012 r. *w sprawie standardów zarządzania zasobami ludzkimi w służbie cywilnej, V. Rozwój i szkolenia.* [Attachment to Ordinance No. 3 of the Head of the Civil Service dated 30 May 2012 on Standards of Human Resources Management in the Civil Service, Chapter V. Development of Skills and Training].

185 *Strategia zarządzania zasobami ludzkimi w służbie cywilnej 2011–2020*, Chancellery of the Prime Minister, Warszawa, 2011, p. 8.

Service himself does not undergo assessment as such but submits to the Prime Minister his/her annual report from the execution of tasks and awaits for its acceptance. To this day there has been no incident of the report not being accepted. It seems, however, that a rejection of the report would lead to the dismissal of the Head of the Civil Service.

- The right to remuneration. Without a doubt, taking up employment entitles to remuneration as provided under the Labour Code. In the case of the civil service, the legislator differentiates between the remuneration for civil servants and civil service employees. The salary of a civil service employee consists of two components: the basic salary foreseen for that specific position and a pay supplement or bonus for years of employment in the civil service. The salary of a civil servant consists of three components: the basic salary foreseen for that specific position, a pay supplement or bonus for years of employment in the civil service (5% of basic monthly salary after five years' service increased by 1% for each subsequent year up to the level of 20% of the basic monthly salary) and a civil service pay supplement according to his/her service rank.[186] The Act does not provide for a function-related pay supplement for a civil service corps member.

There has been a noticeable real drop in salaries in the civil service corps (in 2009 by 2%, in 2010 by 1.2%, in 2011 by 0.7%) despite a real rise in salaries in the national economy in the same period (in 2009 by 1.1%, in 2010 by 0.8%, in 2011 by 0.9%).[187]

Civil service corps members may be granted additional pay for additional tasks assigned to them by their superiors, from remuneration fund resources, for the duration of the performance of the task. In 2011 payment appropriations for additional tasks in the civil service at the ministries (including the Prime Minister's Chancellery) accounted for 1.9% of the total appropriations intended to cover remuneration of civil service corps members, whereas in voivodship

186 The Civil Service Act of 21 November 2008, Art. 85.

187 M. Dąbrowski, 'Zatrudnienie i wynagrodzenia w korpusie służby cywilnej w 2011 r.', *Przegląd Służby Cywilnej*, p. 13; The highest average monthly remuneration was recorded in the Civil Aviation Authority, the State Mining Authority, General Directorate for National Roads and Highways (GDDKiA), Chief Inspectorate of Environmental Protection, and the Energy Regulatory Office; the lowest in the HQ of Polish Border Guards, Agricultural and Food Quality Inspection (GIJHAR-S), National Police HQ and the Office for Foreigners, source 'Sprawozdanie Szefa Służby Cywilnej', 2012, op.cit., Table 12.

offices they accounted for 1.2%. This suggests that offices and ministries are not very keen on using this component of remuneration.

Years of employment in the civil service that entitle to a length-of-service bonus or supplement comprise all previous years of employment and other proven periods recognised under separate regulations as those that entitle to the various workers' rights and benefits. Periods of employment with the communist party (the Polish Workers' Party or the Polish United Workers' Party) are not considered, the same as employment in state security organs as prescribed under Article 2 of the Act of 18 October 2006 on the Disclosure of Information About Documents of State Security Organs in the Period 1944–1990 and Their Contents.[188]

Nine service ranks have been established for civil servants. Civil service pay supplement rates are assigned to the particular service rank held. Salaries of civil service corps members are calculated using the base amount multiplication factor – its value set down in the Budget Act that takes into account the average national salary. In 1999 the Prime Minister set down by way of a regulation the multiplication factors for the calculation of the basic salary, multiplication factors for the calculation of the civil service pay supplement, the service ranks in the civil service, groups of official posts and the required professional qualifications in those positions.[189] On 31 December 2011 around 43.8% of civil servants had the 1st service rank, around 39.2% – the 2nd service rank, around 13.8% – the 3rd rank, around 2% – the 4th rank and 0.5% – the 5th service rank or higher.[190]

The remuneration system in the civil service is based on the valuation of job positions thus enabling the determination of the relative value of particular positions in the organisation and provide the basis for their comparison and salary-setting for employees more objectively. The job valuation process is intended

188 Ustawa z dnia 18 października 2006 r. *o ujawnianiu informacji o dokumentach organów bezpieczeństwa państwa z lat 1944–1990 oraz treści tych dokumentów*, Dz. U. No. 63, item 425, as amended.

189 Rozporządzenie Prezesa Rady Ministrów z dnia 29 października 1999 r. *w sprawie określenia stanowisk urzędniczych, wymaganych kwalifikacji zawodowych, stopni służbowych urzędników służby cywilnej, mnożników do ustalania wynagrodzenia oraz szczegółowych zasad ustalenia i wypłacania innych świadczeń przysługujących członkom korpusu służby cywilnej*, [Regulation of the Prime Minister of 29 October 1999 on the Determination of Positions of Officials, Required Qualifications, Civil Service Ranks, Multiplication Factors for Calculation of Remuneration and Other Benefits Due Members of the Civil Service Corps], Dz. U., No. 89, item 996.

190 'Sprawozdanie Szefa Służby Cywilnej', 2012, op.cit., p. 33.

to create a rational basis for establishing and maintaining a just and rational remuneration structure in the civil service, facilitate management of reporting lines between the various positions within the organisation, facilitate consistent decision-making concerning rank and pay rates, development of models for the comparison of position valuations to assure equal remuneration for work of similar value.[191]

Despite the implementation of the valuation system, there still remains a disparity in remuneration between the different offices. Employees of voivodship offices occupying similar positions as employees of ministries earn around 50% less, although their job positions have a similar valuation total. Moreover, the remuneration system is not adjusted to the local labour market. For example, if the average salary in the Mazowsze (or Masovian) Voivodship Office is not much higher than in the voivodship offices in Rzeszów or Olsztyn, it obviously cannot attract highly qualified cadres while the latter are attractive employers on their local labour markets.[192]

A similar discussion on the remuneration system as in other European countries is taking place in Poland. The dispute revolves around the concept of justice – in the past, the career-based system was considered to be just – carrying with it guaranteed remuneration rising along with years of service in public administration. Today, many believe that remuneration should be differentiated reflecting individual input, or performance. The implementation of a pay system linked to achievements in work seems an attractive proposition, yet it also raises many doubts. As Ch. Demmke notes, the expectation to be treated individually conflicts with the expectation to be treated equally.

- Special or ad hoc bonuses and jubilee awards. The jubilee bonuses are awarded for a minimum 20 years and up to 45 years of work, 75% and 400% of

---

191 Zarządzenie nr 1 Prezesa Rady Ministrów z dnia 7 stycznia 2011 r. *w sprawie zasad dokonywania opisu i wartościowania stanowisk pracy w służbie cywilnej,* [Order No. 1 of the Prime Minister of 7 January 2011 on the Principles Governing the Valuation of Posts in the Civil Service], M. P., No. 5, item 61, *Strategia zarządzania zasobami ludzkimi w służbie cywilnej 2011–2020,* KPRM, Warszawa 2011, pp. 26–27.

192 The frustration of civil service corps members is the more so due to the disproportions in remuneration among civil service corps in the different ministries, central and voivodship offices; civil service corps members receive the highest remuneration in the Ministry of Finance, Ministry of Regional Development, Ministry for Sport and Tourism and such central institutions as the Energy Regulatory Office or the Civil Aviation Authority, and the lowest in Agricultural and Food Quality Inspection, Bureau for Chemical Substances, the Subcarpathian and Opole Voivodship Offices.

monthly remuneration, respectively. Accounting for 3% of planned staff remuneration, awards for special achievements in work are at the disposal of the director-general of office who can use them to motivate and award civil service corps members.[193]

- The right to additional annual pay. Under separate provisions guaranteed by the legislator, civil service corps members are entitled to additional monthly salary so-called 'thirteenth-month pay'.
- The right to one-time severance pay. On termination of employment due to retirement or incapacity to work and acquisition of a disability pension, the civil service corps member is entitled to a lump-sum severance pay equal to three months' remuneration and if he/she has been employed in the civil service for at least 20 years – to six months remuneration.
- The right to payments in consideration of official transfer, travel expenses and additional days of leave. The employer covers travel expenses and transfer-related costs and other costs connected with the transfer of a civil servant to work in another town, such as commuting costs. The transferred civil service member is entitled to accommodation appropriate to the size of his/her family and to reimbursement of renting costs. He/she is also entitled to a one-time benefit equal to three months' remuneration.

A civil servant reassigned to another office in another town is also entitled to reimbursement of travel costs for him/her and members of his/her family resulting from the transfer as well as transport costs of their property and 4 days leave on account of the transfer.[194]

The Regulation of the Prime Minister provides that the distance (between the place of residence of the civil servant, transferred pursuant to Article 63.2 of the Act) and the place where he/she is transferred that entitles to accommodation or reimbursement of rent needs to be at least 30 kilometres between the administrative borders of the towns in question. A flat at the disposal of the office to which the civil servant is relocated is made available to him/her on the day of his/her arrival. The usable floor area of the living quarters provided to the transferred civil servant depends on the number of family members moving with the civil servant, including him/herself, and is for: 1 person – from 25 to 40 $m^2$, 2 persons – from 35 to 50 $m^2$, 3 persons – from 45 to 60 $m^2$, 4 persons – from 55 to 70 $m^2$, 5 persons – from 65 to 80 $m^2$. Should the move involve more persons, the top

193 See more in J. Itrich-Drabarek, 'Status i ochrona praw pracowników służby cywilnej w Polsce i na świecie', *Zeszyty Politologiczne*, No. 3, Białystok, 2001, p. 68 et seq.

194 Civil Service Act of 21 November 2008, Art. 95.

and bottom indicators are moved up by 10 $m^2$ per each additional person. If a member of the transferred civil servant accompanying him/her is a disabled person or over the age of 75 and requiring constant care, additional 10 $m^2$ are added to the top and bottom indicators of the indicated floor area.

The transferred civil servant has the right to submit a written declaration of resignation from the provided quarters and in the cases when a flat is not made available or the civil servant resigns from the one he/she is offered, he/she receives a monthly allowance to cover the costs of a rented flat. The maximum sum appropriated to cover monthly rent for accommodation depends on the number of family members moving with the transferred civil servant, including him/herself, and is due in Warsaw, Gdańsk, Gdynia, Katowice, Kraków, Poznań, Szczecin and Wrocław for 1 person – PLN 1646 and is proportionally increased to PLN 3396 for 6 persons or more. In other towns the sum is PLN 1235 for 1 person and increased proportionally to PLN 2264 for 6 persons or more.[195]

Transfer-related travel costs of the relocated civil servant and his/her family members moving with him/her as well as transport costs of their property are calculated from their place of residence to the destination of the transfer and back. The reimbursement of travel costs of the transferred civil servant and members of his/her family is made in accordance with provisions concerning the amount and terms of calculating sums due employees of state or self-government entities on a business trip in Polish territory; however, not more than fifty percent of the base amount applied in determining the remuneration of civil service corps members set down in the Budget Act for the budget year in which the transfer takes place. The costs of transporting property to and from the location of the transfer are reimbursed as documented with receipts; however, the amount cannot exceed the sum of two base amounts applied in calculating the remuneration of civil service corps members and set down in the Budget Act for that budget year.

The one-time benefit due at the time of the transfer is calculated in pursuance to provisions regulating the setting of the cash equivalent of paid annual leave.[196]

---

195 Rozporządzenie Prezesa Rady Ministrów z dnia 8 czerwca 2009 r. *w sprawie świadczeń przysługujących urzędnikowi służby cywilnej przeniesionemu do pracy w innej miejscowości,* [Regulation of the Prime Minister of 8 June 2009 on Benefits Civil Servants are Entitled to When Transferred to Work in Another Location], Dz. U., No. 93, item 763.

196 Ibid.

- Non-wage employee benefits. Data indicate that among the benefits applied for most frequently in the civil service take the form of co-financing holiday leave (80% of total employed), co-financing studies or courses (45% of total employed), benefits connected with sports (38% of total employed) as well as the use of parking space (21% of total employed).[197]
- The right to regulated working time. The working time of civil service corps members cannot exceed 8 hours per day and 40 hours per week, on average,[198] within a clearance period of not more than eight weeks. Whenever the type of work or its organisation require a different working time schedule, it is admissible to extend the daily working time to 12 hours per day. In these cases, however, the weekly working time cannot exceed 40 hours per week, on average, within a clearance period of no more than 12 weeks.
  For overtime work assigned by his/her superior, civil service employees are entitled to time off work of equivalent duration. Civil servants are entitled to compensation in the form of equivalent free time for overtime during night-time only. For work on Sundays civil servants are entitled to a day off work during the week following and for work on a public holiday another day off.[199]
- The right to annual paid leave. The duration of annual leave is regulated under the Labour Code. Weekdays that are not days of work in the office are not included in paid leave holidays. Additionally, the Civil Service Act provides for a greater number of days off work for civil servants. Civil servants are entitled to additional paid leave holidays each year – 1 day extra after 5 years of work in the civil service. The paid leave holidays increase by 1 day for each subsequent year, until reaching 12 days. Only years of work in public administration entitle to receive additional days of paid leave holiday.

197 'Wynagrodzenia w służbie cywilnej w porównaniu do wynagrodzeń w pozostałej administracji publicznej oraz podmiotach biznesowych', in A. Przybysz (ed.), *Przegląd Służby Cywilnej,* 2011, No. 2 (11), p. 8.

198 Civil Service Act of 21 November 2008, Art. 97.

199 This system has been criticised by the Council of Europe as in breach of the European Social Charter which as early as in 1996 provides for additional work to be compensated in the form of extra free time or additional pay. Compensation should not differentiate between civil service employees and civil servants. The Council called on Poland to make the appropriate changes in the provisions, but the advised changes have not been made. European Social Charter of 18 October 1961, Art. 4 para.2. In 2011 about 953 721 hours have been recorded in overtime, of which 47% was overtime in the tax and duties administration, in 'Sprawozdanie Szefa Służby Cywilnej', 2012, op.cit. p. 37.

- The right to convalescence leave. Civil servants with a minimum 10 years of service can be granted paid convalescence leave for a period of up to 6 months at a time. The duration of this leave – with a total duration of up to 5 years – is counted as part of the period of employment in the civil service.
- The right to unpaid leave. Civil servants are entitled to unpaid leave for the duration of performing certain tasks, of taking up duties in certain positions or performing functions outside the civil service 'in cases justified as being in the public interest', such as running for local council or performing the functions of an elected local council member, also when running for parliament but not when holding a mandate as a member of parliament (whether of the lower house or senate).
- The right to retirement pension. Civil service corps members are entitled to retirement or disability pension from the Social Insurance Fund (ZUS), as provided under relevant provisions. In cases when termination of employee relationship with a state office is due to the liquidation of his/her office or its reorganisation, the civil service corps employee is entitled to a retirement pension on reaching the retirement age of 65 (for men) or 60 (for women) on condition of having the required length of employment of 25 and 20 years, respectively. This applies to persons born before 1 January 1949.
- The right to reinstatement. Should the employment of a civil servant cease due to him/her being taken into temporary custody, the director-general of office, where the civil servant was employed, is required to take him/her back, taking into consideration his/her professional qualifications, if penal proceedings against him/her are discontinued or there is an acquittal, and the civil servant expresses his/her desire to return to work within seven days from the date the adjudication comes into force. This rule does not apply in cases when criminal proceedings are discontinued under the statute of limitations or amnesty or due to conditional discontinuation of proceedings. If reemployment in the civil service is denied, the case can be appealed in a labour court.

The list of entitlements of the civil service corps is quite extensive. The legislator took into account the numerous duties of civil service members and decided to compensate them indirectly through remuneration, severance pay, occasional bonuses, inclusion of unpaid leave periods in the calculation of length of service, the principle of the length of service entitling to the different employee rights being the sum of the different periods of employment. Undoubtedly, in the case of a part of the rights and duties, there still remain questions the answers to which are not all that clear, such as where are the limits of loyalty to the government or the right to freedom of expression and its limitations, especially with respect to government policy.

## The Duties of Civil Servants and Civil Service Employees

There are several typologies of classifying the duties of civil service corps members. The first, depending on the specific nature of work, distinguishes between constitutional and employee duties. The scope of employee duties is regulated under Article 100 of the Labour Code that regulates such matters as the length of working time, workplace regulations and fixed schedules, adherence to work and fire safety rules and regulations, compliance with regulations concerning statutory secrecy, abiding by the rules of social coexistence in the workplace[200]. Constitutional duties of civil service corps members include the duty to abide by the Constitution of the Republic of Poland and other legal acts, never to succumb in their daily duties to any particular or group interests, to protect state interests, human and civil rights and to rationally manage public funds.

Another classification reflects the scope of tasks of civil service corps members and, in consequence, the division into general, official and those outside of official duties. Successive civil service acts specify the duties of civil service corps members and, in the scope of general duties, impose the following:

- The duty to take the oath. By taking the oath the civil servant commits him/herself to the observance of the Constitution of the Republic of Poland and other legal acts,[201] and each successive civil service act does not derogate from the obligation of taking such oath.[202]
- The duty of loyalty. Every civil service corps member has the duty to remain faithful to the Constitution[203], which means that he/she is required to protect the interests of the state, human and civil rights. The concept of loyalty contains the commitment to democracy and a civil society and not to the political

---

200 Labour Code, Art. 100.

201 The text of the oath of a civil servant is as follows, 'I shall serve the Polish State, observe the Constitution of the Republic of Poland, fulfil the duties of a civil servant conscientiously and impartially, to the best of my knowledge and will'.

202 Civil Service Act of 5 July 1996, Art. 33.1, Civil Service Act of 18 December 1998, Art. 39.1, Civil Service Act of 24 August 2006, Art. 29.1, Civil Service Act of 21 November 2008, Art. 50.1.

203 In accordance with the Civil Service Act of 5 July 1996, Art. 47.1, Civil Service Act of 18 December 1998, Art. 67.1, Civil Service Act of 24 August 2006, Art. 47.1 and the Civil Service Act of 21 November 2008, Art. 76.1.

parties currently in power. The observance of law is linked to the principle of legitimacy of the public authorities in place as one of the basic principles of a democratic state and the rule of law. Loyalty to the Constitution means the observance not only of the Basic Law but also the law that derives from it. It allows us to trust that a civil servant upholds the law and is subject to that law at the same time.

- The duty to protect national interests. This duty refers to intangible interests such as the defence of the independence and sovereignty of the country, internal and external security and territorial inviolability.
- The duty to manage public funds wisely. This duty refers to material interests, that is the spending of funds in accordance with public objectives and tasks and their rational use.[204]
- The duty to protect human and civil rights. Civil service corps members should protect human and civil rights with attention to the principles of a democratic state and the rule of law.[205]
- The duty of impartiality. Neutrality and impartiality, the requirements of upholding the rule of law are expected of Polish civil service corps members. A civil service corps member is required to observe neutrality towards political parties, trade unions, pressure groups, parliamentary and non-parliamentary lobbies and individual interests. Each and every administrative decision should be devoid of any influence of any groups of interest. Adherence to this principle provides a guarantee that all citizens, irrespective of their political convictions and party affiliations, sex, race, religion, social status and wealth, receive equal treatment.[206] Civil servants have to resolve issues in the public interest, state interest and individual interest. Conflict of interests and partiality takes place when a public official, who is responsible for resolving a matter or is in any way involved in this process, has or can be suspected of having material or other interest in how the matter is resolved. Conflict of interest is

204 Civil Service Act of 5 July 1996, Art. 47.3, Civil Service Act of 18 December 1998, Art. 67.3, Civil Service Act of 24 August 2006, Art. 47.3 and the Civil Service Act of 21 November 2008, Art. 76.3.

205 Civil Service Act of 5 July 1996, Art. 47.2, Civil Service Act of 18 December 1998, Art. 67.2, Civil Service Act of 24 August 2006, Art. 47.2 and the Civil Service Act of 21 November 2008, Art. 76.2.

206 Civil Service Act of 5 July 1996 – Art. 47.4, Act of 18 December 1998 – Art. 67.4, Civil Service Act of 24 August 2006 – Art. 47.4, Civil Service Act of 21 November 2008 – Art. 76.4.

always there when own particular interests take precedence over concern for the common good.

- The duty never to succumb to individual or group interests.[207]
- The requirement of political neutrality. This means that civil service corps members are not allowed to be active politically. A civil service corps member cannot establish or take part in the work of political parties[208] or combine work in the civil service with the mandate of a local council member[209] (unless on unpaid leave). The ban on the manifestation of political convictions does not apply when the civil servant is on unpaid leave and running for local council. The ban on combining work in the civil service with the mandate of a local council member does not apply to civil service employees[210], so they do not have to take unpaid leave for the duration of the mandate but should refrain from manifesting their political convictions. A civil service corps member cannot hold a parliamentary mandate (MP or senator). If he/she wins such a mandate, then within a fortnight they should submit their declaration of resignation from the post of a civil servant – if he/she fails to do so, their parliamentary mandate (MP or senator) will be terminated after that period. The requirement of guaranteeing political neutrality means the fulfilment of the principle that a civil servant corps member cannot be guided, in particular, by political interest.[211]
- A ban on strike action. Work in the Polish civil service is of a continuous character. This means that the civil service corps works for the common good and its members cannot participate in strike action or protest that would interfere with the functioning of the office.[212] Under the Act of 18 December

---

207 Civil Service Act of 5 July 1996 – Art. 49.1), Civil Service Act of 18 December 1998 – Art. 69.1, Act of 24 August 2006 – Art. 49.1, Civil Service Act of 21 November 2008 – Art. 78.4.

208 Civil servants when performing their duties cannot be guided by their political or religious convictions, particular or group interests. Section 2 – they cannot manifest publically their political convictions, Civil Service Act of 5 July 1996 – Art. 49.1–2; Civil Service Act of 18 December 1998, Art. 69; Civil Service Act of 24 August 2006 – Art. 49.2 and 5.

209 Civil Service Act of 24 August 2006 – Art. 49.4; Civil Service Act of 21 November 2008 – Art. 78.1.

210 Civil Service Act of 18 December 1998, Art. 70.

211 Ibid., Art. 69.

212 Civil Service Act of 5 July 1996 does not take up the issue of the right to strike, Civil Service Act of 18 December 1998 – Art. 69.4, Civil Service Act of 24 August 2006 – Art. 49.3, Civil Service Act of 21 November 2008 – Art. 78.3.

1998 a civil servant could not also perform any functions in trade unions[213]; however, the Act of 21 November 2008 restricts this ban only to civil service corps members in senior positions.

Representatives of the civil service corps perform their duties as required in their posts, including:

- The duty of complete commitment to the service. A civil service corps member is required to implement the tasks entrusted to him efficiently and in a timely manner. Full commitment does not narrow down to the regular showing up at the office but means full engagement in the accomplishment of duties. Public officials have to exercise their duties in accordance with the respective civil service act. Their conduct should never undermine the public's confidence and trust in public administration. Without the approval from the director-general, civil servants and those in senior positions cannot take up additional paid activity or function.[214]
- The duty to be conscientious and impartial. Civil service corps members cannot take official action in their own interest, in the interest of their family or friends, other persons or groups.[215] In order to avoid any suspicion of partiality or action in one's own interest, reporting lines in the civil service between wife and husband or between persons in a family relationship up to second degree relatives are not permissible.

  Polish civil service law has not gone so far as that of the UK or Germany and its regulations do not directly ban the acceptance of gifts from third parties, but a provision to that effect can be found in the 2002 Civil Service Code of Ethics.[216]

---

213 Civil Service Act of 5 July 1996 does not take up the issue of trade union rights, Civil Service Act of 18 December 1998 – Art. 69.4, Civil Service Act of 24 August 2006 – Art. 49.6, Civil Service Act of 21 November 2008 – Art. 78.1.

214 Civil Service Act of 5 July 1996 – Art. 51, Civil Service Act of 18 December 1998 – Art. 72, Civil Service Act of 24 August 2006 – Art. 51, Civil Service Act of 21 November 2008 – Art. 80.1. In 2011 there were 1204 applications concerning additional employment submitted, of which 96% were granted, in 'Sprawozdanie Szefa Służby Cywilnej', 2012, op. cit., p. 36.

215 Civil Service Act of 5 July 1996 – Art. 49.1, Civil Service Act of 18 December 1998 – Art. 69.1, Civil Service Act of 24 August 2006 – Art. 49.1, Act of 21 November 2008 – Art. 78.1.

216 The Code is no longer in force since 2008. Zarządzenie Nr 114 Prezesa Rady Ministrów z dnia 11 października 2002 r. w *sprawie ustanowienia Kodeksu Etyki Służby*

- The duty of obedience and loyalty. Civil service corps members have the duty to obey official orders of their superiors and follow the general guidelines. The legislators set down the limits to this obligation in order to preserve the legitimacy of such orders and the scope of line of duty relationships.[217] If a civil service corps member considers the order to be inconsistent with the law or displays signs of error, he/she has the duty to inform their superior of this in writing. If the order is reconfirmed in writing by the superior, he/she is required to obey it but is then released from personal responsibility. A civil service corps member does not obey an order if its execution could result in committing an offence or a minor offence and has the duty to report this without delay to the director-general of the office he/she is employed in.[218]
- The duty to protect classified information. The civil service corps is bound by the Act on the Protection of Classified Information which determines the principles of protection of information the unauthorised disclosure of which would or could cause a threat to the fundamental interests of the Republic of Poland or expose those interests to a substantial damage, also during the course of its preparation, and irrespective of the form and way it is expressed.[219] Classified information can be entrusted exclusively to persons providing a guarantee of secrecy and only in the scope indispensable for them to perform their tasks or the execution of duties required at their post or other similar assigned tasks. Facts and circumstances that are general knowledge are not protected under the law.
- The duty of professional development. Civil service corps members are required to continuingly raise their qualifications, professional and general knowledge through continuing education and participation in training programmes.[220] Participation in training programmes is considered just as important as the performance of the official duties. There are specific regulations

---

*Cywilnej,* [Order **No. 114 of the Prime Minister dated 11 October 2002** on the Establishment of the Civil Service Code of Ethics], M. P., No. 46, item 683.

217 E. Zieliński, *Administracja rządowa w Polsce,* Warszawa, 2001, p. 106.

218 Civil Service Act of 5 July 1996 – Art. 48, Civil Service Act of 18 December 1998 – Art. 68, Civil Service Act of 24 August 2006 – Art. 48, Civil Service Act of 21 November 2008 – Art. 77.

219 Ustawa z dnia 5 sierpnia 2010 r. *O ochronie informacji niejawnych,* Dz. U. No. 182, item.1128, Chapter 2.

220 Civil Service Act of 5 July 1996 – Art. 47.6, Civil Service Act of 18 December 1998 – Art. 67, Civil Service Act of 24 August 2006 – Art. 47.6, Civil Service Act of 21 November 2008 – Art. 76.6.

regarding the duty of civil servants and civil service employees to take part in training programmes – the director-general of an office has the duty to establish a schedule of professional development for each civil servant.

- The duty of cost-effectiveness. Civil service corps members are required to manage public funds rationally.[221]
- The duty to move to another town or office. The transfer of a civil servant within the same office in the same town, taking into account his/her professional qualifications, can be made by the director-general.[222] If it is required in the 'interest of the civil service', the Head of the Civil Service may transfer a civil servant to another office in the same town and, if a particular interest of the civil service so requires, the Head of the Civil Service may transfer a civil servant to another office in another town for a period of up to two years.[223]
- The duty of keeping working hours – start and end work punctually. If the circumstances require it, a civil service corps member has the duty, when ordered by his/her superior, to perform tasks outside the normal working hours and in exceptional cases – also at night, on Sundays and holidays.
- The duty of abiding work safety regulations and principles. Civil service corps members should also be acquainted with work safety regulations and principles, attend training in those subjects, conduct their work in accordance with those regulations, take due care of furnishings and equipment and keep order in the workplace, apply group safety measures, appear for medical examinations.

Civil service corps members also have duties outside their official duties. This category includes the duty of conduct in a dignified manner when at his/her post as well as at all other times.[224] Civil servants should conduct themselves in a way which earns them respect. This means that the actions of a civil servant as a private person, outside his/her working hours, should never undermine the trust in public administration or tarnish the good name of the institution that employs them.

---

221 This duty is of particular importance as it concerns accumulated public funds from fiscal revenues.

222 Civil Service Act of 21 November 2008, Art. 62.

223 Ibid., Art. 63. In 2011 the Head of the Civil Service exercised his right to have a civil servant transferred once. 'Sprawozdanie Szefa Służby Cywilnej', 2012, op. cit., p. 27.

224 Civil Service Act of 5 July 1996 – Art. 47.7, Civil Service Act of 18 December 1998 – Art. 67.7, Civil Service Act of 24 August 2006 – Art. 47.7, Civil Service Act of 21 November 2008 – Art. 76.7.

The Civil Service Act precisely determines the scope of duties of civil servants and civil service employees. The list of duties is longer than foreseen by the Labour Code. The decision to seek employment in the Polish public administration means the conscious resignation from certain civil rights, such as the right to establish or join a political party (in the case of civil servants), to strike, to manifest publicly one's political convictions, the right to participate in election campaigns, to hold a function in trade unions or the incompatibility of positions.

The specific character of work in government administration means that the duty of the civil service corps is first of all to the state and society, the duty to abide by the constitution and other legal acts and succumb to limitations that being a state official entail.

If we look through the consecutive legal provisions of all the civil service acts that had been put into force to the present day, we will notice a certain regularity in the case of duties imposed on civil servants. First of all, the vast majority of policy-makers never had any doubts as to the importance of duties imposed on civil servants. Secondly, the July 1996 Act limited only the duties imposed on civil servants; other legislation increased the scope of duties imposed on the civil service corps, both the civil servants and civil service employees in government administration. This meant that, whereas in 1997 the imposed duties concerned 115 persons, as of 1998 they applied to 110 000 to 120 000 persons.

It would seem that the duties set down in legal acts and codes of ethics provide sufficient guidelines for public officials to follow. In reality the concepts of responsibility and responsible choice (Z. Bauman) in the modern world that 'used to reside in the semantic field of ethical duty and moral concern for the Other moved or have been shifted to the realm of self-fulfilment and calculation of risks. (…) "Responsibility" means now, first and last, responsibility to oneself'.[225] Effects of actions that are not subject to moral evaluation tend to be achieved by substituting 'responsibility for others' with 'responsibility to oneself' and 'responsibility for oneself'.[226]

## Professional Development in the Civil Service

Professional development of civil service corps members should be the responsibility of directors-general of offices whose task is the organisation of the process of establishing individual schedules of professional development of civil service

---

225 Z. Bauman, *Does ethics have a chance in a world of consumers?*, Cambridge, MA: Harvard University Press, 2008, pp. 52–53.

226 Ibid,. p. 53.

corps members in their offices. Directors-general of offices are also responsible for the approval of individual professional development programmes for persons in senior positions in the office.

One of the methods of human resources management in the civil service is the system of training programmes aimed at raising the effectiveness, competency, knowledge and skills of its members. The process of managing public administration institutions involves the management of those employed in the civil service. It is particularly important to provide training to those employed in managerial civil service positions, as it is their task to take the civil service through the difficulties encountered during the period of social and systemic transformation, changing laws, the implementation of new methods of management, electronic public administration and the establishment of relations with politicians.

Training and education of employees is intended to turn an employee, who has successfully completed the competition tests with the goal of finding a job and means of living, into a professional who is conscious of the mission of public service, has a sense of public responsibility and respect for moral values and is an actively engaged citizen. Public administration 'in order to achieve true professionalism has to be a virtual, self-educating organisation'[227].

In light of the above, training programmes need to adapt their subject matter to the challenges facing the administration. It seems that, although the approach of the Polish legislator changed along with the political changes taking place, the need for enhancing professional qualifications of the civil service remained among the priorities. Successive acts on the civil service have been upholding the principle of continuing training of civil service corps members. The training programmes should be available to all civil service corps members and address complex issues in various fields, such as ethics, administration, law, organisation and management, and interpersonal skills[228].

Apart from training organised by individual institutions in Poland, there were centrally planned training programmes that in 2011 addressed the issues of the 'Quality improvement of managerial competence of cadres managing inspection units in government administration in order to enhance professionalism in the

227 H. Kisilowska, 'Pojęcie profesjonalizmu we współczesnej administracji', in A. Dębicka, M. Dmochowski and B. Kudrycka (eds.), *Profesjonalizm w administracji publicznej*, Białystok, 2004, p. 109.

228 In 2011 various types of training courses were organised for about 25 thousand employees of ministries, central and voivodship institutions, in 'Sprawozdanie Szefa Służby Cywilnej', 2012, op. cit., p. 35.

execution of supervisory tasks' and 'Modern leadership in public organisations geared to changes – the role of senior positions in the civil service'.[229]

The answer to the question of the value of training, its effectiveness and quality is not that straightforward. The decentralisation of training brought on a profusion of firms providing training of unequal quality. The firms that win organised competitions are often those that simply have better-developed marketing skills, yet the effectiveness of their training programmes has never been the subject of discussion. As a result of the lack of a professional knowledge management system in the Polish civil service, the transfer of experience and conclusions from the training is also lagging behind.

The Department for the Civil Service in the Prime Minister's Chancellery in its attempt to combat the negative processes in the training systems pointed out that, first of all, staff training requirements should be properly identified by the offices themselves. Efforts to motivate their staff to take part in training courses 'should not be confused with the mere distribution by personnel offices of information about available courses – this may lead to self recruitment, a process that reduces the quantifiable benefits of training courses (this applies to 'soft' skills training in particular)'. Efforts aimed at encouraging participation in training should reflect the staff management policy implemented by the office and should be directed not only to its staff but their superiors as well. Decisions regarding the participation of particular persons in training courses should use merit criteria. The training should be organised in such a way as to avoid situations 'in which several persons holding key positions in the particular office participate in training at the same time'.[230]

In civil service systems, where the career based model is the dominant one, for the state to have the means to select the best qualified staff, it is important to provide, within its own capacity, the facilities, institutions that would prepare and train the prospective candidates for work in the civil service. Announcing a change in the approach to the question of human resources management in public administration in Poland was the establishment of the National School of Public Administration (KSAP) modelled on the French ENA. KSAP was established by virtue of a resolution of the Council of Ministers dated 30 May 1990. Its

229 Ibid, p. 34.

230 A. Tomaszewska, 'Informacja nt. raportu końcowego dotyczącego ewaluacji wybranych działań szkoleniowych realizowanych w ramach projektu "Wdrożenie strategii szkoleniowej"', *Przegląd Służby Cywilnej,* 2012, No. 1 (16), p. 30.

status is governed by the Act of 14 June 1991[231] and its statute of 23 August 1992, conferred by the Prime Minister.

The 1991 Act lays down the legal foundations for the school's operation, the rights and duties of its students. In accordance with its provisions, the school and its director are directly subordinate to the Prime Minister. This was probably intentional on the part of the legislators to ensure the school board's autonomy and stress the importance placed by the Third Republic of Poland on the training of personnel employed in public administration. In February 1991 the Council of the National School of Public Administration was established and teaching activities commenced on 4 September 1991. Among the school's activities, as provided in its statute, particular stress is placed on the education of candidates for senior positions; preparation of programmes and organisation of training for public administration personnel, the civil service in particular; cooperation with public administration, institutions of higher education, other institutions as well as foreign and domestic organisations. The school is also entitled to verify the command of selected foreign languages of public administration employees and persons performing public functions.

The training curriculum of the School is interdisciplinary in nature and focuses mainly on the development of practical skills. The primary programme consists of practical classes in the form of training sessions and research workshops while traditional lectures comprise approximately 20% of all classes. The status of the school's students has more in common with that of a public administration employee than with a typical university student (for example, students are entitled to holiday leave instead of a vacation). In the course of their education the students are bound by the same principles as state officials. The school offers full-time studies with no division into terms. The programme includes intensive courses in two western foreign languages. The school's statute also provides for internships with relevant public administration institutions at home and abroad (of 8–9 weeks duration). Classes are held in small groups.

An important part in the students' curriculum is the mandatory hands-on experience, one gained in a ministry or central institution in Poland and another in administrative institutions abroad, in countries such as the USA, France, Germany or the UK. The objective is for the students to become knowledgeable about the latest trends in the administrations of highly developed countries. There is a side effect to this as, while some students become closely acquainted with the career-based model, others gain the experience of the position-based

231 Ibid.

model, with both groups becoming fervent proponents of the respective models, thus very probably perpetuating the debate on which model would be best for Poland to adopt. Another effect of this is an attempt at combining the two in theory and everyday practice in public administration.

The entrance exam to the National School of Public Administration comprises the following elements:

- a written test on the candidate's knowledge of issues of public administration,
- a foreign language fluency exam to check the candidate's ability to perform during his/her internship abroad,
- a written assignment presenting arguments and a commentary to a played lecture on a broad area of issues of public administration (including international),
- an interview with the candidate by the commission.

In 2009 there was a change in the requirements for candidates wishing to sit the exam to KSAP concerning the knowledge of foreign languages; only one of three – English, French or German – is now required. The School's graduates are exempt from preparatory service. The Head of the Civil Service determines and publishes in the Civil Service Bulletin a sample application form for nomination to be used by KSAP graduates. KSAP graduates who are civil service employees, have an MA degree or its equivalent, know at least one foreign language, are reservist soldiers or exempt from general defence duty, submit their applications for nomination to the Head of the Civil Service from 1 January to 31 May of the given calendar year (similarly as all other participants in the qualification procedure).[232]

The Prime Minister indicates the first work posts of successive classes of KSAP graduates in the civil service, presented to him by the Head of the Civil Service, with the exception of senior posts. KSAP graduates are first in line for nomination. The total number of KSAP graduates since 1991 has reached almost 920 persons. The graduates are obliged, under Article 5.1 of the KSAP Act, to take up employment after graduation and they should provide information of their place of employment on the day of receipt of their diplomas, at the latest.

232 In the opinion of J. Jagielski and K. Rączka, this approach is not proper, nor necessary, as the language implies some sort of initial verification procedure whether the candidate meets the requirements, whereas 'checking whether conditions are met [by the candidate] is an integral element of application processing by the competent nominating authority', in J. Jagielski and K. Rączka, *Ustawa o służbie cywilnej. Komentarz*, Warszawa 2010, p. 213.

They are obliged to work off five years in public administration in positions at the disposal of the Prime Minister, including the civil service.

At the end of 2011 there were 678 KSAP graduates employed in the civil service corps, nearly 66% of all the School's graduates, of which the largest group were employed in posts in an independent capacity.[233] Almost 25% of senior positions in the civil service were occupied by KSAP graduates, although they accounted for less than 9% of all civil servants in 2010.[234]

When summing up the achievements of the School, one has to take into account a variety of factors. First, one should take a closer look at how policy-makers view it. Has the political vision regarding the School changed? It certainly seems so. In the early 1990s the majority of Polish politicians were convinced that the establishment of the National School of Public Administration would bring about a profound change in the rules and the philosophy governing the functioning of public administration and its human resources management that would guarantee KSAP graduates senior posts in the civil service (in the majority of cases, from department director to director-general, in the so-called 'attractive' ministries, such as the Ministry of Foreign Affairs, the Ministry of Finance or the Ministry of the Economy). However, after 2001 – undoubtedly due to the new left wing government, reluctant to pursue the concepts of their predecessors of a different political option, the School's graduates had something to worry about. The situation did not get any better under subsequent governments that did not share the enthusiasm of their predecessors in the 1990s for the School. The number of attractive posts offered to KSAP graduates dropped while distrust and even hostility towards them from the other public administration employees, who were not graduates of the School, rose. They were accused of many deficiencies: insufficient skills, insufficient professionalism and experience and disproportionate ambitions. The costs of the whole education process in the School were considered too high, the graduates too young and their privileges too many (for example, the right to select the place of employment, automatic nomination to the lowest civil service rank, fast track promotion to managerial positions).

There is a discussion currently underway on the future of the National School of Public Administration. In the opinion of the majority of directors-general, who in April 2012 had the opportunity to evaluate its curriculum and educational methods, the full-time curriculum does reflect the needs of public

233 Sprawozdanie Szefa Służby Cywilnej, 2012, op. cit., p. 27.
234 <http://www.ksap.gov.pl/ksap/file/pdf/co_z_ksap/Odpowiedz_Dyrektora_KSAP_4_kwietnia_2012.pdf> – accessed 4 July 2012.

administration, and the changes in the curriculum introduced in the years 2008–2011 have taken account of the changing needs of that administration. In evaluating the individual components of the curriculum, the dominant view was that they serve their purpose quite well. The classes in the 'Public administration and management' course were appraised most highly, while classes in the 'European Union and foreign policy' course and internships abroad received the lowest scores.[235] One of the most frequently raised issues is the need to adapt the student profiles to the individual requirements of institutions. Despite criticism, the National School of Public Administration is still considered a useful and valuable component in the functioning of the civil service. Only the form in which the education is provided remains a topic of discussion, yet the best solution seems to be the conversion of the School into one that provides training to those who already make up the civil service cadres.

235 < http://www.ksap.gov.pl/ksap/content/view/746/94/ >, accessed 21 June 2012.

# Chapter 5: Modern Methods of Managing Public Institutions

## Quality Management

The level at which administration performs is determined by many factors, of which the quality of its cadres is among the most important.[236]

Quality management is a method for ensuring that all the activities necessary to design, develop and implement a product or service are effective and efficient in relation to the system and its performance. The quality management system (QMS) outlines the policies and procedures necessary to improve, control and integrate the processes eventually leading to a better performance. Quality management systems determine the optimal conditions that allow organisations to adapt themselves to the continuously changing society they serve; they are an attempt at making management aware of who their customers are, their requirements and how these can be balanced with political imperatives, demonstrating at the same time clear commitment to citizens/customers and other stakeholders.[237]

QMS highlights those key activities or results where satisfactory performance is essential in order for an organisation to succeed. Key performance results are the results the organisation is achieving with regard to its strategy and planning related to the needs and demands of the different stakeholders (external results) and the results in relation to its management and improvement (internal results). In turn, the concept of competence includes knowledge, skills and attitudes of individuals used in practice in a job situation. Thus, the quality management system is a 'set of interrelated or interacting elements used: to establish policy and objectives, to achieve those objectives and to run and supervise an organisation in terms of quality'.[238]

The factors that affect quality include the so-called hard factors, or in other words, a documented quality management system based on ISO standards, tools and quality techniques, processes and self assessment, and the soft factors in the

236 P. Szreniawski, *Nauka o polityce administracji*, Rzeszów, 2008, p. 123.

237 The Common Assessment Framework (CAF 2006): Improving an organisation through self-assessment, p. 8.

238 M. Lewandowski, *System zarządzania jakością według ISO 9001:2008: wdrażanie i organizacja*, Warszawa 2010, p. 28.

form of increased efficiency of the staff, teamwork, training, commitment and communication between them.[239] These components complement each other.

Quality in the public sector is 'maximizing the value of products and services for all stakeholders within a political and financial framework'. Quality management in public administration helps to reduce 'passivity, resulting from legal regulations, in favour of greater engagement in the formulation and implementation of quality policy objectives'[240] through the process of 'continuous participation and cooperation of individuals who are aware of and acquainted with such a policy'.[241]

Total Quality Management (TQM) 'focuses on procedures and processes that are deemed instrumental in promoting quality'. Quality control, in turn, means checking the 'organisation's ability to create professional quality in the services it offers and delivers. It is systematic in that the results emerge from a planned, deliberate effort. Some organisations choose a system for quality control based on a quality manual or process manual. Quality control systems usually contain a select collection of guidelines for implementing quality controls in practice and how quality is measured and improved'.

TQM is a customer-oriented management philosophy that seeks to continuously improve business processes using analytical tools and teamwork involving all employees. There are several TQM models, the most commonly used being the EFQM, the CAF, the Malcolm Baldrige (USA), ISO 9004.

The civil service takes advantage of the achievements of the International Organisation for Standardization (ISO). ISO identifies 'what International Standards are required by business, government and society, develops them in partnership with the sectors that will put them to use, adopts them by transparent procedures based on national input and delivers them to be implemented worldwide. ISO Standards specify the requirements for state-of-the-art products, services, processes, materials and systems, and for good conformity assessment, managerial and organisational practice'.[242]

---

239 T. Thiagarajan and M. Zairi, *A review of total quality management in practice: understanding the fundamentals through examples of best practice applications – Part I*, http://www.deepdyve.com/lp/emerald-publishing/a-review-of-total-quality-management-in-practice-understanding-the-c3yEl0cQTO, accessed 12 January 2012.

240 B. Kożuch, 'Modele zarządzania publicznego', in T. Białas (ed.), *Dylematy i wyzwania współczesnego zarządzania organizacjami publicznymi*, Gdynia, 2007, pp. 17–20.

241 K. Dajczak, 'Zarządzanie jakością a jakość zarządzania', in T. Wawak (ed.), *Komunikacja i jakość w zarządzaniu*, Vol. 1, Kraków, 2010, pp. 442–445.

242 CAF 2006, op. cit., p. 46.

The ISO 9000 family is a collection of four standards, thus forming a coherent set of quality management system standards.[243] The introduction to this category is ISO 9000: 2008, which specifies the basic terminology to achieve consistency in communications and to eliminate ambiguity of the concept of 'quality'. A uniform definition and shared understanding of terms within the international environment is intended to contribute to a more effective implementation of the system (E. Kreier, *ISO 9001: Effective Method of Obtaining a Quality Certificate)*. ISO 9001: 2008 is focused on customer needs and maximum effectiveness in their achievement with the efficient use of resources of the institution.

The ISO 9001: 2008 standard is the most commonly used (certified to by nearly 800 thousand entities in 161 countries) and discusses the practical aspects of implementing quality policy. It also sets out the requirements that must be met to ensure consistent satisfaction of customer expectations. These include: the principle of focusing on a customer whose needs should be defined, understood and fulfilled by all employees of the organisation and the insistence on effective exchange of information with the customer, which is the most important measure of success in this category;[244] the principle of establishing leadership, which requires management to focus on the development of the organisation and change their attitude from that of a supervisor to that of genuine leader. This principle points to the importance of the proper identification of objectives, indication of the direction to follow and a skilful creation of the company's image, which encourages greater involvement by the staff, strengthens the leadership position and helps to tackle the problems with quality that in 80% are the result of bad organisation and human resources management.[245] Another of the principles is that of involvement of people 'where it is important that they fully identify ideologically with the mission of the organisation they are working for and express their full involvement through conscientious execution of their duties'.[246] The Standard recommends, among other things, participation not only in compulsory internal courses necessary for the maintenance of entitlements

243 A. Jazdon, *Doskonalenie zarządzania jakością*, Bydgoszcz, 2001, p. 30.

244 J. Zymonik, 'Czynniki ewolucji znormalizowanych systemów zarządzania jakością, in *Nowe prądy w ocenie systemów zarządzania jakością*, conference materials of the Wrocław University of Technology, Wrocław, 2005, p. 14.

245 W. Sokołowicz, *ISO – system zarządzania jakością*, Warszawa, 2004, p. 32.

246 A. Springer, 'Znaczenie postaw i kompetencji pracownika w zarządzaniu zasobami ludzkimi w organizacji', in T. Wawak (ed.), *Komunikacja i jakość w zarządzaniu*, Vol. 1, Kraków, 2010, pp. 72–76.

but also in extra courses in interpersonal skills such as those that teach effective communication and modern management methods.

Another standard in the ISO 9000 family is ISO 9004 that includes elements of ISO 9001 as well as marketing issues, costs associated with quality, safety, responsibility for services delivered and assessment of the quality management system installed, in order to maintain the organisation's process of self-development by continuously improving efficiency and satisfaction of all involved, both the institution and citizens/customers, the recipients of decisions. Another standard, ISO 19011, refers to the group of users involved in the implementation of quality management systems, in the certification process and in the conduct of audits, thus being the last point of control in the implementation of the quality management system.

The implementation of the service quality Standard, known in Poland as ISO 9000, means the introduction of changes in the management of an office in order to make it more functional and customer-friendly. The first Polish office to implement a quality management system in accordance with ISO 9000 was the Town Hall in Dzierżoniów. In November 1999 it obtained the certificate confirming the implementation of the new system aimed at raising the qualifications of its staff, addressing the needs and expectations of the local community in its programmes and development plans, settling citizen problems in keeping with procedures and time limits prescribed by law.[247] Next to follow in its footsteps was the Town Hall in Kwidzyń that only a few months later obtained the ISO 9001 certificate for the reorganisation of work at its offices to better adjust it to the needs of the town's residents. This involved specifically the establishment of a customer service office and a free customer helpline where callers can obtain information about such things as what documents need to be submitted in a specific case. It was not long for other public administration offices to follow in towns such as: Sopot, Bielsko-Biała, Gliwice, Śrem, Toruń, Pabianice, the Municipality Office of Warszawa-Ursynów, the Poviat Office in Pruszków, the Voivodship Office for Małopolska and more.

The civil service also applies the methods of the Common Assessment Framework (CAF) regarding:

a) consensus, which is about 'reaching agreement and usually follows an initial self-assessment when individual assessors get together to compare and discuss their individual assessments and individual scores. The process usually

247 S. Wysocki, 'Jak poprawić jakość działania administracji publicznej?', *Służba Cywilna*, No. 2, 2001, p. 27.

ends with individual assessors reaching agreement with a combined overall score and assessment for the organisation';
b) network, as an informal organisation connecting people or organisations that may or may not have a formal line of command; members of the network often share values and interests;
c) balanced scorecard, which is a set of quantitative and qualitative measurements to evaluate the extent to which the organisation is successful in achieving its mission and strategic objectives. These measurements take into account four aspects: innovation and learning, internal processes, customers and financial management. The indicators of each approach are linked to each other through a cause-effect relationship.[248]

The experience acquired through CAF enables the skilful use of strategic comparative analysis when the organisation seeks to improve its overall performance by examining the long-term strategies and methods that had contributed to the success of organisations recording good results. The analysis includes a comparison of such aspects as core competencies, the development of new products and services, a change in the balance of activities or the development of skills necessary to deal with changes in the external environment. It also includes the implementation of a variety of practices such as, for example, a brainstorming session in which the most important rule is to avoid any kind of criticism during the ideas development phase,[249] the application of the PDCA cycle (Plan-Do-Check-Act) as an improvement programme for public administration operation (including the civil service), in which it is crucial to start with careful planning, followed by effective action subject to verification and possible correction, and to move on to another cycle that again begins with careful planning. The CAF method may improve communication in all directions, both top-down and bottom-up, raising awareness of the importance of organisational values and developing a code of conduct as well as installing more transparency, more accountability and more empowerment.[250]

The main features of 'good governance' in the public sector are determined by the appointed framework of authority and control. They include 'the reporting obligation on the goals achievement, transparency of actions and decision making process to the stakeholders, efficiency and effectiveness, responsiveness to

248 CAF 2006, op. cit., p. 43, 44, 47.
249 Ibid, p. 44.
250 P. Staes et al., 'Five Years of CAF 2006: From Adolescence to Maturity – What Next?', European (EIPA) CAF Resource Centre, p. 27.

the needs of society, anticipation of the problems and trends and respect of the law and rules'.

Excellence is an element of CAF and it includes: results orientation, focusing on the needs of both present and potential citizens-customers, leadership and constancy of purpose, management by processes and facts (the desired result is achieved more efficiently when the related resources and activities are managed as a process and effective decisions are based on the analysis of data and information), involvement of people and their development (creation of a working environment of shared values, a culture of trust, openness, empowerment and recognition), continuous learning, innovation and improvement, mutually beneficial partnerships (public sector organisations can achieve their goals only by working together with other organisations) and corporate social responsibility (compliance with the principles of sustainable development and environmental protection).[251]

Of particular importance from the point of view of public service is the evidence, or information that supports a statement or fact, which is essential in forming a conclusion or a judgment. There is a follow up once the self-assessment process is completed and changes introduced. Then there are the intermediate outputs (products delivered from one department to another within an organisation) and final outputs (products or services delivered to someone outside the organisation), which are the immediate results of production in the form of products and services. Effectiveness is the relation between the set goal and the impact, effect or long-term outcome achieved. Cost effectiveness is the relationship between the effects that are implied by the goal of the organisation and the costs of achieving them (possibly including the full social costs).[252]

Innovation is defined as 'the process of translating good ideas into new public services, processes, tools, systems and human interaction. An organisation may be described as innovative when an existing task is performed in a way new at the workplace, or when the organisation offers its customers a new service in a different way such as self-service via the Internet'.[253]

Suggestions for improvements to the CAF model refer to the further development of e-communities, creating an off-line version of CAF e-tools, greater availability of information about CAF, support at political level, an accurate

251 Ibid., p. 32.
252 CAF 2006, op. cit, pp. 45–47.
253 Ibid, p. 46.

description of best practices, promotion of learning from others and avoiding mistakes that others have made.

## Knowledge Management

The civil service should make use of comparative analysis (benchmarking) and/ or knowledge analysis (bench learning). In practice, comparative analysis usually involves: 'regularly comparing aspects of performance (functions or processes) with those organisations which are considered to be good practitioners (applying good practices); sometimes reference is made to "best in class", but as no one can ever be certain as to who is best, the term "good" is preferred; identifying gaps in performance; seeking fresh approaches to bring about improvements in performance, following through with implementing improvements, following up by monitoring progress and reviewing the benefits'.[254]

In European public administrations benchmarking usually focuses on the aspect of learning through the sharing of knowledge, information and even risk. This, in turn, links it with knowledge analysis (bench learning), in which greater emphasis is placed not on comparison but on the learning process based on an analysis of the strengths of other institutions, as well as on learning from their mistakes (and avoiding them in later practice). Knowledge analysis involves employing good practices.[255]

Knowledge management is the method of exploiting accumulated experience, potential and 'institutional memory' by the civil service corps. It may be institutional in form – the management of accumulated knowledge and experience by a public institution, for example, in the form of a developed organisational culture or the institution of good practice which is the sum of its accumulated experience through trial and error. It may also be individual in form – the management of knowledge of people employed in the civil service. Knowledge management conceived as a public good means the duty to share it within a public institution (internally) as well as with other public institutions (externally). As a public good it requires support from the state – beginning with a system of financing university studies, through investment in professional development of civil service corps employees and civil servants, and ending with the adequate equipment of offices.

The essence of knowledge management is 'gathering data and information, their selection and conversion into knowledge embedded in the culture of the

254 Ibid., p. 44.
255 Ibid., p. 40.

organisation. Knowledge so produced becomes the primary resource of the organisation that enables it to achieve the established goals.'[256]

The OECD uses the term 'knowledge management' loosely to refer to 'a broad collection of organisational practices related to generating, capturing, disseminating *know-how* and promoting knowledge sharing within an organisation and with the outside world, including: organisational arrangements (decentralisation of authority, opening up bureaucratic divisions, use of information and communication technology etc.); personnel development (mentoring and training practices, mobility etc.) and management of skills; transfer of competencies (databases of staff competencies, outlines of good work practices, etc.); managerial changes and incentives for staff to share knowledge (staff performance assessment and promotion linked to knowledge sharing, evolution of the role of managers, etc.)'.[257]

Knowledge, according to OECD experts, can be divided into four categories. These include: knowledge about facts, close to what is normally called information – it can be broken down into bits and communicated as data; knowledge about principles and laws of nature or society; knowledge about those with knowledge and the description of that knowledge, provided that they have the social ability of cooperation and communication with experts on the outside and, finally, knowledge with regard to skills, intuition and experience of people employed in the organisation (*know-how*).[258] *Know-how* is considered as knowledge 'partially embedded in organisations, structures and institutions. This does not rule out the possibility that an organisation's competence may be dramatically weakened by the departure of key persons. Nonetheless, a layer of knowledge (shared codes of communication, shared routines, commonly shared methods for problem solving and searching) would normally remain.'[259]

S. Mazur distinguishes three types of knowledge: strategic (understood as knowledge essential to create reflexively meta-rules for programming principles and to design state development policy steering instruments); tactical (understood as knowledge applicable in the development of public policies and programmes for the achievement of the development policy goals of the country);

---

256 S.Mazur, 'Zarządzanie wiedzą w polskiej administracji publicznej', in A. Haber, M. Szałaj (eds.), *Środowisko i warsztat ewaluacji,* Warszawa: PARP, 2008, p. 51.

257 OECD (2003) 'Conclusions from the Results of the Survey of Knowledge Management Practices for Ministries/Departments/Agencies of Central Government in OECD Member Countries', Paris: OECD – PUMA, p. 4.

258 Knowledge Management in the Learning Society, OECD, 2000, p. 14 et seq.

259 Ibid., p. 19.

and operational (knowledge allowing both the effective, efficient and responsive implementation of public policies and programmes as well as delivering standard public services).[260]

Knowledge management is a 'structured and continuous sharing of acquired knowledge with other interested government administration institutions and the use of accumulated knowledge and experience that is the result of cooperation with analytical-advisory institutions using modern communication tools'.[261]

The knowledge management system in the Polish civil service is still barely in its initial stage. 'This system is overloaded with data, incomplete resources of information and so a limited knowledge potential that could otherwise provide the basis for economically and socially rational decisions by the state and its institutions. The primary drawback is its low capacity to generate knowledge useful in decision-making processes.'[262]

Knowledge management, its quality and transfer speed are crucial factors affecting the efficiency of services offered by the civil service, and the level of its development requires the use of ever newer techniques of collecting, processing, transfer and use of its resources.

Knowledge generation and management in the civil service is a process of mutual interaction between politicians, people employed in the civil service, customers of the office as well as public institutions. Knowledge is generated not only in the office but by universities, education and training systems, experts, political parties, private companies and the media.

Tools that support knowledge management in the civil service include: e-learning, distance learning, the knowledge base (law, standards, good practices etc.), the 'community of practitioners', expert groups, innovation and research management, learning from others as well as drawing conclusions from the mistakes of others, management of documentation (description of processes, procedures, instructions, etc.), management of citizen/customer relations, intellectual capital management.

260 Mazur, op. cit., p. 60.

261 *Wytyczne dla urzędów administracji rządowej w sprawie wzmocnienia potencjału analitycznego służby cywilnej poprzez wykorzystanie potencjału środowisk naukowych i eksperckich,* 26 July 2011, Warszawa 2011, < http://dsc.kprm.gov.pl/sites/default/files/wytyczne.pdf >, accessed 6 July 2012.

262 Mazur, op. cit., p. 51.

Knowledge management components are often referred to as six core processes: knowledge identification, acquisition, development, sharing and distribution, utilisation and retention.[263]

The main aim of knowledge management is to 'increase the efficiency of the organisation and in terms of strategic benefits – to increase the satisfaction of stakeholders (individual and institutional) with the level of implementation of tasks'.[264] In accordance with the human resources management standards introduced by the Head of the Civil Service in the civil service in May 2012, directors-general are required to determine the principles and implement knowledge management tools in their offices to facilitate knowledge sharing by employees and improve access to knowledge held by other people in the office.[265]

Examples of good practice in knowledge management already in place include: regular meetings of human resources management employees (initiative of the Ministry of National Defence), exchange of in-house trainers between offices (the Mazowsze Voivodship Office – Ministry of the Economy – Civil Rights Ombudsman), meetings of experts at the National School of Public Administration, interdepartmental expert task groups.

There are several interlinked factors that impact the practice of knowledge management in the Polish civil service. These include: funds deficit, personnel restrictions, the organisational structure of government administration, access to and use of information and communication technology (ICT), the influence of policy-makers on the knowledge management system in the civil service, the impact of the time factor in the process of knowledge management, the operation of closed and open knowledge management systems in the civil service and the loss of resources.

The cause of funds deficit may be the fact that the civil service has at its disposal budget resources allocated for a particular year. Financial resources for knowledge management should be planned in a long-term perspective that takes into account both a negative option, an economic crisis for instance, and

---

263 G. Probst, S. Raub and K. Rombardt, *Managing Knowledge*, John Wiley & Sons Ltd., 2000, p. 35.

264 K. Mroczka, *Zarządzanie wiedzą jako element systemu zarządzania zasobami,* Mazowiecki Urząd Wojewódzki w Warszawie, Warszawa, 2012.

265 Załącznik do Zarządzenia Nr 3 Szefa Służby Cywilnej z 30 maja 2012 r. *w sprawie standardów zarządzania zasobami ludzkimi w służbie cywilnej, V. Rozwój i szkolenia.* [Attachment to Ordinance No. 3 of the Head of the Civil Service dated 30 May 2012 on Human Resources Management Standards in the Civil Service, Chapter 5 – Development and Training]

a positive one – a period of economic growth. Otherwise resources of accumulated knowledge may be lost, or part of the financial resources may be wasted on processes not relevant to knowledge management. It is essential to analyse the costs and effects that the implementation of knowledge management brings. Should there be a reduction in the appropriated funds, it is necessary to decide which resources are of particular importance in terms of institutional continuity and, should the budget appropriations be higher, which knowledge management processes should be strengthened in the civil service in order to improve its efficiency and the rationality of its performance.

A deficit of financial resources bears its impact on the use of ICT solutions to manage knowledge in the civil service. Modern technologies are costly, budgetary resources limited, the staff not always prepared to use the available resources. Another drawback is the lack of a uniform integrated government IT system that would not only be at the disposal of the entire civil service and allow, for example, the electronic circulation of documents within its framework but would include all the institutions that could enhance that knowledge – universities, analytical centres, expert groups. The civil service should consider the formation of new communication networks. The idea of the departure from a strictly hierarchical system in favour of such a network is not too popular, whether among the decision makers or the civil service corps itself.

Smart application of ICT solutions helps to improve levels of services provided by the office, to increase customer satisfaction and earn the sympathy of citizens. Their efficient application reduces the number of administrative procedures and helps in their simplification, stimulates continuing learning and training of new personnel.[266] The office then operates like a modern enterprise with a separate customer service department responsible for collecting orders electronically. In charge of the implementation of such a system is a team responsible for internal administrative procedures that automatically process the data entering the system. To ensure the electronic exchange of information between the various institutions in a safe way, it is necessary to have compatibility between the different IT systems.[267] The use of information and communication technology allows the office to shorten customer service time and benefit citizens financially as well as lighten the burden of civil servants and civil service employees.[268]

---

266 See M. Kleiber, *W kierunku nowoczesnego urzędu*, Warszawa, 2004.

267 A. Pawłowska, 'Od wirtualnej administracji do elektronicznych urzędów', *Służba Cywilna*, No. 7, 2003/2004.

268 For more on this issue see Chapter 6.

In the civil service, knowledge management requires the preparation of the corps members for the new tasks. It may necessitate the employment of new people who already have the skills required for the task, provided that they are available on the labour market. It is also possible to find people already working in the civil service who are sufficiently equipped for the challenge of knowledge management or possibly only require some additional training in this field. However staffing problems increase during periods of economic crisis due to the lack of resources, higher personnel turnover and loss of institutional memory. Weakening or loss of part of knowledge management components may also take place during administrative reforms involving the reduction of part of organisational structures and the resulting layoffs of employees.

The impact of the political system on knowledge management in the civil service, as a result of tenure of politicians elected in general elections and of their treatment of the civil service as loot that I have written about more than once, means, among other things, frequent changes in the strategic goals of the civil service, lack of a monitoring system of the implementation processes of strategies adopted by the civil service, the confusion of strategic objectives with tactical ones by politicians, etc. Politicians focused on achieving rapid success may not see the benefits of a long-term and consistent knowledge management policy.

The influence of the time factor in the civil service increases with the use of the knowledge management method there. Time verifies the meaning of knowledge management processes and perpetuates the good practices in this regard. The phenomenon of 'crowding-out time', or the return to lost or abandoned practice, may also occur. The pressure of time in the civil service restricts the exchange of information not only between departments within a single ministry or voivodship office but also between the different ministries and the voivodship offices as well as across the whole of the civil service.

A pilot study on knowledge management has been conducted under the Learning Ministries (MUS) project, an analysis of the potential of 'public governance' implementation. The four ministries that took part in this project were: the Ministry of Economy, the Ministry of Regional Development, the Ministry of the Environment and the Ministry of Infrastructure. The study showed that knowledge management did exist in these ministries but was fragmented and its particular components unnamed and unidentified. Because of this there was a dispersion of functions and lack of coordination of the management process. All agreed that the negative observable fact was the 'lack of feedback loops' in the circulation of information on performance at the level of employee-superior.

Employees become disoriented as they don't know whether they have performed their tasks properly. The lack of a structured and formalised information-sharing network results in weak institutional memory. In addition, 'the lack of collective reflection leads to a focus on corrective action and reaction (a single-loop learning). Double-loop learning to strengthen the effectiveness and rationality of efforts (and hence the strategic use of knowledge)' is not taking place, in the opinion of the respondents.[269] The prevailing practice in the surveyed ministries is learning from their own mistakes, and the current system is focused on procedures and processes, rather than on functions and goals these processes and procedures should serve to achieve. In a situation where the goals are unclear, 'the reference point required to identify the necessary sources of information, categories of analysis and principles for the identification and correction of errors, as well as to seek growth opportunities and define alternative solutions disappears.' It is true that there are informal groups of knowledge-sharing in the offices, but they only operate within a division or a department. This signifies that there is personal development and learning in these ministries, but there is a lack of institutional learning. Another problem is the weakness of the learning processes; there is no regular performance analysis, no institutionalised form of interaction with outside institutions, and only ad hoc expert solutions are applied.[270]

The authors of the MUS report suggest that changes aimed at the creation of a knowledge-based system should be of partial scope, from the bottom-up, based on small, relatively simple tests and improvements which should be followed with a verification of the effects of the incremental changes. It is necessary to take measures designed to determine objectives at the level of ministries, which requires major structural changes; the introduction of self-reflection tools in working teams (self-assessment techniques, discussion animation and self-reflection on a regular basis at the level of departmental divisions and progressing to the level of departments); strengthening the potential of the management cadres as promoters of change; investing in IT tools, databases and libraries.[271]

Thus, in the Polish civil service one observes a strong tendency to build closed management systems within a single ministry or office with little desire to share good practices and experience with others coupled with just as little activity in seeking out good models to exploit. Lack of openness may occur in institutional form, which means that a public institution is building its own knowledge

269 See K. Olejniczak et al., 'Polskie ministerstwa jako organizacje uczące się', *Raporty i Analizy EUROREG* 1(4)/2010, pp. 50–54 et seq.

270 Ibid., loc. cit.

271 Ibid., p. 53.

management system and does not benefit from the practice and experience of others, as well as in individual form, when there is no exchange of knowledge between people employed in similar positions in various ministries and offices.[272]

## Management by Objectives

Management by objectives as the method used in the management of human resources in an organisation was defined by Peter Drucker in his book *The Practice of Management*, first published in 1954. Management by objectives is the identification of the organisation's objectives beginning at strategic level and through to the operational level. 'A clear indication of objectives to be achieved by each employee and their harmonisation with the organisation's objectives will not only substantially increase motivation of our people but also bring order into the organisation itself and allow identification of bottlenecks and excess capacity. The mechanism of agreement (negotiations) of objectives also provides loop feedback at every level about the feasibility of the set objectives.[273]

Management by objectives can therefore be an effective tool in showing employees at all levels how to proceed in their work. But, according to P. Drucker, whether they will want to do this depends on the spirit of the organisation that 'motivates, that calls upon a man's reserves of dedication and effort, that decides whether he will give his best or do just enough to get by. It is the purpose of an organisation to make "common men do uncommon things" – this phrasing is Lord Beveridge's.'[274]

Management by objectives is a tool intended to improve the operation of the office in line with the mission and the purpose for which it was set up. An interesting example of good practice in the field of management by objectives is the functioning of the Mazowsze Voivodship Office in Warsaw (MUW). True to the mission that 'the voivod is government closer to the people' the office set down its priorities for 2009 to be professional and timely customer/citizen service, rational and efficient use of resources, improvement of quality management and an open information policy.

---

272 An example of an office developing a knowledge management system is the Energy Regulatory Office – see M. Krawczyk, *Problematyka zarządzania informacją i wiedzą w instytucjach sektora publicznego na przykładzie Urzędu Komunikacji Elektronicznej*, KNWS 2010.

273 http://www.mhr.pl/mhr-zarzadzanie-przez-cele – accessed 6 June 2012.

274 P. F. Drucker: *The Practice of Management*, Harper Business, 2006, pp. 144–145.

The process of the annual setting of objectives in the MUW is a hierarchical one. The voivod, who stands at the head of the office, is the person responsible for setting down the office's strategic objectives. Next, the heads of divisions determine the objectives and the quantitative measurements for their divisions. The director-general of office endorses the goals and measurements for the divisions and the voivod accepts the goals and measurements for the divisions. And this is exactly how the MUW prepared its annual strategic objectives for the years 2010–2012. In 2010, the goals were to achieve greater efficiency in the implementation of tasks, the reduction of the number of outstanding administrative procedures, and cuts in staff. In 2011, they were to improve levels of customer/citizen satisfaction, increase task implementation efficiency and completion of any outstanding administrative proceedings, and in 2012 – staff reduction, improvement of timeliness of issuing decisions and time-reduction of verification procedures.[275]

The document that the heads of divisions receive from the voivod is called the Annual Action Plan (AAP) and describes in detail how the objectives are to be achieved, defines the quantitative measurements that determine the degree of their progress at the division, the office and even at particular task levels. This document is prepared once a year and consists of the AAPs of individual divisions and the Consolidated Action Plan of the Office. Implementation of the objectives specified in the AAP is monitored and assessed in quarterly cycles. The AAP consists of the following components:

- priority tasks for the division, specifying: task name, objective, progress measurements, planned quantitative measurements, task performance cost, planned measures to attain the objective,
- the project budget, specifying: task name, objective, progress measurements, planned quantitative measurements, planned task performance cost, determination of measures to attain the objective,
- strategic objectives: improvement of timeliness of executed tasks; measurement: the relationship between the number of decisions issued past their deadline and the total number of decisions,
- planned quantitative measurements – measures facilitating the achievement of the objectives. Serving these objectives is time-reduction of verification procedures; measurement: average duration of verification procedures, planned quantitative measurement, measures taken to achieve the objective.

275 E. Stanisławska, *Zarządzanie przez cele. Doświadczenia Mazowieckiego Urzędu Wojewódzkiego*, Warszawa 2012.

Improvement of timeliness of executed tasks, measurement: the relationship between the number of decisions exceeding the deadline and the total number of decisions made, planned quantitative measurements, measures taken to achieve the objective,[276]

- increased levels of customer/citizen satisfaction, survey of delivered services, service users, planned satisfaction levels, measures taken to achieve the objective.

A management facilitating tool for organisations from the point of planning, implementation, monitoring and control of strategy implementation is the Balanced Scorecard. The BSC uses a coherent system of measurements for the evaluation of the extent the organisation is effective viewed from four perspectives: financial, customer, internal processes, potential and development; it enables the assessment of past activities and anticipation of future results; and by integrating strategic and operational objectives, it enables easy transmission of strategy to lower organisational levels.

The Mazowsze Voivodship Office in Warsaw

Balanced Scorecard

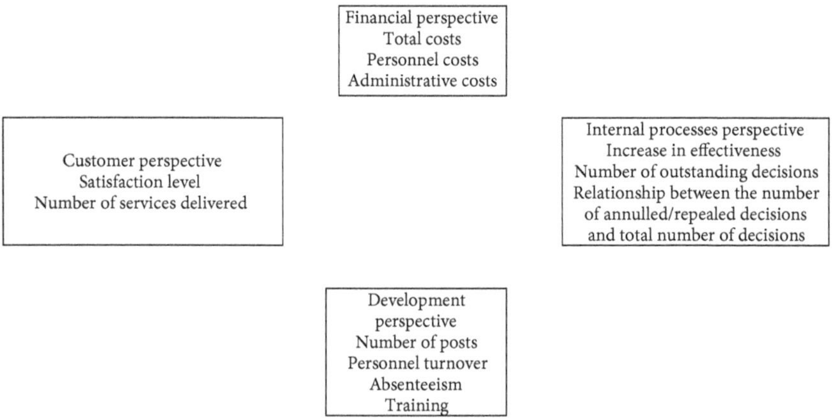


Source: E. Stanisławska, *Zarządzanie przez cele.*

The benefits of implementing management by objectives at the Mazowsze Voivodship Office are:

276 Ibid.

- definition of measurable and concrete operational objectives, broken down by particular tasks (services), and of measurements of their realisation;
- alignment of operational objectives with overriding strategic objectives;
- involvement in the implementation of set goals at all levels of management;
- the possibility of making financial and organisational decisions on the basis of concrete data;
- the possibility of an objective (based on 'hard' measurements) performance evaluation at all levels;
- easier identification of areas that require improvement or corrective action;
- improved effectiveness despite a decrease in personnel;
- significant improvement in the quality of services delivered by the office; the effect: an improved perception of the office.[277]

Due to the use of modern management tools consistent with quality policy, such as transparency, wise and well-planned costs management, annual action plans, the Mazowsze Voivodship Office succeeded in introducing an organisational culture focused on achieving results. The effectiveness of used resources and the quality of customer service also improved. In the same period, staff was reduced (at the office and consolidated units) from 1447 people in 2007, 1505 in 2009, to 1365 people in 2011.[278]

## Ethical Management in the Civil Service

Ethical standards in public administration are shaped by the ethical infrastructure, or in other words such processes, mechanisms, legal standards, ethics and institutions that encourage the maintenance of a certain canon of ethical values and limit undesirable behaviour. In determining the ethical standards of public administration, the following should be taken into account:

- the professional and social specificity of public administration,
- the success criterion, which is not a financial one, but the satisfaction of the needs of citizens,
- the political empowerment of citizens, who are not merely consumers of public services,[279]

277 Ibid.

278 http://www.mazowieckie.pl/portal/pl/2/8698/Polska_Prezydencja_o_MUW_na_konferencji.html – accessed 29 September 2011.

279 D. Długosz, 'Kadry w administracji publicznej', in J. Hausner (ed.), *Administracja publiczna*, Warszawa 2006, p. 235.

- the functioning of public administration in conformity with rule of law principles, including serving as an example for other sectors – economic and non-governmental organisations – to follow and thus select such canons of ethical values that constitute the basis of good governance, give legitimacy to public administration performance, prevent unethical behaviour, corruption in particular, develop positive values in public life and make taking difficult decisions easier.[280]

The implementation of selected, clearly defined canons of ethical values relies on ethical management that – by observing norms and values, including the criterion of social responsibility and the development of ethical principles among public administration employees (with particular emphasis on senior positions) – ensures the application of the idea of public ethics in practice. 'Public ethics may be defined as common values and norms in the public services. The moral nature of these norms refer to what is judged to be right, wrong, good or bad behaviour.' Public ethics answers the question whether the behaviour of a civil servant is 'legally and morally correct in a given situation'.[281]

Public service ethics is a set of 'common values and norms to which public servants subscribe in carrying out their duties. The moral nature of these values/ norms, which may be stated or implicit, refer to what is considered to be right, wrong, good or bad behaviour. Whereas values serve as moral principles, norms may also state what is legally and morally correct in a given situation'.[282] It is within this framework that the mission of an office is defined, in line with what the 'organisation should achieve for its stakeholders. The mission of a public sector organisation results from a public policy and/or statutory mandates. It is the organisation's "raison d'être"'.[283]

Ethics in public life is positioned 'between normative ethics (a set of moral norms) and applied ethics (the application of these norms in practice) and refers to values such as public good, public interest, justice, equality before the law, equal opportunities and freedom. The discrepancy between civic and bureaucratic ethics is most evident in the attitude to returning favours, making preference for

280 Ibid., p. 251.

281 *Ethics in the Public Services of the European Union Member States, under the Irish Presidency* 2004, Ch. Demmke and D. Bossaert, EIPA, Maastricht, January to June 2004, p. 14.

282 CAF 2006, p. 45.

283 Ibid., p. 47.

friends, the right to participate in political party organs, the freedom of running a business and the right to privacy'.[284]

Ethics in the case of government administration applies to 'a set of duties and rights that derive from an individual's particular position in his/her official, professional and organisational relationships (…) when we speak about an ethical attitude, we are speaking about values, duties and tasks that we are committed to professionally, officially and organisationally'.[285]

The basic values that public administration abides by are shaped by the political system in which it functions, the system's 'fundamental ideological, cultural and organisational strategies as well as the culture, tradition and the history of that society'.[286] These values vary depending on the level of social development and wealth, the tradition of a pragmatic culture (as in the UK) or a rational one (as in Germany).

The identification of ethical responsibilities and the definition of prohibitions and requirements, to which civil servants should subscribe, is a task for contemporary professional ethics.

Professional ethics is especially important in those professions where, first, the professional works for the greater good of the customer, and second, the customer has little possibility of controlling the actions of the professional.[287] Does a public official fit in this category? The answer seems to be 'Yes', if by the term of greater good, we understand all the important matters that affect the functioning and satisfaction of a human individual: freedom, private property, equal opportunity, knowledge, social security, the right to justice, freedom of speech, etc. These goods require constant care and effort: 'they are perishable and at the same time constantly desired'.[288] Despite legislative effort to improve controls over the work of civil service corps members by introducing, for example, greater citizen access to information on the activities of public administration, these efforts seem insufficient. And although government and self-government officials are controlled by many internal and external control institutions, in

---

284 B. Kudrycka, '*Etyka w życiu publicznym*', *Kontrola Państwowa*, No. 2, 1998, pp. 3–5.

285 B. Kudrycka, *Dylematy etyczne pracowników administracji*, Warszawa, 1995, p. 47.

286 I. Macek, '*Aksjologiczne uwarunkowania procesu decyzyjnego w administracji publicznej*', *in* L. Habuda (ed.), *Administracja i polityka. Proces decyzyjny w administracji publicznej*, Wrocław, 2000, p. 81.

287 See more on the subject in P. Łuków, *Granice zgody: autonomia zasad i dobro pacjenta*, Warszawa, 2005.

288 See more on the subject in T. Romer and M. Najda, *Etyka dla sędziów. Rozważania*, Warszawa, 2007, p. 8 et seq.

direct politician – public official – customer contact, it will always be the professional or official who has the upper hand.

The first principle of professional responsibility is *primum non nocere*, or the principle of: 'Above all, not knowingly to do harm.' This principle is the basic rule of professional ethics and the basic rule of an ethics of public responsibility.[289] A professional is required to have skills based on theoretical knowledge, training and education, a test of the competence administered by a professional body, and his/her career path is dependent on the existence of a formal professional organisation that has the power to regulate entry to the profession and on the existence of a code of ethical conduct.[290]

There are many factors that influence professional ethics of civil servants such as:

- general ethics guidelines,
- civil service traditions,
- the environment in which the civil service is functioning, including the living conditions and needs of society, as well as the constitutional position of the civil service, the socio-political system, Europeanisation and globalisation,
- the nature and social rank of the tasks performed by civil servants,
- the position of civil servants in the social hierarchy,
- the rights and duties of civil servants,
- the role and responsibilities of senior civil servants within the framework of the civil service corps (in public administration in general).

Studies conducted in 29 OECD countries in 2000 and 2009 identified political neutrality and impartiality as core public service values, with legality following right behind. Also found to be in high regard were transparency and integrity/honesty while efficiency and professionalism seem to be increasingly gaining importance.[291]

The European Code of Good Administrative Behaviour adopted by the European Parliament on 6 September 2001 can serve as a benchmark for national solutions. The Code was prepared with the intention to explain in more detail what the right to good administration – Article 41 of the Charter of Fundamental Rights of the European Union – should mean in practice. The right enshrined

---

289 P. F. Drucker, *The Essential Drucker*, Collins Business Essentials 2001, p. 65–66.

290 M. Armstrong, *A Handbook of Human Resource Management Practice*, London, Kogan Page Ltd, 8th edn, 2001.

291 *Government at a Glance*, OECD, http://www.oecd.org/dataoecd/36/3/43926778.pdf – accessed 6 July 2012.

in Article 41 of the Charter includes the right of every person to be heard, before any administrative measure that could affect him /her adversely is taken; the right of every person to access his/her files and the right to receive from the administration reasons for its decisions.

The Code contains principles of European administrative law governing the behaviour of government administration officials, including: absence of abuse of power, principles of legality, absence of discrimination, impartiality and independence, objectivity, fairness and courtesy. It also speaks of a reasonable time-limit for taking decisions and the duty to state the grounds of those decisions as well as the responsibility of informing the public of the provisions of the Code, of promoting it and making it available to citizens.

Another important document having influence on the quality of personnel of public administration is the Recommendation of the Committee of Ministers of the Council of Europe, which recommends that the governments of member states apply principles that are apolitical and based on merit in the recruitment of candidates to public posts,[292] and the Recommendation of the Committee of Ministers of the Council of Europe to member states, which sets a model code of conduct for public officials.[293] The main purpose of this Recommendation was to introduce standards of conduct for public officials to follow so as to carry out their tasks professionally, fairly, in a way that earns the trust of citizens and is politically neutral. The model code contains a number of provisions that help avoid the possibility of conflict of interest such as taking up employment or economic activities outside the public service; offering or accepting benefits; how to react to attempts of offering gifts, favours or other benefits; and how to proceed in cases of unlawful or unethical acts.

The professional standards for members of the Polish civil service comprise the following values:

- high professional competence: solid education and necessary professional experience, knowledge of law and administrative procedures, discharging one's duties in accordance with the law, pursuit of professional development,
- concern for the public good,

---

292 Recommendation No. R (2000) 6 of the Committee of Ministers of the Council of Europe to member states on the status of public officials in Europe; T. Górzyńska, '*Służba nie drużba. Rekomendacja o statusie pracowników publicznych w Europie*', *Rzeczpospolita* 2001, No. 75, p. C3.

293 Recommendation No. R (2000) 10 of the Committee of Ministers of the Council of Europe to member states on codes of conduct for public officials.

- political neutrality and impartiality,
- professional loyalty to superiors and co-workers,
- transparency of actions taken,
- when it comes to customer service and relations with external entities: the maintenance of high quality standards of services, appropriate, friendly relations with customers (professionalism and efficiency).[294]

A good civil servant should not only be honest, truthful,[295] impartial and reliable, but also competent (it seems that in the case of public officials, competence takes on a moral character). Next to professional ethics, the most frequently cited source of moral duty is the dignity of the profession, the essence of which is membership in the professional group.

The ethical conduct of officials is shaped by professional ethos understood to mean a set of norms and values acquired and accepted by a group of people (such as a professional group) that regulate the behaviour of its members.[296] It is a 'method or style of satisfying the need of dignity. Social, professional, workers', institutional ethos comprises a distinctive for that subculture set of norms, symbolic penalties and rewards associated with it as well as rituals, ceremonies, signs and symbols that embody for the members of the group or community the meaning of dignity'.[297]

It seems difficult to define the ethos of the Polish civil service at this stage because the way values held by this professional group are applied is undergoing continuous evolution, the result of the enactment of new legislation and the dynamic socio-political changes taking place in Poland since 1989.

There have been dramatic changes in the hierarchy of values held by public administration officials – especially those who had been employed before 1989 and those employed after this symbolic date. The hierarchy of values they were meant to be guided by was repeatedly changed with each successive act of parliament that formally replicated certain principles, but their interpretation remained in the hands of the successive political fractions in power. Despite the fact that

294 C. Trutkowski *(ed.)*, '*Postawy członków korpusu służby cywilnej wobec kwestii etycznych. Raport z badań*', *study report,* Warszawa, 2004.

295 M. Ossowska included speaking the truth among the moral standards that are required to gain trust.

296 S. Dziamski, *Wykłady z nauki o moralności,* Poznań, 1994, p. 7.

297 M. Kosewski, '*Etos pracowniczy w urzędach państwowych i samorządowych*', *Służba Cywilna*, 2003/2004, No. 7, pp. 79–80.

members of the civil service corps declare having a sense of a civil service ethos or general guiding principles that apply to them and determine their professional identity, they nevertheless 'demonstrate poor capacity to translate their sense of belonging to this professional group into specific rules of conduct and poor capacity to clearly identify situations that are atypical'.[298]

Studies indicate that the values most commonly accepted by members of the civil service corps are honesty and integrity. Considered unethical, on the other hand, is conduct that breaches professional rules, namely: the failure to uphold high competence at work, failure to take due care to protect public goods, politicisation and partiality, lack of professional loyalty, lack of transparency of actions.[299] Examples of unethical behaviour include: acceptance of gifts from clients as an expression of gratitude (some officials believe that a show of gratitude when expressed after a matter had been considered is acceptable because it had no effect on the process); use of knowledge and information acquired at work to conduct training or engage in public speaking for profit; recruitment of staff members (competition procedures raise much doubt); political engagement and participation in the election of members of the civil service corps; pressure exerted on civil servants by their superiors, including political pressure; the use of institutional resources for one's needs (use of office supplies and equipment, use of office time to see to private matters, the use of office phones for private purposes); corruption connected with the organisation of competitions to fill posts in the administration; abuse of or bypassing required procedures.[300]

The ethical identity of those employed in the administration is institutionalised in the form of codes of professional ethics. There were many reasons for interest in codes of ethics in public administration in the 21st century. They include external circumstances such as the political culture of a society, the adopted forms of responsibility or systems of social values and internal circumstances such as the culture of an organisation and the ethics of civil servants.

One of the many reasons for the emergence of new ethical codes or for the modernisation of the old ones are the continual social changes. Corruption scandals that hit many democracies initiated a fresh push for the formation of codes of ethics. Representatives of professions traditionally associated with public administration decided to lay down sets of rules to protect the reputation of their profession and to establish principles of conduct. Another reason for the

298 Trutkowski, op. cit.

299 Ibid.

300 Ibid.

formation of ethical standards in the form of codes in the public domain is the increasingly educated society and public awareness as to the consequences of non-compliance with the values and ethical standards. Finally, interest in the ethics of public officials rose with the right of citizens to good administration; and citizen access to information on the activities of public administration increased the quality and transparency in the public sphere.

Codes of ethics are a promotion tool for an office, which means that the declaration of conduct in accordance with specific ethical standards is perceived as attributing to a better quality of services delivered by the office and its civil service to their country and the public. The codes influence the formation of organisational culture in the civil service based on concrete values, standards and principles. They constitute in fact a declaration of conduct, a model that civil service corps members should aspire to. The civil service code of ethics is not only there to create a positive image of civil servants and civil service employees but also to earn the institution greater recognition in the eyes of citizens.

Consequently, we see that a code of ethics also affects the lives of civil service corps members outside their office work, often influencing the way they conduct themselves in private.

There is no doubt that codes of ethics strengthen the professional identity of those employed in the civil service by stressing their distinctness, uniqueness (not everyone can serve their country and the public), and they strengthen the sense of a mission (representing the authority of the state) by giving them a sense of having influence on the course of important social events. All this, provided that civil servants and civil service employees are acquainted with the provisions of the code, understand their meaning and identify with them. If a given code is just another document, a formality without practical import, then, from a common sense point of view, we might as well do without it.

The necessity of the existence of codes of ethics in public administration does not derive only from the belief that ethical action in the public sphere should be inherently moral nor is it the result of a trend (because many developed countries have adopted such codes) or a political view point (because the code of ethics is a conscious act of the authorities sending a clear signal to society that they pay serious attention to the ethical conduct of their administration), but – what should not be overlooked – codes of ethics combine that which is moral with that which is legal by law. Violations of ethical standards by public officials destroy confidence in the idea of democracy and the democratic state, and violation of those standards by professional groups in which society places special trust, such as the civil service corps, result in the erosion of a civil society.

It was during the Third Polish Republic that the first codification of rules regarding the civil service corps was made. This was the Civil Service Code of Ethics of 11 October 2002.[301] It constituted a development on principles under Article 153 of the 1997 Constitution of the Republic of Poland. And so, apart from the principle of public service, it addressed in detail the principle of public service, its integrity, professionalism, impartiality and political neutrality.[302]

The code was formally repealed with the entry into force of the Civil Service Act of 21 November 2008. Despite that fact, the code continues to be regarded by civil servants, civil service employees as well as the public as a source of reference in ethical dilemmas. New guidelines regarding compliance with the principles of the civil service and the ethics of the civil service corps were laid down in the Prime Minister's Order No. 70 of 6 October 2011.[303]

The Order is subdivided into two parts: guidelines for the civil service and the ethics of the civil service corps. In the case of the guidelines for the civil service, the Prime Minister specified nine major civil service principles, as follows:

1. The principle of legality, the rule of law and reinforcement of the trust citizens place in public administration authorities.
2. The principle of human and civil rights protection.
3. The principle of selflessness.
4. The principle of openness and transparency.
5. The principle of not disclosing confidential information protected under law.
6. The principle of professionalism.
7. The principle of responsibility for action taken or the failure to act.
8. The principle of rational management of public resources.
9. The principle of openness and competitiveness in recruitment.

In turn, in accordance with the mandate provided under Article 15.10 of the Civil Service Act of 21 November 2008, which requires the Prime Minister to

---

301 Zarządzenie Prezesa Rady Ministrów *w sprawie nadania kodeksu etyki służby cywilnej*. [Order of the Prime Minister on the establishment of the civil service code of ethics].

302 Ibid., Paragraphs 2–5.

303 Zarządzenie nr 70 Prezesa Rady Ministrów z dnia 6 października 2011 r. *w sprawie wytycznych w zakresie przestrzegania zasad służby cywilnej oraz w sprawie zasad etyki korpusu służby cywilnej*, M. P., No. 93, item 953. [Order No. 70 of the Prime Minister on guidelines for compliance with the principles of the civil service and ethics of the civil service corps]

determine the ethics of the civil service corps, the Order lists the following principles of ethics for the civil service corps:

1. The principle of dignified conduct.
2. The principle of public service.
3. The principle of loyalty.
4. The principle of political neutrality.
5. The principle of impartiality.
6. The principle of reliability.

Order No. 70 is addressed to the most important entities of the civil service: the ministers and top management in government administration, the Head of the Civil Service, the Civil Service Council, the National School of Public Administration (KSAP), the director-general or head of the office in charge of tasks of director-general of an office, as specified in the Civil Service Act of 21 November 2008, and members of the civil service corps, managers of members of the civil service, their subordinates. The order is addressed to ministers and the top management in government administration because they report to the Prime Minister, due to which the guidelines can be addressed to them and they have the duty to cooperate with the Head of Civil Service in ensuring the observance of the principles of the civil service, including the consideration and respect for civil service principles in relations with members of the civil service corps.

The guidelines addressed to the Head of the Civil Service require him to take up necessary action – the organisation, execution and supervision – with respect to directors-general of offices in order to achieve the objective of raising the ethical standards of members of the civil service corps. They also require him to cooperate in this respect with other public administration authorities, social partners, non-governmental organisations and representatives of the mass media.

In turn, the Prime Minister instructs the Civil Service Council to respect, in the course of its work, the civil service principles referred to in the Order. The National School of Public Administration, on the other hand, is required to include the study of civil service principles in its curriculum. The Prime Minister also requires directors-general to take up necessary action – the organisation, execution and supervision – with respect to members of the civil service corps employed in their offices. Finally, the Prime Ministerial guidelines are addressed to the members of the civil service corps in charge of subordinate members of the civil service corps to ensure the observance of the civil service principles by all its members.

The principle of legality, the rule of law and reinforcement of the trust citizens place in public administration authorities means that members of the civil service corps have the duty of loyalty to the Constitution,[304] which is to protect the interests of the state as well as human and civil rights. The concept of loyalty combines the adherence to the ideals of a democratic state and civil society rather than the political parties currently in power. Respect for the law is connected with the principle of the legality of public authority actions – one of the fundamental principles of a democratic state under the rule of law.

Work in the Polish civil service is continuous in nature. This means that the civil service corps works for the common good, and its members are not allowed to participate in strikes or any acts of protest that could disrupt the functioning of the office.[305] The principle of loyalty to the Constitution means loyalty to both the Basic Law and the laws enacted in compliance with it. This allows us to trust that a public official is there to uphold the law while at the same time being subject to that law.

The principle of protecting human and civil rights means that a member of the civil service corps should protect the interests of the state but never at the expense of human and civil rights.[306]

The next principle is that of professionalism, which combines a number of factors. Effective administration requires effective management of human resources, an organisational culture within which the development of knowledge and skills must extend to all aspects of the professional life of a civil servant or civil service employee, the modernisation of the selection, appointment and evaluation processes of the managerial cadres in the civil service, the establishment of channels of mobility of cadres within the framework of the civil service, devising a system that shows a clear link between an employee's assessment and the development of his/her career.

Professionalism is understood as management of competent officials in such a way as to make them fully aware of what is meant by a public service mission and to use their knowledge, qualifications and skills to accomplish that mission. Professionalism means placing demands and assessing their performance, developing a sense of responsibility as well as management through self-assessment and the setting of clear objectives. A modern public administration organisation is there to 'provide a specific service to society'.[307] Public service requires

304 Civil Service Act of 21 November 2008, Art. 76.1.

305 Ibid., Art. 78.3.

306 Ibid., Art. 76.2.

307 Drucker, *The Essential Drucker*, op. cit., p. 51.

professionalism and this requires the maintenance of an education system that can provide a high level of learning. 'Staffing of posts should be done on merit-based competitions conducted by objective and professional committees, in keeping with ethical standards at the highest level, the implemented standards of proper conduct of officials, under the scrutiny of professional associations.'[308] 'The modern official receives a professional training which unavoidably increases in correspondence with the national technology of modern life.'[309] In the civil servant – citizen relation, professionalism means the provision of services to the customer/citizen, or in other words, to the taxpayer who is interested in the public services being provided and their effects.

A professional official shares and respects the values that make up the idea of public service because respect for these values is an important element of self-identification of every professional civil servant and motivates them to put public interest before their individual interests.[310]

The foundations of professional public administration are primarily based on legal principles, but political decisions and ethical canons also play an important role. The professionalisation of public administration is 'a much wider task than implementing civil service regulations and introducing personnel management improvements'.[311] The principle of professionalism encompasses the principle – specified by the no longer existent Office of Civil Service – of continuous improvement of professional qualifications that includes the duty to enhance one's knowledge and professional qualifications, the planning of one's professional development, the ability to analyse one's training needs, monitoring developments in the area of one's tasks and applying them at work, putting into practice the knowledge acquired during training, learning by drawing conclusions from one's mistakes as well as from opinions and comments of experienced colleagues, engagement in new projects.[312]

---

308 H. Kisilowska, 'Pojęcie profesjonalizmu we współczesnej administracji', in A. Dębicka, M. Dmochowski and B. Kudrycka (eds.), *Profesjonalizm w administracji publicznej*, Białystok, 2004, p. 107.

309 M. Weber, *Economy and Society. An Outline of Interpretive Sociology*, University of California Press, Berkeley-Los Angeles-London 1978, p. 1401.

310 B.Guy Peters, *The Politics of Bureaucracy*, London: Routledge, 2001.

311 OECD (1990), 'European Principles for Public Administration', *SIGMA Papers*, No. 27, OECD Publishing, p. 26.

312 Twinning Project PHARE, PL03/IB/OT/06.

The competence of an administration is its 'capacity to make socially relevant and accurate decisions, the ability to organise the conditions of social life'.[313] Administrative competence combines constitutional and statutory laws that refer to the administration's discharge of responsibilities (its legal competence), the conviction of public administration officials and employees that they are acting within the law and social responsibility, qualified personnel – their recruitment and promotion based on merit, a system that encourages seeking further improvement of qualifications and ensures stability, as well as the use of independent, competent, reliable, unbiased and responsible advisers.

The idea of meritocracy[314] is based on the belief that posts should be staffed by the most competent people for competence is a special type of merit. People deserve to fill posts that correspond to their qualifications.[315] Competence also defines the scope of what authorities can do. Competence, as Ewa Łętowska points out, is not restricted only to rights but also to the duties that go along with them. The point, therefore, is about correlating that which is allowed and can be done with what needs to be done.[316]

Professionalism means the organisation of work and the achievement of results where the execution of tasks is planned, organised and supervised by first identifying the priorities and objectives on the basis of the optimal use of available resources. Professionalism of public managers is when a superior skilfully assigns and coordinates tasks to get the best results, determines the requirements, defines the goals in a precise way, identifies and sets priorities and responsibilities for their implementation, adjusts plans and organisation of work to changing circumstances, effectively manages time (timely execution of task), assesses the work in terms of planned results, knows and is able to assess the potential of his/her subordinates, employs new technologies in order to improve effectiveness.[317]

The skill of working in a team is another feature of the principle of professionalism. In accordance with provisions adopted by the Polish civil service, this skill

---

313 T. Mołdawa, 'Konstytucyjny system wartości a jakość administracji publicznej – wybrane problemy, in *Praworządność-sprawność-rozwój lokalny a samorząd terytorialny,* Zeszyty Naukowe CSSTiR, No. 8, Warszawa, 2004, p. 16.

314 See M. Young, *The Rise of the Meritocracy 1870–2033*, Baltimore, 1961.

315 M. Walzer, Spheres of justice. A defense of pluralism and equality, New York: Basic Books 1983.

316 E. Łętowska, *Kompetencje o niekompetencji*, Krzysztof Brunetko i Michał Nawrocki talk with prof. Ewa Łętowska, Justice of the Constitutional Tribunal, *Tygodnik Powszechny* 2002, No. 35.

317 Twinning Project PHARE, PL03/IB/OT/06, op. cit.

involves: identifying clear objectives, encouraging and motivating colleagues or subordinate staff to achieve results, providing support to others, sharing information and knowledge with colleagues, submitting constructive proposals that improve teamwork, skilfully diffusing conflicts in the workplace, ensuring a friendly atmosphere, making fair and objective assessments of employees, respecting the privacy of others and being discrete, resolving conflicts effectively and impartially.[318]

The principle of reliability means timeliness, the adherence to statutory deadlines. 'Delay of public administration in making decisions and taking action can cause frustration, injustice and severe harm for both the public interest and for private interests. (…) civil service with a recruitment scheme based on merit, and regularly providing training, can reduce incompetence within public administration, and works for the value of reliability.'[319]

The role of the employer, in this case – the state, is the application of law which is particularly relevant in the assessment of administrative institutions that represent it. Accountability of civil servants for the execution of tasks is defined by law and is inalienable. Accountability is 'the obligation to answer for responsibilities that have been conferred and accepted, and to report on the utilisation and management of resources entrusted. The people who accept accountability are responsible for answering questions and reporting on resources and operations that are under their control to those people who have to hold accountability. So both parts have their own duties'. Corporate social responsibility is 'a commitment by private and public sector organisations to contribute to sustainable development by working with employees, their families, local communities and society to improve the quality of life. The aim is to bring benefits both for organisations and the wider society'.[320] Competency means 'an expressly and legally bestowed power to decide on a given matter or issue of public interest, which legally enables the public authority not only to take decisions on the matter but also obligates it to take responsibility. A competent public authority cannot abdicate this responsibility'.[321]

Accountability, separated from discipline, restricts individual rights, according to G. Lipovetsky, only to such an extent as to strengthen an individual's life and creative potential, the potential of freedom and achievements. The ethics of accountability means that bureaucratic inertia is considered a personal enemy

---

318 Ibid.

319 OECD (1990), 'European Principles for Public Administration, op. cit., p. 12.

320 CAF 2006, op. cit., pp. 43 and 45.

321 OECD (1990), 'European Principles for Public Administration, op. cit., p. 10.

that needs to be fought and defeated; dialogue is becoming the basis for actions by members of the civil service corps, its effect being a better pace of work and increased output, and the more there is horizontal cooperation and coordination, the greater the moral pressures.[322]

Accountability of members of the civil service corps is associated with the confidence that the execution of tasks that are consistent with one's views enables positive self-assessment, including self-assessment in his/her capacity as a member of a professional group and at the same time means being fully conscious of both legal and ethical consequences of the lack of such consistency.

The principle of rational management of public resources means an obligation of members of the civil service corps to administer public funds in a way that is cost-effective and in consideration of economic interests, which means spending in accordance with public goals and tasks yet wisely at the same time.[323] It imposes on members of the civil service corps the duty to have due regard for the interests of the country and its citizens, to aim to achieve the designated objectives and be ready to account for due diligence when managing public resources and property.[324]

The recruitment process to the civil service should enable the selection of candidates who demonstrate good communicative skills, the desire to achieve results, the ability to work and cooperate within a group, analytical and synthetic thinking as well as anticipation and planning skills. However even the recruitment of best presenting candidates does not guarantee that they will become good civil servants in the future. That is why there is so much stress put on the need for continuous training and retraining of civil servants.[325]

The principle of dignified conduct means that civil servants and civil service employees are expected to conduct themselves at work and in private time in a dignified manner. During work the principle demands that members of the civil service corps execute their duties with respect for the rules of social conduct and propriety and respect for the dignity of other people, including subordinate staff, colleagues and superiors. It requires members of the civil service corps to treat others with fairness and courtesy and take due care to avoid conflicts – the rule also applies in their relations with citizens/customers, which means that a public

---

322 http://www.opoka.org.pl/biblioteka/I/IK/etyka_odpowiedzialnosci.html – accessed 12 June 2012. Excerpt from G. Lipovetsky, *Le crépuscule du devoir*.

323 Civil Service Act of 21 November 2008, Art. 76.1(3).

324 The Prime Minister's Order No. 70 of 6 October 2011. Ibid., Para. 9.

325 I. Macek, 'Zarządzanie zasobami ludzkimi w administracji publicznej', in A. Ferens and I. Macek (eds.), *Administracja i polityka. Wprowadzenie,* Wrocław 1999, p. 134.

official should not distance him/herself from the customer/citizen by displaying what some call a chilly bureaucratic attitude. The principle of dignified conduct off duty means that in private life civil service corps members are bound by certain restrictions in their behaviour if that behaviour could have a bearing on the perception of the state, the civil service or their office. The attitude of people employed in the civil service should inspire respect. This means that a public official even in private cannot by his/her behaviour undermine the trust in public administration or tarnish the good name of the institution he/she works for.

The Prime Minister's Order does not list specific cases of unwarranted behaviour but, as mentioned earlier, one of the statutory requirements for those working in the civil service is that of impeccable reputation and its loss can cost that person his/her job (Article 71.1(3) of the Civil Service Act).[326]

The principle of public service emphasises the fact that work in government administration is, as the name implies, 'being at the service of' and indicates the two recipients of that service – the Polish state and its citizens. Public service means putting the common good of citizens before personal, individual or group interest. Serving the state means protecting its interests and facilitating its development, concern for its image abroad and among its citizens as well as a positive image of its administrative authorities and institutions, including the civil service. Public interest requires sometimes difficult and even socially unpopular decisions on various issues.[327]

The duty to protect the interests of the state refers to intangible interests – the protection of the independence and sovereignty of the state, its internal and external security and the inviolability of its territory.

Pursuant to Order No. 70 the principle of loyalty signifies that members of the civil service corps owe their loyalty to the Republic of Poland which means that they must abide by the law and respect the constitutional authorities of the state, which is in accordance with the preamble to the Constitution of the Republic of Poland that speaks of all citizens being equal in their responsibility for the common good; with Article 82 of the Constitution, which states that every Polish citizen owes his/her loyalty to the Republic of Poland and has the duty to care for the common good; and with the words of the oath taken by every civil servant.[328]

---

326 D. Długosz and W. Zawadzki, 'Etyczny drogowskaz urzędników. Zasady etyki w praktyce administracji', *Przegląd Służby Cywilnej*, Special Edition No. 1, Warszawa 2011, pp. 10–11.

327 Ibid., p. 11.

328 I swear to serve the Polish State, observe the Constitution of the Republic of Poland.

Members of the civil service corps owe their loyalty to the government which means that they realise its program loyally and faithfully, regardless of their own convictions or political views, to the best of their knowledge and will, without obstruction. It is a conscious and conscientious service to a lawfully constituted government.

Members of the civil service corps are expected to be loyal to their office and superiors which means being ready to carry out their orders with attention to compliance with the law and care to avoid making errors. Particularly important in the concept of reliability is the interpretation of the principle of loyalty to one's superiors which means that in the case when a superior authority, despite the civil servant's protest, takes a decision believed by him/her to be wrong, he/she nevertheless carries it out – at the responsibility of the superior – conscientiously and carefully as if he/she were fully convinced of it being correct. According to M. Weber, the whole apparatus would collapse if it were not for this moral discipline and self-renunciation, in the strictest sense of these words.[329] Thus, loyalty of civil servants to their superiors aims to prevent arbitrary decisions or opinions on their part and enforces compliance with the standards and legal norms in a democratic state based on the rule of law. Nevertheless, a public servant should not passively watch the mistakes or errors of his/her superior but, on the basis of his/her experience and understanding of the situation, should seek their rectification.

Loyalty to the superior means never withholding from him/her any significant information in a given matter or acting in any way that could indicate an intention to 'obstruct rational decision-making by the superior and the effective implementation of those decisions as such acts constitute a violation of the duty of loyalty at elementary ethical level'.[330]

There is however a limit to the duty of loyalty in the civil service and that is compliance with the law. Should the superior's command bear any attributes of an offense, and its result would be a breach of law, the civil servant has the duty to immediately inform the director-general of office in writing of his/her refusal to execute the command. The civil servant can, and even should, refuse to execute the command.

However, should the superior's order raise questions of a moral nature or the suspicion of bias or of having negative social impact, the civil servant may try

329 M. Weber, *Economy and Society.*, op. cit.

330 I. Bogucka and T. Pietrzykowski, *Etyka w administracji publicznej,* Warszawa, 2009, p. 235.

to refuse execution of his/her superior's order. Nevertheless, if the superior confirms his/her order and requests its implementation in writing, the civil servant is required to carry it out. There is an ongoing discussion in the literature on the subject on the issue of the correctness of such behaviour by a civil servant. The Civil Service Act of 21 November 2008 states clearly that a member of the civil service corps has the duty to execute orders of his/her superiors but, should the command be in breach of the law or bear signs of error, he/she must inform the superior of this in writing. If the order is confirmed in writing, he/she is required to execute it.[331] In some opinions, however, even if the order is not by any means an offence but is against public interest, the civil servant should nevertheless consider whether to refuse to carry out this order.[332]

Loyalty to the superior means that a member of the civil service corps is obliged to provide his/her superior with objective advice and opinions to the best of his/her knowledge and will when drawing up proposals concerning action plans for government administration., blind loyalty however can be unethical should it lead to hiding irregularities. Loyalty to subordinates, on the other hand, means 'applying just, merit-based criteria in making quantitative and qualitative evaluations of work they put in and of their interpersonal conduct.'[333]

Loyalty is also expressed in restraint in expressing opinions about one's work, especially if they are negative and could undermine public confidence in these institutions. Discretion is not synonymous with the prohibition of expressing – in the public interest – critical opinions about the work of an office, provided that they are intended to help eliminate irregularities, not to undermine citizens' trust in the office's management or staff.[334]

Political neutrality, just as 'incorruptibility and professionalism, has become a foundation of the civil service in all EU Member States'.[335] One may ask, however, whether it is a goal to be achieved or already a fact. Despite many reforms in countries that have a civil service, civil servants are regarded by society as an executive arm of the state that should be politically neutral when carrying out

331 Civil Service Act of 21 November 2008, Art. 77.

332 Bogucka and Pietrzykowski, op. cit. p. 237.

333 Długosz and Zawadzki, 'Etyczny drogowskaz', op. cit., p. 12.

334 Ibid.

335 T.G. Grosse, 'Służba cywilna w Polsce i możliwości jej rozwoju', *Służba Cywilna*, No. 2, 2001, p. 86.

government work. Critics of the civil service believe however 'that the classical model of public administration was shaped in a world that no longer exists'.[336]

The principle of political neutrality of civil service corps members can be deduced from the constitutional principle of equality of all citizens before the law. That is why civil servants are bound to treat all citizens equally, regardless of their political views, race or religion. Public administration is required not only to be politically neutral but also objective, in a broad sense of the word.[337]

The neutrality of persons employed in the civil service means that actions of the administration are politically neutral and endowed with a large dose of objectivity. This means that 'policy-makers cannot influence the actions of the civil service.[338] Political neutrality means the elimination of factors that could influence the corps' activities, such as their personal political, religious or ideological convictions, and the dissociation from different party or group interests. Authors of the commentary to the civil service law stress the fact that political neutrality means independence from the influence of not only party politics but also from any community organisations such as trade unions or local self-governments. 'The attitude of a civil servant and his conduct are to be impartial and distanced.'[339] A politically neutral corps member does not have to agree with the decisions of the government or its policies but has the duty to act in accordance with the political line of the freely elected officials now standing at the head of the administration. He/she has the duty to carry out their orders with due diligence.

Neutrality can also be understood as a willingness to be active and diligent in implementing, 'regardless of the civil servant's personal views and assessment of the people who represent them', programmes and political plans of his/her superiors.[340]

As we analyse the different interpretations of the concept of political neutrality, we can detect some contradictions, mutual exclusions and signs of chaos. In short, we could define political neutrality as a state in which members of the civil service corps refrain from any action that could be detrimental to the political leaders.

---

336 D. H. Rosenbloom, J. Dolan (eds.), *Representative Bureaucracy*, ME Sharpe 2003, as in Ch. Demmke, *Working towards common elements in the field of ethics and integrity*, EIPA, Maastricht, September 2004, p. 17.

337 B. Kudrycka, *Neutralność polityczna urzędników,* Warszawa, 1998, p. 49.

338 M. Rocki, 'Polityka zamiast neutralności', *Rzeczpospolita*, 3 July 2005.

339 J. Jagielski and K. Rączka, *Komentarz do ustawy o służbie cywilnej z 1998 r.* Warszawa, 2001, p. 17.

340 Bogucka and Pietrzykowski, op. cit., p. 230.

Other attributes of a politically neutral civil servant or civil service employee are similar to those of an apolitical public servant, which means that he/she does not manifest publicly his/her opinion and political sympathies, does not cause tension in the workplace due to political convictions, does not discriminate nor favour subordinates, colleagues or citizens on political grounds, does not allow political pressures influence the recruitment, selection and promotion processes in the civil service, does not succumb to pressures from professional organisations, local self-governments or any other social organisations. A politically neutral civil servant or civil service employee loyally and faithfully implements the strategy and program of a democratically elected government, regardless of his/her personal beliefs and political views. The separation between politics and administration relies on the division of the public sphere into two parts which, 'although closely interdependent, are different in nature, have a different underlying logic and have different sources of legitimacy. Politics is based on public confidence expressed in free political elections and validated after each political term. Administration is based on merit, and professional capability of civil servants is verified in open competition for entering the civil service, in accordance with the terms laid down by law'.[341]

The question of confidence in the civil service corps seems to be crucial for the understanding of the concept of political neutrality. The idea of political neutrality has to build a system of public confidence in the state, which does not mean – contrary to what part of public opinion and of the scientific community believe – that the administration is a closed system to which policy-makers have no access. The separation between political and administrative positions and the exclusion of political sympathies and antipathies in the work of the administration – deeply rooted not so much in law as in culture and custom – is the correct realisation of the essence of political neutrality of civil servants.

The Order of the Prime Minister confirms the fact that members of the civil service corps are – as all other citizens – entitled to enjoy the guaranteed human and citizen freedoms and rights, including the right to participate in public life. The Order clearly specifies what conduct befits the principle of political neutrality and that is to: refrain from manifesting personal political views and sympathies in public, distance oneself from political influences and pressures that could lead to biased decisions, refrain from public activities that directly support political action, not give rise to suspicion of favouring any political parties and to make sure that relationships with people holding public functions are open and

341 OECD (1990), 'European Principles for Public Administration', op. cit., p. 21.

transparent so that they do not undermine confidence in the political neutrality of civil service corps members.[342]

The essence of the principle of impartiality is based on the distinction between actions in the public sphere, aimed at the protection of public interest, and the private sphere. Members of the civil service corps have the duty to maintain neutrality with respect to political parties, trade unions, pressure groups, parliamentary and extra-parliamentary lobbies as well as individual interests. Every administrative decision must be free of affiliation with any particular group of interest. Compliance with this principle guarantees that all citizens, regardless of their political and party affiliations, gender, race, religion, social or material status will be treated equally.[343] A civil servant decides on issues relating to public interest, state interest and the interest of the individual. Conflict of interest and bias occurs when the public official deciding on a matter, or involved in decisions affecting a matter, has or may have a personal or vested interest in how it is resolved. Conflict of interest always occurs when concern for private welfare outweighs concern for the common good.

The principle of impartiality means the equal treatment of all parties whose cases are being considered by the office and not giving in to pressures from any of the parties involved. 'In order to eliminate suspicion of succumbing to such pressures, civil service corps members should avoid manifesting their familiarity with people active in public life, whether in the sphere of politics or business, or the social or religious spheres.'[344]

The principle of reliability means the conscientious and meticulous execution of tasks and active performance of duties with the best of intent and in the interests of society 'which means more than simply abiding by the law', as well as taking up difficult issues and being accountable for the way they are resolved. The rules of reliability include working conscientiously, striving to achieve the best results and taking into account the rule of law, accountability standards, the good of society and the good of one's government.

The expression of reliability of the corps is their performance of the duties they are entrusted with by the legislator in accordance with the Constitution, the civil service act, relevant regulations and the code of ethics. The Polish legislator decided, as in other democratic countries, that once separate regulations for civil servants had been laid down, it was necessary to spell out clearly the rights

---

342 Długosz and Zawadzki, 'Etyczny drogowskaz', op. cit., pp. 12–13.
343 Civil Service Act of 21 November 2008, Art. 76.1(4).
344 Długosz and Zawadzki, 'Etyczny drogowskaz', op. cit., p. 13.

and duties of civil servants. Reliability, integrity of the civil service affects the perception of the state. The Preamble of the 1997 Constitution of the Republic of Poland speaks of ensuring 'diligence and efficiency' in the work of public bodies, thus imposing on them the duty to perform their tasks with reliability and efficiency. The current concept of public administration holds that policymakers share responsibility with persons working in public administration; as a consequence civil service employees often perform as both the representatives of the authorities as well as employees of the state. Accountability is 'instrumental in showing whether principles like the rule of law, openness, transparency, impartiality, and equality before the law are respected'.[345]

The concept of reliability, according to PHARE, consists of strategic and creative thinking. This means that in daily practice civil service corps members should encourage others to be innovative, use creative thinking to build logical concepts, strategic visions and effective solutions in order to implement positive changes. They have to be able to identify strategic priorities and promote them among their co-workers, subordinates and citizens. They are committed to the tasks of the administration and to their implementation. They are not discouraged by difficulties, determine ways of solving them, predict long-term effects of action and decisions taken and are capable of adapting to changing conditions.[346]

---

345 OECD (1990), 'European Principles for Public Administration', op. cit., p. 13.

346 This definition of the principle of reliability in Polish conditions seems too broad. I am, however, presenting the PHARE project criteria to draw the reader's attention to the variety of interpretations of the concept. It is also written in the project that a reliable member of the civil service corps is one who is a competent and effective communicator, in other words, effectively receives and passes on information, manages it, skillfully negotiates and convinces, speaks and writes properly, communicates clearly and convincingly, actively pursues information, communicates – not just passes on information, tries to understand the opinions, arguments and views of others, applies a range of techniques of argumentation and persuasion to convince others to his/her opinion, presents solid arguments in support of his/her opinions, provides critical comments in a constructive manner, adapts his/her language of communication to his/her interlocutors, shows respect to his/her interlocutors, shares own knowledge and information – necessary for the execution of the task – with the team, has an open attitude to the customer, gives encouragement and support to others, makes use of available information channels, does not use clerical jargon. For example, reliability and decision-making are two distinct principles and concepts. The civil servant may reliably carry out the work but the decision is up to his/her superior. Twinning Project PHARE, PL03/IB/OT/06.

From the point of view of public administration supervision, reliability includes the assessment of actions for 'due diligence in the performance of functions and in the execution of substantive tasks' as well as 'attentiveness to instructions from higher disposition centres' and 'compliance with established standards, rules and parameters in the particular field'.[347]

An analysis of 450 questionnaires completed by civil servants and civil service employees in the first half of the 1990s shows that Polish civil servants are guided by ethical determinants in the following order: law, organisational culture, personal ethics, professional ethics, social ethics. Meanwhile in the USA and in England, the order is slightly different: law, professional ethics, the ethics of a democratic society, organisational culture and personal ethics.[348] According to the author of this study, we should also bear in mind the political circumstances and the influence of politicians on the decisions and the functioning of public administration. There is no permanent hierarchy of values – they depend on the circumstances and experience, the organisation and ethical maturity of civil servants. According to Barbara Kudrycka, when the determinants are not contradictory, whenever they support, complement, reinforce each other and are based on a similar system of values – they pose less ethical dilemmas to civil servants.

We should not forget that codes of ethics and guidelines not only remind civil servants of their responsibility to society but are also designed to protect the citizen against unreliability and dishonesty on the part of the administration. Codes/guidelines are a means of bridging the gap between legal standards and professional ethics. The fact that all the ethical rules have been collected in a single document facilitates their interpretation and prevents conflicts between superiors and their staff. The importance of the rules should not however be overestimated as the conduct of civil servants is shaped in their day-to-day practice. The code nevertheless serves as a guide to what they should aspire to.

## Management Tools in the Civil Service

The Polish civil service has a number of management tools at its disposal, however, not too clearly interlinked yet, thus giving the impression of some chaos and raising uncertainty as to their validity. These tools, applied pursuant to legislative acts and implementing regulations, include internal control, activity based budgets and audits.

---

347 J. Jagielski, *Kontrola administracji publicznej*, Warszawa 2007, p. 52.

348 Ibid., p. 255.

Internal control reveals an institution's management system, focuses on the key areas of management, system quality control and evaluation of the effectiveness of action taken. Internal control has its normative legitimacy in the Act on Public Finances of 27 August 2009 and in internal control standards for the sector of public finances.[349] In accordance with this Act, internal control 'means the whole of operations involved in ensuring the implementation of the goals and tasks in compliance with the law, in an efficient, cost-effective and timely manner'.[350] Internal control standards correspond to a certain degree to ISO 9001 quality standards, but in their case the intention of the legislator was to exert pressure by means of a legal norm to induce improvements in the functioning of administration.

The Act defines the key objectives of internal control, which include: compliance of activities with applicable laws and internal procedures, effectiveness and efficiency of operations, reliability of reports, concern for resources, observance and promotion of the principles of ethical behaviour, efficiency and effectiveness of the flow of information, and risk management. The legislator specified those responsible for achieving the above objectives as well as the duties associated with internal control.

When setting internal control standards[351] use was made of the Guidelines for Internal Control Standards for the Public Sector updated by the International Organisation of Supreme Audit Institutions INTOSAI in 2004, the Revised Internal Control Standards for Effective Management of the European Commission adopted in 2007[352] and Enterprise Risk Management – the framework of the Committee of Sponsoring Organisations of the Treadway Commission (COSO). The standards do not create specific guidelines but provide a reference model, indicating for example that any documentation that contains rules, procedures, orders, etc. is documentation of internal control.

A new element of internal control is risk management. Risk management is a method of creating a context, identification, evaluation of control processes and

---

349 Ustawa z dnia 27 sierpnia 2009 r. *o finansach publicznych* [Act on Public Finance], Dz. U. No. 157, item 1240 as amended; Communication No. 23 of the Finance Minister of 16 December 2009. Dz. U. Min. Fin. No. 15, item 84.

350 Ibid., Art. 68.

351 See J. Drabarek and K. Drabarek, 'Standardy kontroli w Europie', in *Rola projektów europejskich w rozwoju regionalnym i lokalnym,* conference materials SGGW, Warszawa 2004.

352 The Revised Internal Control Standards for Effective Management SEC (2007) 1341 Appendix 1.

information of risk in a way that enables the organisation to minimize its losses and maximize opportunities. Accomplishment of goals and tasks involves a certain level of risk and its identification and assessment can provide justification for stricter control of an institution or unit.

Another tool used in the civil service is an activity-based budget, which is a method of managing public finances geared towards achieving greater effectiveness and efficiency and transparency in the spending of public funds. The method involves, first of all, the preparation of the state budget on the basis of the objectives of an activity-based budget which consist of tasks and measures/indicators of their results (including results of their components) and the degree of their achievement in terms of their efficiency and effectiveness; monitoring and evaluation of the individual tasks of the activity-based budget by applying the indicators, thus providing information on the effects that improve the quality of the allocation of financial resources in the planning of the budget in subsequent planning periods; practical application by the government of the information about the effects in the budget planning process as well as their use during parliamentary discussions and work on the Budget Act.

The activity-based budget principles are based on the principle of good governance (determining the priorities, long-term planning, efficiency, effectiveness), the principle of transparency (planning documents in a coupled classification system – budget and justification), the principle of consolidation – public expenditure assigned to the tasks of a minister financed from different sources (the state budget, target funds, government agency funds). Thanks to an activity-based budget, it is possible to specify targets for tasks, that is, enable assessment of their effectiveness and assign costs to tasks, thus allowing the determination of their efficiency.

An activity-based budget is being implemented in Poland since 2008 and the completion of this process is planned for mid-2013. The activity-based budget provides information on the basis of which, on the one hand, politicians and those in senior positions in the civil service can make more informed and rational decisions and, on the other hand, citizens can verify the effects of implemented policies and see concrete evidence of the implementation of planned objectives. The definition of the objectives and their costs can generate a very important side effect from the point of view of the rationalisation of expenditure and activities of the administration – it can indicate the duplication of objectives pursued by various institutions and lead, if not to their elimination, then at least to their reorganisation.

Another important tool is the organisational audit, the aim of which is to improve the efficiency in areas that are key to an efficiently running office – its personnel, finances and public procurement – through the introduction of changes in management. The audit facilitates the prioritisation of process and organisational issues within the office; there is additional support provided for the processes being implemented with software tools; systemic issues are organised[353] and mechanisms for the development of knowledge and exchange of experience between offices are reinforced.[354]

353 For example, the analysis and recommendations for the improvement of mandate economy processes in 16 voivodship offices – including legislative, process and other changes, in *Audyt organizacyjny i wdrożenie usprawnień zarządczych*, Deloitte, Warszawa 2012, p. 5 et seq.

354 Ibid., pp. 4–6.

# Chapter 6: Several Aspects of Civil Service Operation

## The Politicisation of the Polish Civil Service

To say that in decision making within the civil service it is not possible to separate the political realm from the administrative seems an old truth. All the same, this is exactly the purpose of insisting on political neutrality, to protect the administration from becoming politicized, and consequently, its employees from becoming pliable, submissive and partisan. So what is meant by politicisation? We can say, it is 'the substitution of political criteria for merit-based criteria in the selection, retention, promotion, rewards and disciplining of members of the public service.'[355]

In the modern world the influence of politics over the administration has become increasingly pronounced as, on account of their function and remit, civil servants work together with politicians (who are Members of Parliament, or work in public administration), and with other bureaucrats. Political neutrality, like 'incorruptibility and professionalism have become the backbone of the civil service in all European Union member states.'[356]

The degree of political control over the bureaucracy varies from country to country across the globe, depending on the arrangements adopted in each one of them. In France and Japan, for instance, a considerable degree of autonomy ensures the high status of their experts; senior civil servants in the US deal not so much with political as strategic matters concerning the state; while in Poland, or more broadly, in Central-Eastern European countries, widespread politicisation has taken place, leading to senior official posts being filled with political appointments.

Let us remember that among the functions of public administration is the implementation of administrative tasks, understood as the duty to manage state matters. Following from this idea is the predominant view that the vast majority of civil servants should be involved exclusively in administrative duties (A. Heywood and Ch. Demmke). Thus, depending on the way politicians

355 B.G. Peters and J. Pierre, *Politicization of the Civil Service in Comparative Perspective*, London: Routledge, 2004, p. 2.

356 T.G. Grosse, 'Służba cywilna w Polsce i możliwości jej rozwoju', *Służba Cywilna*, No. 2, 2001, pp. 85–88.

perceive the role of the state, we see the function of the administration grow and intensify in a variety of areas (from social to economic issues) or the reverse tendency takes place – the administration's role becomes limited to an indispensable minimum.

One of the functions of the administration is consultancy: it should provide political advice, since 'the political significance of the bureaucracy stems largely from its role as the chief source of the policy information and advice available to government.'[357] As to the political role of civil servants, Andrew Heywood argues that it boils down to two tasks: outlining the policy options available to ministers, and reviewing policy proposals in terms of their likely impact and consequences.'[358]

Another function of the administration is to articulate and aggregate interests since it is the bureaucracy which comes into contact with interest groups by virtue of its duty of policy implementation. Similarly, maintaining political steadfastness by safeguarding stability and continuity in the political system is especially important in developing states where the existence of qualified and professional civil servants is a guarantee of an orderly and credible government.[359]

Across different countries the problems encountered by the civil service in implementing these functions are at once different and similar. Indubitably, among EU's 'old fifteen', the evolution of the civil service towards higher specialisation and reduced dependence on political power is a growing problem which opens the door to the relaxation of political control over civil service members. This, in turn, breeds the excessive professionalisation of civil servants making them more elitist and isolated from the rest of society. By contrast, the most controversial issue in countries that have joined the European Union after 2004 is the protection of the independence of civil servants from undue political interference – which is borne out by the numerous and often-altered civil service acts, frequent amendments and the many attempts at 'circumventing' these laws by politicians.

It transpires from this analysis of the development of the civil service in Poland that from its inception the influence of politics on the operation of this service has been of utmost importance for politicians and civil servants, as well as the mass media (public opinion).

Going back to the interwar years in Poland, specifically, the 1922 Act on State Civil Service, we find that Article 25.2 carried a provision which read: 'Civil

357 A. Heywood, *Politics,* Houndmills Basingstoke: Palgrave Macmillan, 2007, p. 363.
358 Ibid., 364.
359 Ibid.

servants shall not enter into associations or conspiracies that may interfere with the process of state governance or normal functioning of the office.'[360] In the Third Republic of Poland, the principle of political neutrality of the civil service featured strongly in public debates and prompted attempts at anchoring it in the law. In order for this principle to operate several guarantees were established in the constitution, statutes, institutions and codes.

In terms of constitutional guarantees (the 2 April 1997 Constitution) the following provisions can be found: 'A corps of civil servants shall operate in the organs of government administration in order to ensure a professional, diligent, impartial and politically neutral discharge of the State's obligations'(Art. 153) and 'All persons shall be equal before the law[...]. No one shall be discriminated against in political, social or economic life for any reason whatsoever' (Art. 32) and 'Polish citizens enjoying full public rights shall have a right of access to the public service based on the principle of equality' (Art. 60).

Furthermore, all successive acts concerning the civil service reiterate the constitutional provision that the civil service is established in order to, among other things, safeguard the politically neutral implementation of state duties (Art. 1).[361]

Similarly, the no longer valid Civil Service Code of Ethics of 2002 devotes considerable attention to political neutrality. It suggests that civil servants and employees of the civil service corps in Poland should loyally and diligently implement the government's strategy and programme, irrespective of their own convictions and political views. The Code also commands the civil service corps members to distance themselves from all political pressure and influence, which could potentially lead to partiality, and refrain from involvement in activities which could serve party purposes. Taking care to ensure the clarity and transparency of their own relationships with persons performing political functions was yet another task the civil service corps was changed with.

Political neutrality also features amongst a raft of ethical principles binding on the civil service as outlined in Order No. 70 of the Prime Minister on 6 October 2011.

---

360 Ustawa z dnia 17 lutego 1922 r. *o państwowej służbie cywilnej* [The Act on State Civil Service of 17 February 1922].

361 Ustawa z dnia 5 lipca 1996 r. *o służbie cywilnej*, Ustawa z dnia 18 grudnia 1998 r. *o służbie cywilnej*, Ustawa z dnia 24 sierpnia 2006 r. *o służbie cywilnej*, Ustawa z dnia 21 listopada 2008 r. *o służbie cywilnej* [Civil Service Act of 5 July 1996, Civil Service Act of 18 December 1998, Civil Service Act of 24 August 2006, Civil Service Act of 21 November 2008].

In theory, the guarantees for preserving genuine political neutrality in the civil service comprise of recruitment procedures, the nomination system, durability of employment and change in the employment relationship. Recruitment procedures in Poland have always stirred the most controversy since on numerous occasions the principles of equality and impartiality were violated and competition as the means of recruiting new personnel was often neglected under the watch of repeatedly amended laws and regulations.

Political neutrality enjoyed the institutional guarantee provided by the post of the Head of Civil Service mentioned in many laws. The post was established on the strength of the 5 July 1996 Act, considerably strengthened in law by the 18 December 1998 Act, only to be abolished under the 24 August 2006 Act and then re-introduced by the 21 November 2008 Act leaving the position of Head of Civil Service weaker than what the 18 December 1998 Act provided for. It is in the last mentioned Act that the institution of the Civil Service Head is at its strongest, with the expansion of his/her competencies to include an assessment of the degree to which civil service principles are complied with, including the principle of political neutrality.

In the same way, under the 1998 Act, the Civil Service Head could influence the political neutrality of the civil service by a whole raft of measures: developing preparatory service programmmes; consenting to admit for competition to senior civil service posts persons other than civil servants; running qualifying procedures for civil service employees applying for nomination to civil servant status; selecting examining teams for the procedure; appointing competition teams and managing the running of new competitions. These competences enabled the Head of Civil Service to oversee that members of the civil service corps and those holding high-ranking positions within the service met the requirement of political neutrality.

Another position designed to uphold the principle of political neutrality in the Polish civil service was the institution of the director-general of office, as the head of the civil service corps, whose task it was to oversee compliance with this principle. The director-general was charged with securing the professional development of civil service members and ensuring that the principle of political neutrality is observed by corps members. This meant that they had to respect the ban on the following activities: political party membership, sporting party symbols, participating in political party election campaigns and publicly expressing their political views. Sadly, on the back of the 2 August 2006 Civil Service Act, the position of director-general was transferred from the civil service to the State Staffing Pool thus becoming the subject of political play. What is more, this move meant that a politically appointed director-general was to oversee the political neutrality of civil servants, which seemed an absurd arrangement.

The responsibility of ensuring that the civil service complies with the principle of political neutrality rests with the Civil Service Council (in 2006–2008 called the Public Service Council). Its brief includes overseeing recruitment, the qualifying process for nomination to the civil service and the filling of senior posts in the civil service.

Analysing the legislative process in regard to the civil service yields the obvious conclusion that politicians attach high priority to 'their' civil service. The first post-1989 civil service bill was rejected by the Sejm in its first reading 'with the justification that the Polish People's Republic (PPR) was not successfully overthrown, only to see legal guarantees provided for PPR's administrative employees.'[362]

The situation is confounded by politicians who have little or no knowledge of the civil service and yet pass acts or legislation of a lower order concerning this very issue. This is borne out by the sheer number of bills, acts and amendments proceeded in the Third Republic. The legislation process itself is at odds with European Union policy which recommends that a bad law be replaced by a better one. In Poland the opposite tendency has taken hold irrespective of which political party comes out victorious in the elections (as exemplified by the 24 August 2006 Civil Service Act). Even current legislation (21 November 2008 Act and regulations) falls short of meeting EU recommendations. Several issues still raise concern, for instance the ambiguous regulations providing penalties for violations of the ban on accepting gifts by civil servants; the failure of existing legislation to define the way to proceed and the ethical principles to follow when civil servants resign and leave the service; or the absence of a guideline on what sanctions to apply to persons who enter the civil service, gain experience, information and valuable contacts only to resign and take up employment with commercial institutions and companies, offering their expertise to their new employers.

The following relationship emerged in Poland: in those organisations where employees enjoy long-term employment irrespective of position, they impact the decision-making process to a far higher degree than those who work in organisations where considerable fluctuation of personnel occurs – there politicians wield greater influence. From the perspective of the professional status of

362 M. Kulesza, *Opinia na temat systemu funkcjonowania służby cywilnej w obszarach projektowanych ustaw,* (Forms Nos. 552, 553 and 553-A), Biuro Analiz Sejmowych, Warszawa 24 July 2006.

senior management in government administration, Article 38 of the Council of Ministers Act turned out to be paramount.[363] It provides that in the event of the President's acceptance of a government's resignation the secretaries and under-secretaries of state, voivods and their deputies automatically submit their resignation and it is up to the Prime Minister to accept or reject their resignations within three months from the date of the appointment of the Council of Ministers. Applied for the first time in 1997, this provision led to four different replacements of several hundred-strong managerial staff. Personnel fluctuation in 2009 regarding senior posts in the civil service was 13.5% and at the middle management level – 14.6%.[364]

The principle of open and competitive recruitment was violated many times by Polish politicians of all colour. Although high-ranking posts in the civil service were, indeed, filled through competition, the process was faulty, competition commissions were charged with being politicised, information on recruitment itself was not available and recruitment procedures were deemed unreliable. Each consecutive government accused its predecessor of using negligent and politicised recruitment procedures in regard to the corps and within it. Some governments (the AWS as well as the SLD-PSL governments) devised a unique way of evading the provisions of the Civil Service Act by introducing the function of 'acting manager' which paved the way for entrusting managerial posts in the civil service to individuals who despite not meeting formal requirements and lacking appropriate experience were delegated to work on the basis of political nominations.

Another example of the violation of the recommended recruitment principles was the opening up of officials' positions in the civil service to state office employees, self-government employees and those working in the Supreme Audit Office (NIK) by means of secondment rather than competition (under the PIS/LPR/*Samoobrona* coalition government). On the back of the 24 August 2006 Act, competitions for senior posts were abolished and instead discretionary appointments introduced. In 2008, the PO/PSL government embarked upon 'sweeping recruitment' whereby the final decisions on employment in managerial positions were made by the political management of a given ministry or central office.

Studies conducted in 2005 reveal that only 6% of the persons polled were able to describe recruitment conditions to the civil service. Out of this number, more

---

363 Ustawa z dnia 8 sierpnia 1996 r. o Radzie Ministrów [Act on the Council of Ministers of 8 August 1996] Dz.U. 1996 No. 106, item. 392, Art. 38.

364 A. Kalita and M. Masłowski, '*Ogólna diagnoza sytuacji w zakresie zarządzania zasobami ludzkimi w służbie cywilnej*', *Przegląd Służby Cywilnej*, No. 2 (5), 2010, p. 12.

than half called the recruitment procedure 'dishonest', and there was not a single person who viewed it as 'decidedly honest'. Those who applied for jobs in the civil service viewed the recruitment of employees as dishonest more frequently than others, possibly because they failed to be recruited.[365] In 2012 in an evaluation carried out by the Supreme Audit Office the recruitment procedure was deemed as complying with the premises of the Act.[366]

In 2006 the post of Head of Civil Service was abolished, thereby depriving the civil service of a self-regulatory mechanism. What is more, supervision over the civil service was transferred to the Head of the Prime Minister's Chancellery, a strictly political body. Even though the institution of Head of Civil Service was reinstituted in 2008 its decision-making status declined substantially in comparison to that provided for under the 18 December 1998 Act.

It is thought that in order to maintain political neutrality the civil service should commit itself to implement decisions which are taken by politicians and not the civil service. In practice, this is tantamount to separating strategic decisions from executive ones. Politically neutral civil servants are required to implement the government's programme and strategy loyally and with due diligence irrespective of their own political views and convictions. The value of political neutrality, which is achieved by making the system of recruitment and promotion independent from the change of government, resides in the strengthening of institutional memory and the more effective implementation of public tasks, those in particular, with long-term significance. Another way of rendering the civil service independent from politics is when political positions are unequivocally specified, publicly known and decidedly separated from bureaucratic ones, that is those which are filled exclusively on the basis of fair and open competition.

A technical arrangement which serves to make the Polish civil service independent from current political shifts is the nomination of civil servants, the stabilisation of their employment relationship as well as the provision of legal guarantees for their professional career paths. Sadly, however, the percentage of nominated civil servants is very low, while the nomination procedure itself has come under political attack.

What is equally important, excessive politicisation hinders or even precludes the implementation of the idea of professionalism in the pragmatics of the Polish

365 Report from the PBS Omnibus study for the Civil Service Office, *Urzędnik państwowy w oczach obywateli. Badanie realizowane z klientami urzędów administracji państwowej. Porównanie wyników I i II fali*. Sopot, September 2005, p. 36.

366 NIK, Informacja o wynikach kontroli *Funkcjonowanie służby cywilnej w ramach obowiązujących regulacji prawnych*, Warszawa 2012, p. 25.

civil service. The degree of politicisation changes in step with changing governments. It must be said, however, that to date there were many cases in the Third Republic when the civil service was simply treated as political spoils.

## Administrative Interest

The basic interests that motivate those who work in the public administration, including the civil service, are determined by the shape of the political system and are informed by the system's 'basic ideological, cultural and organizational premises as well as the culture, tradition and history of a given society.[367] These interests depend on the degree of social development and society's wealth, and whether it is a tradition of pragmatic (UK) or rationalist culture (Germany). While officials' interest in the USA and the UK focuses on the idea of citizenship, at the heart of which lies the democratic law-governed state and the tradition of constitution, in Germany, for instance, it concentrates on the idea of the state and society treated as a unity, which involves the citizens' full identification with the state and its democratic legal order.

If we were to pinpoint the ideas around which administrative interest oscillates in Poland, we would have to say that in terms of the model pursued it is the development of the idea of citizenship coupled with the idea of a law-governed democratic state. Nonetheless, the most prevalent view among the Polish public is that public service is not identified with the idea of state sovereignty, nor the collective will of the people, but rather with a single interest group or a professional one which passively submits itself to political will and, *en masse*, derives benefits from this arrangement. At the same time, however, it has to incur losses to the work force resulting from the inevitable personnel reshuffles with each new government.

The perception of administrative interest in Poland has been an evolving phenomenon revealing certain patterns over time. For instance, the Second Republic attempted to identify public service, frequently treated as a sacrificial service, with the civil servants' personal interest, putting in place statutory guarantees of high legal and professional status of the civil service corp. In People's Poland, the interest of administrative officials was tied to the ruling ideology in an attempt to demonstrate that it was in their interest to promote socialist ideology as the 'only right way forward' of social and state development.

367 I. Macek, 'Aksjologiczne uwarunkowania procesu decyzyjnego w administracji publicznej', in L. Habudy, (ed.), *Administracja i polityka. Proces decyzyjny w administracji publicznej*, Wrocław 2000, p. 81.

Finally in the Third Republic, administrative interest is conceived as the implementation of the idea of the rule of law and the promotion of civil society, and in this shape it is present in the 1997 Constitution as in many other laws regulating the status of public service officials. Furthermore, the mission of curbing political intervention, which gave rise to the *conception of stalling*, has also been safeguarded by the Constitution and lower-level legal acts regarding personnel management in public administration. But, again, these measures are set off against the political practice based on the thriving patronage system, whereby a narrow group of administrators, tied to the political party currently in government, pursues its own interests.

Administrative interest is multi-dimensional and is susceptible to numerous external and internal influences. In practice we come across the following types of interests: personal, professional, that of the service, public interest, national security interest, political interest and, finally, the interest of the European Union.

As far as personal interest in concerned, members of the civil service share a conviction that work taken up in public administration institutions will serve as a vehicle for the fulfilment of their personal dreams and desires in connection with the work they have been hired to perform. In this framework there are both material and non-material motives, for instance: a reasonable pay which enables them to achieve a stable economic status, additional privileges (free newspapers, free parking places, business car/computer/telephone), additional days off, attractive projects, working for the state as a reflexion of prestige, a sense of satisfaction from the decisions taken, the mission of the public service as an expression of the fulfilment of one's expectations and professional aspirations, and a high social status. In civil service personnel management, civil servants' personal interest should not be overlooked or relegated to the background and assessed on moral grounds as an unwelcome attitude in the workplace. The connection must be made between civil servants' personal motivation and the success of the organisation they work for.

Even so, the professional interest of civil servants and civil service employees is seldom identified with belonging to the civil service corps. Oftentimes it is limited to the narrow interest of individual departments, sometimes to the interest of a single ministry or office. It is rarely associated with coordinating the operation of the executive apparatus, and least often – with the interest of the state. Although civil servants assert the existence of public service ethos, that is principles which make up their professional identity, they 'have a limited ability to translate the sense of belonging to this professional group into specific rules of conduct and, furthermore, a limited ability to unequivocally define atypical situations.'[368]

Some authors think it is justified to highlight the significance of public interest in the definition of public administration.[369] In such cases, public interest is identical with the common good articulated through political will and achieved through the due application of the law.[370] It thus follows that the category of public service includes 'all persons performing functions designed to achieve state goals within the framework of the state's organizations'[371], and their goal is the common weal as a social value.[372] In order for the civil service corps to be able to fulfil the interest of public service in the name of the common good, its legal and social status should be regulated in such a manner that it would be protected by institutional and legal arrangements against political interference, interest groups and individual interests. State bureaucracy, as a 'universal class' or 'thinking class' is capable of fighting off individual interests and reason in terms of society as a whole – as Hegel already noticed, adding that members of state bureaucracy, while belonging to civil society, are at the same time the embodiment of the state and a negation of egoism and individualism of the same society.[373] The category of 'public interest' is a category which seems to be easy to explain in theory but in practice it eludes defining and classifying. Moreover, in the words of Aniela Dylus 'in this day and age, service is a forgotten virtue.'[374]

In the case of the bureaucracy, the concept of political interest is a complex one. Civil servants are bound to encounter many obstacles in their contacts with political power. First of all, they are expected to fulfil the extremely difficult task of honouring different – often contradictory – obligations such as: persevering in their search for better solutions to the problems of community life, abiding by the letter of the law and effectively implementing the political agenda. Administrative

---

368 C. Trutkowski, *Postawy członków korpusu służby cywilnej wobec kwestii etycznych,* PISM, Warszaw 2004.

369 Izdebski and Kulesza, *Administracja publiczna*, p. 96.

370 Ibid., p. 97.

371 W. Mikułowski, 'Sprawność cywilnej służby jako instrument rządzenia państwem', in W. Kieżun, (ed.), *Dobre państwo*, Warszawa 2004, p. 77.

372 L. Dziewięcka-Bokun, 'Dobro wspólne jako cel służby publicznej', in L. Dziewięcka-Bokun and J. Kędzior, (eds.), *Wartości społeczne w służbie publicznej*, Toruń 2009, pp. 29–31.

373 J. Szacki, *Historia myśli socjologicznej*, Warszawa 1981, p. 210.

374 A. Dylus, 'Służba (publiczna): cnota zapomniana', in D. Bak, (ed.), *Etos urzędnika*, Warszawa 2007, p. 27.

power is partially responsible for matters related to a given ministry, and fully responsible for the vital functions of the state, for instance, security matters as well as the social and economic order. In Europe the focus is on separating political tasks from administrative ones within the structure of individual ministries. In the words of Max Weber, 'to be "above parties" – in truth, to remain outside the realm of the struggle for power – is the official's role, while this struggle for personal power, and the resulting personal responsibility, is the lifeblood of the politician.'[375] The administration should not have its own political aims; it has to draw its competences from the decisions made by the political power.

The perception of administrative interest through the prism of national security interest represents, firstly, the loyalty of the civil service corps towards the state and, secondly, compliance with the procedures in order to protect against internal and external threats. It can become warped when in the name of ill-conceived security, officials presume that it is in the interest of state security to pursue greater rights and privileges for themselves and restrict the rights of citizens.

It lies in the broad interest of the civil service corps to perform the duties conferred upon it by the law-makers in accordance with legal acts: the Constitution, civil service legislation and the ethical code. It is in the civil servant's interest to understand the significance of complying with ethical standards (which in Poland are Constitutional), such as reliability, professionalism, impartiality and political neutrality. When we look at the changes in public administration and trends aimed at transforming Max Weber's traditional, classical model into a state management model we would first have to answer the question whether it is in the interest of civil servants to support reforms proceeding in this direction? There are many reasons why Polish civil servants and civil service employees have changed their views on the management of public matters and perceive the category of 'interest' in a new light.[376] Amongst them are: professional contacts with experts; the European integration process, which on top of leading to mutual close contacts and an exchange of experiences between civil servants in the area of public issues management, also started the change of bureaucratic mechanisms in Poland; development of professional skills through training schemes; the level of public administration independence from political control; the length of tenure in given posts; and attitudes conducive to or discouraging change in the system of public administration management.

---

375 Max Weber, *Economy and Society*, G. Roth and C. Wittich (eds.), Berkeley: University of California Press, 1978, p. 1404.

376 B. Guy Peters, *Public Administration in the Political System*, London: Sage Publications, Ltd., 2002.

Several problems arise in the course of the, correctly understood, pursuit of administrative interest in Poland. The idea of the administration's public responsibility towards society is now beyond dispute. Thus, fearful about their position, many employees and civil servants prefer to respect the letter of the law (rather than its spirit), giving no heed to the fact that their work is becoming one-sided and routine. The existence of an *esprit de corps* amongst members of a given office encourages civil servants to unite around an immediate and explicit goal rather than around, what often seems to them, an abstract idea of the common weal. Herbert A. Simon compares this situation to that which exists in the army 'the regimental battle flag is the traditional symbol of this identification in military administration; in civil administration a frequently encountered evidence of loyalty is the cry, "our Bureau needs more funds!"'[377] This is why civil servants take decisions on the basis of the limited goals of the office rather than the wider objectives of the administrative organization as a whole – which are more difficult to grasp. As William Niskanen suggests, the budget maximization of their own office becomes a source of satisfaction, prestige and material profit for civil servants. The heads of office are not alone in their fight for a high budget; they can count on the support of lower grade officials in whose interest lies not only a pay rise but also the chance of promotion.[378]

While on the subject of the changes that affect the interest of the civil service let us refer to Zygmunt Bauman who argues that in the modern world the bureaucracy has undergone a transformation whereby 'responsibility for' (the welfare, autonomy and dignity of another human being) has been substituted by 'responsibility towards' (one's superior, an authority, the cause and its advocates).[379]

There are ways of making sure that the bureaucracy's egoistic behavior is curtailed. For one, the civil service should be representative of society as a whole, especially its higher rungs should reflect existing social divisions; secondly, the influence of interest groups on state activity should be safeguarded; and thirdly, control over political leadership should be instituted.[380] Still, two more conditions should be added to the ones mentioned above, namely, increasing the status of the citizens as the recipients, consumers and partners of public services, and subjecting the administration to careful supervision exercised by these citizens.

---

377 H.A. Simon, *Administrative Behavior*, 4th ed., New York: The Free Press, p. 11.

378 J.P. Gunning, *Understanding Democracy. An Introduction to Public Choice*, Taiwan: Nomad Press, 2003.

379 Z. Bauman, *Szanse etyki w zglobalizowanym świecie*, Kraków 2007, pp. 37–38.

380 See E.C. Page, *Political Authority and Bureaucratic Power. A Comparative Analysis*, New York: Prentice Hall, 1992.

## Is this Administrative Language or Bureaucratese?

In the dynamic situation that the public administration has found itself, caused by European integration, globalization and migrations, the language it uses has become an extremely important tool for communicating with society, and more narrowly, within its own internal units to ensure its proper operation. In order to fulfill its communicative function, the language used by the administration should be clear, distinct, legible, logical and unambiguous.

Contrary to these guidelines, however, in terms of administrative semantics, reality proves to be far more complex. Firstly, civil service corps members use mental shortcuts, key words, or codes for communicating within the department, the ministry or between public institutions. Secondly, linguistic dualism develops when one type of language is used in contacts between civil service corps members and a different type in communicating with citizens, customers or partners. Thirdly, a growing number of terms borrowed directly from other languages, English in particular, seeps into the administrative lexicon. Fourthly, the hermetic language of legal journals finds its way into the language used in contacts with citizens. Moreover, it has been observed that the less public officials have to do with the environment outside the workplace, the more shortcuts and codes they use in communicating.

The language used by members of the Polish civil service corps has been analysed in the Report entitled: 'The Social Image of the Civil Service. An Analysis of Political Discourse: Analysis of Cultural Meaning, Analysis of Oppositions, Analysis of Codes'.[381] If we examine the expressions found in the vocabulary of civil service employees and civil servants we come across a multitude of terms with an inherently negative attitude towards civil service culture. This is exemplified by the list below:

- Anarchy (*anarchia*) – which stands for 'shambles' and 'chaos' in the area of procedures, regulations and employee competences within the civil service. Involves mainly work in treasury area, such as tax offices;
- Backwoods (*prowincja*) – 1) A public administration agency, with a sense of its service, achievements and initiatives being belittled; made up of civil service corps members colloquially called small-fry, beggars or proles; 2) an

381 'Społeczny wizerunek służby cywilnej. Analiza dyskursu publicznego: Analiza znaczeń kulturowych, Analiza opozycji, Analiza kodów', *Strategia Zarządzania Zasobami Ludzkimi w Służbie Cywilnej* [Concluding Report in the Project, *Strategy for Human Resources Management in the Civil Service*], Kancelaria Prezesa Rady Ministrów, Warszawa, 2011.

office subordinate to the central public administration organisation often described as 'lying beyond the Warsaw upper crust'; expression used in internal official-to-official communication with highly negative axiology;

- Boredom (*nuda*) – an emotional condition experienced by civil service representatives stemming from the introduction of precise, unchangeable and predictable regulations governing the conduct of administrative officials. 'Our work is dull and laborious – you would not find any of the sensations here that the media thrive on.' Predictability and standards regulating most types of behavior in the office undermine innovation and a creative approach to problem solving;
- Calling (*powołanie*) – possessing the right predispositions to perform the role of a civil service member; observing high ethical standards of conduct (in a natural and uncompromising manner) in all their dealings with their colleagues and fulfilling themselves in the service of citizens; a term of positive axiology used sporadically in discourse;
- Civil servant (*urzędnik mianowany*) – a public official who under the terms of the Civil Service Act receives a nomination to the rank of civil servant in the civil service corps following a positively graded examination; representative of a limited and elitist group; in most cases an expert, with factual education and mastery of 'soft skills';
- Corrections (*korekty*) – changes and revisions introduced into the documentation of state administration bodies to remedy mistakes frequently made as a consequence of the officials' ignorance of legal regulations and bureaucratic intricacies. Civil servants often speak of corrections as testimony to head-office staff being undereducated. The regular practice of making corrections becomes a remedy for 'patching up' legislation which is faulty from the start;
- Corruption (*korupcja*) – abuse of position to gain material benefits (money, small gifts) in exchange for turning a blind eye to improprieties; solving difficult problems disregarding principles; issuing licenses or authorizations without justification; colloquially – taking bribes; in the documents under analysis the concept of corruption appears in regard to the early 1990s as a form of retrospective narratives and reminiscences. Today, it practically does not occur in the context of the civil service;
- Decision-making paralysis (*paraliż decyzyjny*) – refers to bureaucrats who restrict their decision-making because of mounting fear, substantial ignorance or the introduction of professional responsibility; it is reflected in the imprecisely defined competences of civil service representatives leading them to resort to the postponement of action, delaying tactics or a total procedural

blockage; the sort of conduct which is co-responsible for the lack of effectiveness and efficiency of public administration agencies; a term commonly used in internal discourse (official-to-official) and external (journalist-to-reader or TV anchorperson-to-viewer); represents a strongly negative axiology;

- Experience (*doświadczenie*) – length of service, tenure in the civil service which does not necessarily translate into noticeable gratification or motivation to continue in this activity; often occurs in the negative context of naiveté: the longer one's experience, the more gullible one becomes; the positive sense of the term: with experience one's competencies and, thus, usefulness to the civil service and to the state grow; term belongs to the vocabulary used in internal official-to-official communication;
- Expert (*specjalista*) – the opposite of a paper-pusher; a member of the civil service corps, more often than not a highly competent nominated civil servant who is well-adjusted to modern, increasingly high requirements imposed by the citizens, who in his/her parlance are called 'partners' or 'clients'. A person of high ethical standards; a well-versed expert on the subject of law, regulations and the procedures for law-implementation. One who lives up to ethical criteria and follows ethical guidelines;
- Government (*rząd*) – or, Governments rather, one of the pillars of the 'upstairs' (*Góra*). Members of the civil service have an ambivalent attitude towards politics – it is on rare occasions that they do voice their support for a given political party or world view, treating their political views as their private matter. The 'Government', on the other hand, is synonymous with politics, in other words: mediocre activities taken up in order to play to the gallery, the lack of professionals and reluctance to carry out administrative reforms. Each 'Government' finds the civil service's independence vis-à-vis politics to be obstructive, hence the frequent tampering with civil service acts to make it easier to influence the manning of senior positions. Civil servants place very little confidence in politicians and their deeds, especially those who use lofty rhetoric;
- Head office (*centrala*) – 1) the main and most important, decision- and procedure-making unit of the administration and, according to civil service corps members, one which inaptly supervises other offices subordinated to it; disconnected from the everyday reality well known to the 'province'; 2) area which generates practical directives with specific consequences, usually perceived as absurd by the province (see definition) and one with which the province must somehow cope; area colloquially called *Wielka Polska* ('Great Poland'), '*warszafka*' (contemptuously of the hedged in community

of Warsaw's new swanky elite), or the 'centre of chaos' with the attendant expressions denoting those who work there as: brainless creatures, vultures or rogues; a pejorative term used in internal official-to-official discourse;

- Hysteria (*histeria*) – anxiety, fear and panic over the introduction of the principle of financial responsibility for bureaucratic errors; the hysteria launched a search for insurance companies which would insure bureaucrats' mistakes; according to civil servants, in an environment of bad law this would lead to a fall in the number of decisions taken and total paralysis;
- Ill-adapted (*nieprzystosowani*) – new, usually, young recruits to the civil service, incapable of adjusting to the rules in place and the specific nature of the job. Coupled with their problems in absorbing the basic knowledge related to codes of conduct, official regulations, etc. they are often seen as being clumsy and lacking decent schooling, hence, requiring much of their older colleagues' precious time in order to catch up. They are also lazy – shun opportunities to improve their skills and competencies. This is the effect of nepotism. Great paper-pusher material;
- Informers (*konfidenci*) – members of the civil service who because of their attitude, informal function (for instance, informing on others), and being embedded in employee hierarchies that result from a toxic dependence on their superiors (nepotism), fall short of meeting the high standards required from civil servants in the performance of administrative duties; the term has a pejorative meaning in the internal official-to-official discourse;
- Jack-in-office (*urzędas*) – the baddie of civil service discourse; the type of public official who has all the negative and stereotypical traits of the system: lazy, incompetent, brusque, poorly educated, heartless, ill-mannered, dismissive (he/she serves 'petitioners' rather than 'customers'); a stickler hiding behind the rules of administrative law; on a daily basis, a 'jack-in-office' deals with the juggernaut of bureaucratic ritualism; a stereotype which came into existence at the turn of the 1980s and 1990s – although to a lesser degree, it is still valid today – an opposite of the increasingly predominant expert-technocrat; frequently used in internal discourse;
- Nepotism (*nepotyzm*) – even though corruption rarely appears in the area of the civil service corps, nepotism is an everyday occurrence. It points to the employment or appointment of 'trusted' people, often family members or friends of an employee who has influence over the recruitment competition. It underscores the fact that civil service structures are off-limits to the outside world and underscores the meaning of the notion 'caste of officials'. 'Most people here have some sort of backing' – statement implies that the majority of

those who work for the civil service have a protector who proved helpful in their recruitment for the job;

- Non-nominated official or a civil service employee (*urzędnik niemianowany*) – in the internal fabric of the civil service perceived to be an individual bereft of the skills and ambition to seek nomination into the ranks of civil servants; an idler who often complains, mostly about low pay, but does nothing to improve his/her status (or pay) or relationships with other colleagues in the service; frequent expression in internal official-to-official discourse; negative axiology;
- Old folk (*starzy*) – members of the civil service corps with many years of experience in the profession; on account of their predispositions and long service in the administrative apparatus they belong to one of the two typical groups of bureaucrats: experts (see definition) or pensioners (see definition); the expression appears in internal official-to-official discourse; the axiology is neutral;
- Overstaffing (*przerost zatrudnienia*) – poor management of human resources in public administration units causing a mismatch between existing levels of employment and the actual staff needs, something administrative employees are aware of; often referred to as the 'army', 'grandiosity', or fabric bursting at the seams;
- Paper for everything (*papier na wszystko*) – highlights the universally existing bureaucratic system dominated by paper documents; used interchangeably with the expression: 'Paper is stronger than words';
- Paper pushers (*papierkowi przekładacze*) – colloquial expression to denote those civil service corps members whose main task is to fill out and check paper forms, files and other documents;
- Pensioners (*emeryci*) – older generation of civil service corps members with long service, usually of pre-pension age and fearful of all things new; a synonym of stagnation and lack of involvement, creativity and motivation; wide experience and detailed knowledge of regulations as well as the practical aspect of work in the civil service corps – something 'pensioners' are unwilling or incapable of sharing with others; they represent the burnout syndrome and anxiety over losing their job (subject to rationalization); 'pensioners' perceived negatively by the young (see definition) for blocking access to higher-level jobs and positions and preventing changes for the better in the service; term often crops up in official-to-official communication;
- Petty beggar (*żebraczek*) – a negative designate for a civil service representative, referring to the low pay he/she receives – inadequate in regard to the hard

slave labour being performed; expression used in internal official-to-official communication;

- Pressure (*presja*) – a condition seen in the fabric of the civil service corps caused by the degeneration of individual administrative units created by numerous counts of mobbing, constant stress and uncertainty; it is magnified by the additional tangle of regulations and the introduction of internal control; functioning as it does in public administration it leads to the utter frustration and discontent of the employees; a term of strongly negative axiology used in external communication narratives (journalist-to-citizen/reader, TV host-citizen/viewer);
- Professional accountability (*odpowiedzialność zawodowa*) – civil servants' personal and financial accountability for any deliberate action to the detriment of the citizens. Received with as much surprise as dismay by the civil service, since the majority of its members persist in drawing attention to bad, overgrown regulations which invite ambiguous interpretations, and these in turn can lead to a wave of lawsuits – contrary to the neutral or good intentions of these regulations. Officials feel that the whole responsibility for the unwieldy State has fallen upon their shoulders – 'they've got themselves a whipping boy', they say.
- Prole (*robol*) – a civil servant who in his/her own view is treated as an uneducated person asked to perform dull, taxing jobs in the civil service; an expression often occurring in internal official-to-official communication; negative overtones;
- Promethean attitude (*Prometeida*) – here expression alludes to the aspect of self-sacrifice in the Promethean myth; suffering for the cause of creating a state administration system; 'we are suffering for others', subjecting ourselves to the higher good. For adopting such an attitude, members of the civil service, like Prometheus, are punished and regarded with disfavor by their bosses. Work at the grass-roots level is unrewarding, unprofitable and undervalued but one without which society would not be able to function;
- Promotion-blocking instrument (*narzędzie blokujące awans*) – a colloquial expression for periodical assessments of the quality and efficiency of the work carried out by civil service corps members; performed at least once every two years – treated as an instrument for enforcing obedience; potentially blocking promotions; has little to do with factual status and quality of work; tailored to suit the conditions existing in a given office, often associated with nepotism (ideal tool for promoting 'our own'); used for internal point-scoring (manager-employee); a phraseological expression often used by civil servants;

- Rationalisation (*racjonalizacja*) – construed by the Government, a project of streamlining state administration in order to increase savings. It presumed a 10% reduction in the numbers of all employed in the administration, excluding senior positions (such as managers, directors). A decidedly negative notion, often used in internal discourse in order to negate perfectly rational measures. Considered to be a bad law by civil servants, the 2010 Employment Rationalisation Act[382] is said to have led to the erosion of the civil service and intimidation of its employees ('as many employees as possible are hired under any pretext – just in any case, in order to lay off as many new hirelings as necessary when the Act comes into force'). At the same time, it made it possible to keep 'one's own', while boasting to one's ministerial superiors of accurately fulfilling his/her orders; 'to throw the baby out with the bath-water' – aimed particularly at impressing public opinion, and influencing the governing party's public opinion poll ratings – instead of seeking to improve the administration's performance. It has a rather positive ring in external discourse as 'rationalisation' has been used in the context of making savings, increasing the efficiency of the administration and its agencies, etc. In the end, however, the project was challenged by the Constitutional Tribunal;
- Regulations (*przepisy*) – set of legal acts (statutes, orders, regulations) generally applicable to public administration and members of the public, enacted by the legislative; considered to be a set of ambiguous, sloppy, tangled, irritating and constantly changing directives which tend to generate procedural absurdities and interpretative conflicts; term used frequently in discourse;
- Riff-raff (*doły*) – those members of the civil service corps who are convinced they belong to the irrelevant, inferior and subordinate group of public administration officials treated as slaves; term often used in internal official-to-official communication; the riff-raff toil away and carry out orders: they are not supposed to think or advise; they will take anything – you can always hammer them and increase their workload, you can perform experiments on them (such as rationalisation); negative axiology;

---

382 Ustawa z dnia 16 grudnia 2010 r. o racjonalizacji zatrudnienia w państwowych jednostkach budżetowych i niektórych innych jednostkach sektora finansów publicznych w latach 2011–2013 [Act of 16 December 2010 on the Rationalisation of Employment in State Budgetary Agencies and Selected Units of the Public Finance Sector in 2011–2013]; the Act was adopted by the Sejm but following the 2011 ruling by the Constitutional Tribunal that parts of it were unconstitutional, the Act did not come into force.

- Security (*bezpieczeństwo*) – term related mainly to employment security. In administrative discourse undoubtedly seen as one of the key advantages of working in the civil service as it provides: 1) continuity of employment guaranteed by statute, in practice – immunity to staff turnover; 2) certainty of receiving pay on time, as well as the extras, bonus salaries and awards; 3) absence of change and surprises; predictability, ability to plan the future in no uncertain terms ('barring calamities I know very well where I will be in five years' time'). Without doubt, this context is a crucial existential (Frommian) key to understanding this attitude – forsaking some freedom, consenting to a set of constraints – in return for a sense of stability and security;
- Small fry (*szaraczek*) – 1) a civil servant who in his/her own view is a person of little importance in the public administration system; 2) used for denoting a civil service corps representative in internal official-to-official communication;
- Stagnation (*stagnacja*) – lack of perspectives for professional development in the ranks of the civil service going back to poor human resources management; demotivation; little appreciation for the work carried out, bringing down employees' self-confidence; incorporating complicated and rigid promotion procedures. The other referent pertains to the administrative lull resulting from the negative attitude of the officials themselves who manifest their total boredom, lack of creativity and effectiveness on the job; term rarely seen in external narration (journalist-to-citizen/reader), represents negative axiology;
- Superior (*przełożony*) – refers to a person in a transitionary place between the ruling 'upstairs' and the exploited 'province' (see definition); one who wields genuine influence on individual career paths, remuneration distribution (extras, bonuses and awards) and conducts periodical employee assessments – which is a ticket for applying for a civil service nomination. On account of a malicious attitude to matters concerning his/her subordinates, colloquially defined by them as a 'hardliner', 'reject', 'loser' or 'sacred cow', 'no matter what, it won't harm a hair on his head'; in internal communication used as a synonym of 'employer' alternating with terms such as 'boss', 'ruler', 'His Lordship' with negative overtones – where the degree of negativity is augmented by the rising rank of his/her job in public administration;
- System (*system*) – an abstract existence without a personification which connects activities in all the areas and manifestations of the state bureaucracy. In external discourse it is presented as the Medusa (Gorgona), the elusive cause of all ills, difficult to identify and neutralize. Besides being a symbol of incompetence and irresponsibility, it acts as a brake on development and

reforms in the civil service area, and shields its conformist apologists and destroys innovators. It exists more in the mind than in any real civil service organisation;

- Well-adjusted (*przystosowani*) – (young) people newly employed in the civil service with the appropriate education (often graduates of National School of Public Administration) and interpersonal skills, exhibiting charisma and above-average vitality in their work; represent a rational, innovative attitude; try to improve work quality and the functioning of the civil service corps. People with ambition, which might lead them to seek jobs in the private sector; term occurring in internal official-to-official discourse with positive overtones;
- Yardsticks (*mierniki*)– instruments designed to measure and assess the work of individual offices across Poland; intended to compare the effectiveness and efficiency of office operation and select the best public administration body that adheres to all procedures and directives. It is seen by administration employees as an artificial juggernaut which provides little objective information on the condition of offices and generates more problems than it solves – 'you work for yardsticks, not for the citizens';
- Young (*młodzi*) – team of newly recruited employees with meager experience and not many years of service. According to the 'old folk' the young are represented by two different types of people evaluated in terms of the following: 1) career predispositions: well-adapted (see definition) and ill-adapted (see definition) to work in the civil service; 2) scale of nepotism involved in the hiring procedure itself. Colloquially called 'offspring' or 'young blood'; neutral axiology in internal official-to-official communication.[383]

Another dimension of the language used by representatives of the civil service corps are the mistakes they make, especially lexical mistakes in the form of pleonasms, such as 'true fact' or 'free gift'. Next, is the abuse of certain words, such as 'to implement' *realizować*, another 'to possess' *posiadać* which is the favourite replacement for 'to have' *mieć*. So in a bid to give the language a pompous edge, instead of saying 'have some control', civil service parlance comes up with 'possess some control'. Likewise, the improper use of words regardless of their meaning, for instance 'appointed regulations' *powołane przepisy* to denote 'adopted regulations'. Then there are many syntax errors, for example, in letters in opening expressions the use of a wrong preposition in the Polish equivalent of the English 'with regard to', so instead of '*w związku z*' we have the ubiquitous '*w nawiązaniu do*'. The conjunction 'that' is overused. Finally, errors are notoriously made in

383 Ibid., pp. 30–46.

prepositional phrases ('in regard to' *odnośnie*, 'in order to' *celem*). As for spelling, the most frequent mistakes arise from confusing which words to write together and which to write separately: two separate words are written as one word, or what should be written as one word is separated into two words; equally frequent is the excessive use of capital letters for common nouns. Many mistakes concern punctuation marks: for instance, wrongly placing commas in single independent clauses or failing to place a comma before conjunctions such as 'in order to', 'whether', 'because', 'if' and in expressions with gerund participle clauses, which in Polish necessitate a comma.'[384]

In the bureaucratic jargon, the use of which does nothing to improve the clarity of the message, the customer becomes a 'party' *strona*; instead of 'asking' *prosić* we 'apply' *wnioskować*; and instead of 'paying' *płacić* we 'submit payment' *uiszczać*; or in place of 'selling' *sprzedać* we 'dispose of' *zbywać*.[385]

The authors of the *Report* are of the opinion that among the readership of newspapers, only 18% of the readers of the 'Fakt', 30% of 'Super Express' and 41% of 'Gazeta Wyborcza' would be able to understand an average article on European Funds published in these dailies.[386] The mistakes most frequently committed in administrative language include all sorts of lexical mistakes and unintelligible constructions. The problems include semantic redundancies (pleonasms and tautologies): 'within the time of one year', 'at this point in time', 'it has been, and still is', etc.; extending the range of collocations; wrong use of words; unfortunate metaphors; (unintentionally) using words with negative connotations. Another linguistic mannerism that has crept into Polish bureaucratic language is the overuse of the word 'proverbial' *(przysłowiowy)* to signalise the use of an idiomatic expression and certainly not a proverb, which in English would read: 'this action is the proverbial blessing in disguise'. In the same category are stylistic errors: the style used in documents on European Funds 'is uneven. One could even say the basic features are inconsistency and eclecticism. The most common mistake made by the administration is the abuse of official jargon, bookish expressions, overuse of official language especially in the form of trite constructions (at this point in time, during the course of, in the nature of ), abuse of colloquial language (signalized with quotation marks), or the unintended comical effect (especially

384 <http://www.mazowieckie.pl/wai/pl/2/9107/Jezyk_urzedowy_bardziej_zrozumialy.html>, accessed 7 November 2011.

385 <http://www.emetro.pl/emetro/1,85648,10611732,Wielokrotnie_zlozona_urzedni cza_mowa_trawa.html>, accessed 6 July 2012.

386 J. Miodek et al., *Język tekstów o Funduszach Europejskim*. Raport, MRR, UE Europejski Fundusz Rozwoju Regionalnego, Narodowa Strategia Spójności, Warszawa 2010.

with the use of metaphors)'.[387] Finally, the writing of administrative staff is dominated by overelaborate parallel syntax:

- Excessive number of interpolations usually awkwardly placed in a sentence; lack of agreement between compound nouns and verb; mistakes in the use of prepositions (for instance *dla*/for);
- Frequent use of elliptical constructions (without the dash); frequent omissions of pronouns which refer the reader to the subject in earlier sentences; an unnatural word order;
- The notorious and pretentious abrupt ending of a sentence only to be followed with a gerund clause (with no predicate) – as a conclusion of the earlier statement."

The team headed by Prof. Jerzy Miodek came up with the suggestion that authors writing about European Funds should do so from the perspective of ordinary people, and follow these guidelines:

- Write colloquially, taking an anthropocentric view, embracing personalism, using metaphors, following common sense and the logic of the concrete, etc.;
- Place referential content in the (everyday life) context well-known to the recipient;
- Use words from the basic vocabulary of the Polish language;
- Write in a conversational style (question and answer);
- Assume the role of a good friend/adviser;
- Avoid formal and legal style.[388]

The analysis of the Polish language as it is spoken and written by members of the civil service, carried out by such researchers as Prof. Jan Miodek or Prof. Radosław Pawelec, has not only revealed language mistakes but also underscored the necessity for bringing about change to improve communication between the government and the citizens/clients/applicants. Reports, analyses and strategies produced by government agencies do not have to be easy to read. However, if they are to play an informative function or promote good practice, care should be taken to avoid the use of words such as 'interprogramme manner', 'fragmentation of knowledge' or 'diffusion', legible only to a handful of readers and potentially causing communicative resistance. This is all the more so, since it is perfectly possible to covey the same meaning using simpler terminology.

387 Ibid.
388 Ibid.

## How the Civil Service Influences the Modernisation of Public Administration?

Modernisation represents the 'effective adaptation to change, the continuous quest for quality improvement, efficiency of operation and the satisfaction of the residents'. Modernisation embraces: new public management, implementing and maintaining a system of quality management (ISO standards), strategic planning, long-term financial plans, task budgets, improving public organisations and e-government.[389]

An overhaul of the public administration could follow the outline given below:

- Authorities should be guided by a sense of mission, not only rules. This translates into an awareness of the goals which the administration strives to achieve. The main goal is optimal social and economic development. Reaching this goal requires the following factors: anticipation, modern leadership, change, competitiveness, the licensing of services, investments, cooperation with the widest possible network of partners (social organisations, NGOs), continuous promotion of activities and aims.
- Authorities should pursue a policy focused on goals rather than the means of achieving them.
- Public authority should be decentralized.[390]

The modernisation of the civil service implies that the civil service should use the premises of the Common Assessment Framework creatively, in other words, it should develop and provide services and products addressed to the citizens/customers by means of the following: 'involving citizens in the development and improvement of services and products (in the form of interviews, feedback, focus groups or questions in which citizens are asked about the usefulness of services and products taking account of the diversity of their needs based on their gender, among other things); incorporating the citizens and other interested parties in designing the quality standards of services, products and information conveyed to the citizens; creating clear, legible and simple legal rules; incorporating citizens into the designing and shaping of information sources and channels; providing access to appropriate and credible information by way of offering help and support to the citizens; widening access to the organisation (flexible office hours, diverse forms of documents: in different languages, including Braille,

389 Ibid., p. 107.

390 S. Wysocki, 'Jak poprawić jakość działania administracji publicznej?', *Służba Cywilna*, No. 2, 2001, pp. 28–32.

e-documents, posters, pamphlets, etc.); promoting electronic forms of contact and interaction with the citizens; developing efficient systems and procedures for providing answers and reacting to complaints.’[391]

Published in 1994, the Bangemann Report, drawing attention to the development gap between the states of the European Union on the one hand, and the US and Japan on the other, compelled EU members to adopt the Lisbon Strategy in 2000. The document set out plans to create the most competitive and dynamic economy in the world and a knowledge-based society by the end of 2010. Among the measures recommended, new tasks were drawn up for the civil service, such as introducing and using new technology which affects space-time contraction. In a world which sees the development of information society, network economy and knowledge-driven economy, new technologies serve to improve the efficiency of public administration institutions and the quality of services rendered. New technologies also increase the usefulness, transparency and access to information resources in the administration’s possession, finally becoming an effective instrument for generating change.

Information society has been defined as a ‘new system of society developing in countries with a high degree of technological development wherein the management of information, its quality and the speed of information flow contribute decisively to competitiveness in industry and the service sector alike, while the level of development requires the use of new technologies of storing, transforming, conveying and applying information.’[392] Information is used in the economy, politics and law. The term refers to statistical data, facts and certain categories or phenomena.[393] In information society ‘it is not direct contacts [...] but rather contacts [...] through the mass media that have become the predominant form of social contacts [...] As Japanese studies have revealed, communication through the social media, especially on line has become a more convenient means of communicating for the young generation than direct personal communication.’ The notion of information society, in turn, is primarily historical, defining the typical traits of social relations associated with civilisational development (e-generation).[394]

---

391 Ibid., 27.

392 ePolska – Plan działania na rzecz rozwoju społeczeństwa informacyjnego w Polsce na lata 2001–2006, dokument przyjęty przez Radę Ministrów w dniu 11 września 2001 r. <http://kbn.icm.edu.pl/cele/epolska>, accessed 6 July 2012.

393 For more see, B. Stefanowicz, *Informacja*, Warszawa 2004.

394 For more on the subject see T. Goban-Klas and P. Sienkiewicz, *Społeczeństwo informacyjne: Szanse, zagrożenia, wyzwania*, Fundacja Postępu Telekomunikacji, Kraków 1999.

The concept of electronic public administration (e-administration) belongs to the information society. Because of the ever-increasing use of information in administration many new notions describing this phenomenon are applied, for example: e-government, e-administration, e-services, which besides representing a new approach to management and the application of state-of-the-art technologies are also a sign of the acquisition of new skills in the public services.[395]

The implementation of ICT in the civil service consists of several elements, firstly, launching the strategy of treating the citizens as customers; secondly, introducing a service for citizens/customers under the one-stop shop slogan; thirdly, privatizing certain services through outsourcing; fourthly, making documents accessible on-line; and, finally, implementing the e-management programme. Members of the public are also encouraged to communicate with administrative services via their mobile phones. Accordingly, documents will be made available on mobile phones (pensions, benefits, applications, birth certificates); information will be provided by means of text-messaging (e.g., bus service time-tables, appeals to blood-donors); drivers' licenses and ID cards will be issued and renewed; applying for unemployment benefits will be encouraged through on-line registration services. In view of all these possibilities the Polish civil service faces many challenges and dilemmas, which is not to say that its evolution has failed to follow the trends described in other countries altogether.

Already as a EU-candidate state, and part of the *eEurope* plan, Poland has formulated its own design for developing information society. One of its priorities was the implementation of the project 'Gateway to Poland – public administration for information society', which was to make the provision of administrative services by electronic means more convenient and efficient. In 2000, the 'Friendly Administration' programme was launched, intended to expand citizens' knowledge on government administration and advance the opinion that the administration plays a service role in regard to society. In this context the following tasks were outlined:

- Improving the quality of work in government administration offices,
- Improving the quality of communication between citizens and officials,
- Altering the image of a civil service corps member,
- Introducing improvements into offices tested in terms of quality,
- Simplifying procedures and shortening the time necessary for getting things done,

395 M. Kleiber, *W kierunku nowoczesnego urzędu,* Warszawa 2004, s. 5.

- Increasing officials' competencies,
- Informing the public about the changes introduced.

In 2003, the Civil Service Office and other ministries created an online information service 'Friendly Administration' open to citizens through a network of 'info-mats' or special public terminals. More than a 100 terminals were set up in shopping malls and in seven offices (Bydgoszcz, Kielce, Łódz and others). The service was to aid customers in their speedy search for information on how and where to have things done. Information was provided according to categories, instead of the hitherto set-up based on the competence of a given office.

As well as that, in the National Development Strategy 2007–2015[396] an opinion was put forward that the system of public administration should be efficient, effective and inexpensive and that it required the promotion of flexible and alternative forms of employment in the form of flexi time, part-time jobs or tele-working. The operation of the civil service should be based on social trust, cooperation with citizens and organisations grouping citizens, entrepreneurs and experts. The civil service needs to be 'open, transparent, dialogue-oriented, efficient and adaptable.' Furthermore, 'activities strengthening employee potential as well as technical and technological modernisation are necessary.'[397] The authors of the *Strategy* argued that Polish public administration has failed to introduce the necessary modern management techniques and information systems and, what is more, it also desisted from improving public finance management.[398]

The drawn-out integration process with the EU, the caesura of which (but not its completion) was Poland's membership of this supranational organization, determined and chartered the direction of change in Polish public administration to a considerable degree. It is, however, a determination and direction of a peculiar sort: as required by the principle of procedural autonomy it refrains from creating uniform systemic, structural and operational standards for public administration in individual member states. The civil service corps – through its style of work, manner and mode of decision-making, eliminating or tolerating functional disorders – contributes to the moulding of opinions about the civil service.

Poland ranks very low among European states in terms of the development of e-administration, indicated by, among other things, the accessibility of twenty basic public administration services on-line (which defines the progress made in

---

396 *National Development Strategy 2007–2015* was adopted by the Council of Ministers on 29 November 2006.

397 Ibid., 60.

398 Ibid., 17.

implementing the Lisbon Strategy). Considering the 27 states of the European Union as a whole, the indicator in 2007 was 59 %, whereas for Poland it was a mere 25 %.[399]

The establishment of a modern technical infrastructure is taking place in Poland although there are many obstacles, especially the state's financial capabilities, the lack of modern technologies and poor management. Expenditures for the implementation of IT solutions vary: on average in 2007 they amounted to 1.4% of all public expenditures, in 2008 they fell to 1.25. The percentage of offices which provided ICT training for their employees remained on the same level of 27%. ICT training takes place in the civil service more often than in communal/municipal or district offices.[400] Those who make the most online contacts with the public administration are university graduates, the self-employed and women in the 25–34 age group.[401] Conversely, those who make the least contacts are farmers, people with elementary education, pensioners or people with disabilities and those who are in the 55–74 age group. Only 6% of all internet users in Poland have never searched for information on the public administration's online services. Most frequently the information sought has to do with taxes, jobs and personal matters, such as ID cards, passports, registration, registry office certificates, etc.[402]

There is, however, evidence suggesting that the quality of customer service in the administration offices is improving, as demonstrated by the research project 'The Impact of Computerization on the Streamlining of Public Administration Operation in 2010'. Applying IT technologies in the process of service provision allowed for the following:

- Contracting the time needed to serve a customer/citizen – in the opinion of 75% of office managers;
- Increasing the number of services provided – in the opinion of 48% of managers;
- Simplifying procedures of service – reported in 52% of offices;
- Increased customer satisfaction – as observed by 54% of office employees.[403]

399 Ibid., 38.

400 Departament Społeczeństwa Informacyjnego, Ministerstwo Spraw Wewnętrznych i Administracji, *Społeczeństwo informacyjne w liczbach* 2009, Warszawa 2009, p. 36.

401 Ibid., 40.

402 *Strategia sprawne państwo 2011–2020…* p. 29.

403 Ibid.

In the context of the above analysis, it seems impossible to provide an explicit answer to the question whether the Polish civil service is fully adapted to facilitate the proper functioning of our country in the European Union. Firstly, Poland operates in the EU on various planes, hence, adaptation will have to be looked at from many different angles. Secondly, since the EU itself is subject to continuous shifts we can see in this context that EU member states in general are notoriously ill-adapted to the EU, or, more accurately perhaps, there is on the part of EU members the persistent effort to adapt to the requirements of the ever changing Union.

It seems that Poland's membership in the European Union is leading to a continuous improvement of operational and systemic standards of Polish public administration. This is evidenced by, among other things, the care taken to maintain the relatively high level of the civil service, and very importantly, the continuous functioning of the National School of Public Administration (basically within the same original framework) regardless of changing governments.

The modernisation of the civil service is enhanced by financial projects from European funds. Financial support from the European Social Fund made it possible to include about 2,300 offices in a whole gamut of projects concerned with modernisation, information, training and advising; in 2008–2011, 10,775 employees of the revenue administration were trained (in new human resources management techniques, customer satisfaction management, modern standards of customer service and process management).[404] Examples of what has been achieved are listed below: a competence model was implemented in the Śląsk Voivodship Office; support was given to the goals-management system in the Ministry of the State Treasury; the EMAS community management system was implemented in the Ministry of the Environment; an electronic system of document circulation was implemented in the State Archive in Kraków and the Main Veterinary Inspectorate; a compendium of seven subject areas and educational films (e.g. ethics) targeting civil service corps members was prepared by the Mazovian Voivodship Office; in the Central Office of Measures an integrated management system was implemented based on the ISO-9001:2009 as well as a System of Counteracting Corruption Threats.[405]

In an assessment of the policies mentioned above, what needs underlining is the innovative nature of the projects and the anticipated synergy effect produced

404 Kancelaria Prezesa Rady Ministrów, *Sprawozdanie Szefa Służby Cywilnej o stanie służby cywilnej i realizacji zadań tej służby w* 2011 roku, Warszawa, March 2012, pp. 70–78.

405 Ibid., pp. 77–78.

by these policies while in operation. On the other hand, it is worrying that the project does not include all the offices (with the exception of the Mazovian Voivodship Office project) but rather individual entities, thus preventing the Polish civil service from establishing uniform standards.

About 40% of offices use the electronic document management system (EDMS); 43% of the systems have the archive package-creating modules; moreover, 42% of offices are able to export all data under EDMS. Even so, the use of the EDMS has not been able to eliminate the traditional circulation of documents in paper form. In the majority of offices, regardless of the level, a dual system of document circulation is in place. What is more, 86% of offices indicate that this concerns over a half of all cases dealt with by the offices. In excess of 80% of all offices which have not installed EDMS confirmed their plans for incorporating the system. Roughly speaking, one in five offices had plans to introduce the system by the end of 2011, one in two – in 2012.

The Podlaskie Voivodship Office in Białystok was the leader in the practical implementation of the electronic circulation of documents by June 2012. It was the first office in Poland which replaced paper documents with their electronic versions and introduced the tele-information system (EDMS). The system is 'adapted to comprehensive office service: from the moment incoming mail reaches the office, through creating drafts, acceptance and final endorsement, up to the generation of the correspondence book. The collaboration between organsational cells within a single unit takes place by sharing, which according to the idea of the new office directive, has done away with the buildup of office work in the unit [...]. The EDMS makes it also possible to manage documents: receiving incoming paper documents, lending them and returning – these basic activities performed by employees requires reporting this in the system in order to effectively manage its resources. At the same time, the system enables employees to conduct official business in the traditional manner with paper documents. Still, auxiliary registration, case list management, case sheet generation and preparation of outgoing mail, offered by EDMS – is definitely an advantage of document management, in addition facilitating the supervision of how everyday business is done in the office'.[406]

Undeniably, then, modernisation is responsible for improving the quality of the civil service and the trust it inspires amongst the citizenry. Nowadays as states face many new problems and challenges, civil servants and civil service employees are one of the first to bear the brunt of the changes occurring domestically

406 *Społeczeństwo informacyjne w liczbach 2009*, p. 36.

and in the international environment. Thus, the necessity of modernising the civil service underpins the philosophy of its existence and operation.

The term 'customer' has become the key concept in the process of civil service modernisation. The prominence given to the term was to draw attention to citizens' needs and provide an impulse to start treating members of the public as the private sector treats customers, in other words, as people who pay for the product they buy (here it is taxes). Thus, by implication, the citizens/customers should receive efficient, professional and courteous service.

Transferring the concept of 'customer' from the private to the public sector and making it a symbol of the new relationship between members of the civil service and the citizens, is a purposeful ploy designed to underline the service role of state officials vis-à-vis the citizens. However, there is resistance to this idea in the public sector where it is argued that the concept is inadequate as the public sphere is not the place where offices compete with each other for customers. There are, however, arguments in favour of insisting on this term which has been formally valid since 2000 in all EU member states. It is especially significant in describing the relationship between the administration and the citizens in Central and Eastern Europe. In this part of the world, where states are still undergoing a socio-political transformation, the question of advancing the concept of 'customer' is not mere semantics but rather a symbol of change.

We can be sure that the role of the civil service in Poland will grow. In order for this to happen, however, the civil service needs to identify increasing the effectiveness of different civil service agencies as its prime objective by establishing common principles, regulations and standards. To make the operation of these agencies more efficient other factors are paramount, such as the continuity and quality of operation, procedural culture, appropriate qualifications of all employees, and the increased accountability for any wrong done by the civil service. Hence, these and many others factors must be taken into account when drafting each administrative reform.

What are the obstacles to the modernisation of the Polish civil service? The list includes: the lack of systemic and constitutional guarantees; low political culture; local particularism and excessive party interference; lack of legal culture; difficulties in the process of adjusting Polish administration to that of the European Union (such as inconsistent requirements, too many partners in the decision-making process, the sectorisation of the functioning of the Council of the European Union and European Commission, the variety of issues which the domestic public administration has to deal with in the scope of EU operation); limited funds; and the service's negative image shaped by the media.

In terms of internal barriers to growth the following seem to be of major importance: low level of civil servants' ethics; strained relations with the media (the syndrome of the 'closed fortress'); problems linked to the implementation of e-administration and IT; exempting political cabinets from civil service legislation; fiddling during the recruitment process to the civil service; ill-advised methods of human resources management; no access to expert knowledge; low level of expertise among newly recruited employees; lack of employee mobility; personnel rotation; insufficient professional stability breeding a sense of insecurity; inertia; low and not very competitive pay; de-motivating remuneration system; weak relations between citizens and the civil service. Nor should we forget that the departmental system is an obstacle in the smooth functioning of the civil service as it generates divisions between sections of the administration.

Low, non-competitive pay in the civil service hampers the modernisation of the civil service in Poland. It does not attract the required number of candidates for civil service jobs, especially experts in their own fields. The remuneration system is not of the motivating type and makes a weak causal connection between remuneration levels in the civil service corps and work results. On the other hand, civil service pay is highly competitive in auxiliary posts; in expert positions it amounts to 71% of the pay in the private sector; pay in senior positions (managerial) is the least competitive (for directors-general it is 12% of the pay received in the private sector).[407] Thus 'in the civil service, the higher the position, the less competitive the salary as compared to remuneration in business organisations. In terms of highly qualified specialists and senior managers, the median in the civil service corps constitutes 33–35% of the median salary in similar positions in the business sector.'[408]

Similarly, there are doubts concerning the recruitment mechanisms to the civil service: do they provide the means for identifying potentially dishonest candidates, and if so what are these mechanisms? If this is indeed true, how can these candidates be dissuaded from applying for the job? Another cause for concern is the fact that the current civil service legislation does not eliminate white corruption, that is the – difficult to eliminate – practice of using one's official position to further personal or familial interests. Equally worrying is the fact that civil

407 Hay Group Report, 'Wynagrodzenia w administracji publicznej w Polsce i w Europie. Hipoteza na temat motywacji i jakości służby cywilnej w Polsce', in 'Ogólna diagnoza sytuacji w zakresie zarządzania zasobami ludzkimi w służbie cywilnej', *Przegląd Służby Cywilnej*, No. 2 (5) 2011, p. 12.

408 M. Dąbrowski, 'Zatrudnienie i wynagrodzenia w korpusie służby cywilnej w 2011 r.', *Przegląd Służby Cywilnej*, May-June 2012, No. 3.

service legislation persistently lacks effective legal protection for employees who raise alarm over irregularities they notice in the organisations they work in. Polish lawmakers shied away from establishing the institution of the whistleblower, popular in other democracies, and failed to implement arrangements providing the framework for exposing suspected wrongdoing in a given organisation by the employees and at the same time providing them with protection.

Moreover, the lawmakers did not strengthen the position of directors-general of the civil service by failing to, firstly, extend their term of office (to at least six years) and, secondly, establish disciplinary issues as the only reason for removing them from the post. This move would protect them from the all-too-frequent political interferences. Also, many of the problems plaguing the current management of mainly large departments or offices would be solved if the director-general would have his/her deputy designated statutorily. Substituting the director-general by the head of the department, as it is practiced during the vacation season, does not seem a viable solution.

Similarly, there are doubts whether the Civil Service Act in force indeed provides ample grounds for the application of internal control mechanisms, the coordination of internal policy-making processes within departments, the fostering of appropriate relationships with the representatives of external interests and the effective use of expertise. Will the application of this Act bring to a halt the informal and discretionary forms of control and coordination? Considerable doubts still remain.

The fact that employees attach very little importance to ethical matters seems to impede the development of the Polish civil service. The main problems both civil service employees and civil servants raise have to do with remuneration levels, inter-employee relationships and excessive workloads – ethical questions are left outside their sphere of interest. Of course, when asked about corruption, civil service corps members voice their condemnation for it, claiming, that corruption in public administration is but a marginal phenomenon.[409]

Opinions about the civil service are adversely shaped by the media which show interest in the subject only when a political or corruption 'scandal' erupts. The media do, indeed, exert pressure to expose and counteract irregularities in the civil service but fall short of popularizing information amongst the public on the nature of the civil service, its function, tasks and significance, all of which play a pivotal role in the proper operation of the state and the way in which the state is perceived by the public.

---

409 Trutkowski.

Another negative phenomenon is the use of government advertising for showcasing an 'ironed out' picture of the administration. Government advertising in democracies is a massive and serious employer. Increasing spending to cover the government's self-promotion costs provides all democratically chosen governments with enormous powers of persuasion and a high potential for chicanery. This is illustrated by the work of government spokesmen, press-officers and their press bureaux which project a favourable image of political leaders and government representatives.

One of the reasons of the worsening quality of work in offices, or lack of improvement thereof, is the inertia and reluctance to introduce good practice on the part of the members of the civil service corps. According to the Polish public, the lack of improvement in the way offices operate is caused by the mentality of civil servants and the lack of good will on the part of the authorities (no new regulations initiating improvements are introduced and no new measures from the top which would trigger an impulse for progress).[410]

Likewise, in the process of harmonizing Polish administration to meet EU requirements the Polish civil service comes against difficulties in many areas. Those mainly concern the cooperation/negotiation sphere, where the problems seem to be of a systemic nature. Let us now consider a few examples:

- Inconsistent requirements: on the one hand effectiveness and efficiency, on the other, the (high) quality of views to be formulated;
- The large number of partners in the decision-making process (domestically and in the EU) with different missions, different work methods or even different organizational cultures;
- The sectorisation of the functioning of the Council of the European Union and European Commission, in other words, the focus on issues clearly dealing with separate areas, which complicates the necessary cooperation, hinders the proper and legible separation of tasks and sometimes blurs the criteria for the separation;
- The large variety of issues the national public administration has to deal with in relation to the EU.[411]

---

410 CBOS na zlecenie MSW, *Wyniki badania sondażowego. Opinie na temat funkcjonowania urzędów w Polsce*, Warszawa 2007.

411 See J. Itrich-Drabarek and A. Nowak-Far, 'Polska administracja publiczna w procesie dostosowania do Unii Europejskiej', *Przegląd Europejski*, No. 1, 2008.

A program for reinforcing the civil service was introduced in Poland as part of the country's preparations for the EU presidency, to be implemented 'by improving the skills and qualifications of the cadre of officials and creating a consistent system of human resources management in government administration'.[412] To find the right model of coordinating the implementation of European policies on active rungs still remains a daunting challenge for Poland at a time when the decision-making process is moving away from the working group stage to COREPER. The challenge lies even in answering the question of whether coordination of this sort is at all necessary. The answer should take into account, besides purely systemic matters (the structure of the decision-making process and enforcing one's decisions), the existing potential for securing valuable service on the part of the coordinating agency. This is mainly in terms of the efficiency of the entire administration system. If such an agency due to, say, the inappropriate preparation of its employees for the job to be coordinated (or simply worse than in coordinated units) is unable to guarantee an added value, then the decision should be taken against employing the agency for the job or assigning to it a much reduced task. If, on the other hand, an added value of such an agency is identifiable then its position within the system needs to be strengthened and channels of rapid information flow from the centre of executive power (this should be the Prime Minister's Chancellery) firmly secured. In which case such an agency should find itself incorporated into the Chancellery's structures.

Technical innovation could be perceived as a source of bureaucratic expansion. The sheer scale of purchasing and installing computers, software costs and those of training make the market of software devices and IT arrangements used by the civil service attractive for computer companies (the status of the owner, that is, the administration, is stable, predictable, defined and guaranteed). Thus when vying for state contracts these companies use marketing techniques and lobbying to emphasize the advantages of their wares and conceal the possible faults of their products.

As described in Chapter 1, the fact that Poland lacks a coordinated system of electronic administration that would enable, for instance, the operation of a 'one-stop shop' system, raises questions about the effectiveness of the Polish

412 *Krajowy Program Reform na lata 2008–2011 na rzecz realizacji Strategii Lizbońskiej*, p. 35.

administration. Grassroots initiatives in the area of a single voivodship[413] give rise to additional questions: why can the system be operational in one voivodship and not in another? Why is it not coordinated across the whole country? How are these conditions going to impact the unified administrative actions in areas larger than one voivodship, let alone the whole country?

413 'By the end of 2012 a state-of-the-art IT system will be put in place for the purposes of the unified government administration, encompassing 14 administrative units subordinate to the Śląsk voivod. Toady saw the signing of an agreement on the funding of the project 'Electronic Work Platform of the Śląsk Unified Administration' as part of the Śląsk Voivodship Operational Programme in 2007–2013. As it has already happened in the Śląsk Voivodship Office, this system will make the work of the unified administration more efficient in its provision of e-services, which in turn will facilitate the use of electronic government administration services by the citizens.' <www.katowice.uw.gov.pl> *accessed 21 June 2012.*

# Chapter 7: Dysfunctions in the Civil Service and Tools to Contain Them

## The Source of Violations of Civil Service Ethical Canons

In the study of the irregularities in the civil service and cases of violations of its integrity, I have drawn upon my personal observation and, naturally, the data available. I find that the causes and mechanism which have generated them can be traced back to the ideas predominant at the turn of the twenty first century. I do not believe it possible to point to a single factor that would determine all the others or could be the source of all the difficulties in the civil service. If we assume that the problems experienced by civil servants are representative of the problems throughout all of bureaucracy, and in fact of society as a whole, we can then identify the causes of these problems on several levels.

Structural factors have their effect on the dysfunctions in the civil service, by which we mean the social and organisational structure in which the civil service has to function, the nature of the social structure (democratic or elite) and the depth of social divides. The deeper the social divides and the more hierarchical the organisational structure of administrative institutions, the greater is the threat to the integrity of the civil service. Searching for sources of the various wrongdoings attention should be paid not only to the environment and its impact on the functioning of those employed in the civil service but also to the functional causes and the existence of irregularities within the institutions themselves.

Marshall E. Dimock points out that bureaucratic behaviour is influenced by many factors: those outside the organisation, related to various forms of social life (religion, the military, legislation, higher education), those within the organisation itself (associated with processes such as planning, financing, oversight), those related to the size of the institution (size, age, geographical breakdown) and those associated with the legal status of the entity.[414] Michel Crozier, the author of the theory of the 'bureaucratic vicious circle', indicates that the actions of the bureaucracy are affected by cultural norms within a society, the system of upbringing and education, the political system and the fact that bureaucracy is subject to the specific conditions in which it is operating and undergoing change. Problems affecting the functioning of administration as well as its

414 See also J. Kurnala (ed.), *O sprawności i niesprawności organizacji*, Warszawa, 1972.

employees have been the subject of many studies. While some praise bureaucracy for its orderliness, procedures and strict rules, others – such as Ludwig von Mises – criticise it. When describing public administration, the term bureaucracy is far more often used in a negative sense of the term for its increasing formalisation, excessive red tape with demands of more and more documents, time-consuming procedures and less flexibility of the administrative apparatus, work dehumanization (routine), incompetence, trained incapacity, 'disjunction between bureaucratic acts and morality, even in extreme situations',[415] than in a positive sense – such as professionalism or integrity. Omnipresent bureaucracy destroys citizen initiative, reduces citizen involvement in public life, wastes human resources, controls society and compels people to circumvent the law.[416]

Bureaucracy is a set of negative consequences of the functioning of bureaucratic institutions.[417] The essence of modern bureaucracy, according to John M. Keynes, boils down to the belief that a stable system that provides consistent profits without increasing administrative staff, capital or efficiency, raises fear among those who manage it and is perceived by society as 'dead'. The effect of discipline in bureaucratic institutions, according to Robert K. Merton, is ritualism among public officials, the result being a rigidity in their behaviour, which impedes their performance and creates a chasm between the civil servant and the customer (the caste spirit among civil servants). The mechanism presented by Merton, which runs according to the scheme: rigidity – inability to adjust readily – conflict in contact with the public – the need for controls of behaviour, leads, in his opinion, to an ever greater dysfunction. The way in which 'a vicious circle of dysfunction at the level of expertise and specialisation' (in the words of Philip Selznick) forms in public administration is that the bureaucratic organisation introduces specialisation and separation of roles 'in order to create a more neutral and independent specialist but in doing so generates in him/her the caste spirit'.

Too much formalism, in the opinion of Alvin W. Gouldner, can result in restricting the activities of public administration employees to conformity to the rules, in effect often interfering with the achievement of the purposes of the organisation. This in turn leads to underscoring the formal superior-subordinate relations in the organisation and, as a result, increases the tension between people,

415 S. Pilipiec and P. Szreniawski, *Socjologia administracji*, Lublin, 2008, pp. 66–70.

416 See also A. Tocqueville, *Democracy in America*.

417 Kurnala, op. cit.

with negative consequences for the institution.[418] In the light of the above, one might conclude that 'routine and annoying characteristics of bureaucracy are in fact the result of the resistance on the part of the human against the imposed mechanistic system and are elements of "what could be called a vicious circle" as this resistance only reinforces the operation of the system that provoked it'.[419] Zygmunt Bauman argues that in modern times bureaucracy has undergone a transformation in which 'responsibility for' (for the welfare, autonomy and dignity of another human being) was replaced with 'responsibility to' (to the superior, an authority, the cause and its advocates).[420]

One attempt of compiling a list of problems that the civil service has to cope with specifies the following types of violations of civil service integrity:

1) corruption, including bribing, 'kickbacks', nepotism, cronyism and patronage (with profit for oneself, family, friends, or party),
2) fraud and theft of resources,
3) conflict of private and public interest through gifts (services, promises) or the possession of assets,
4) conflict of interest through jobs and activities outside the organisation (eg. 'moonlighting'),
5) improper use of violence towards citizens and suspects,
6) other improper methods, i.e. improper means for – often – noble causes,
7) abuse and manipulation of information, i.e. unauthorized and improper use of files, leaking confidential information,
8) discrimination and sexual harassment, i.e. indecent treatment of colleagues or citizens,
9) the waste and abuse of organisational resources,
10) private time misconduct, such as domestic violence, drunk driving and private crime.[421]

---

418 E. Masłyk-Musiał, *Społeczeństwo i organizacje: socjologia organizacji i zarządzania*, Lublin 1999, pp. 108–109.

419 Ibid., pp. 109–110.

420 Z. Bauman, *Does ethics have a chance in a world of consumers?*, Cambridge, MA: Harvard University Press, 2008, p. 53.

421 L. Huberts, M. Kaptein and K. Lasthuizen, 'Leadership and Integrity Violations at Work: A Study on the Perceived Impact of Leadership Behaviour on Integrity Violations within the Dutch Police Force', paper for IRSPM VIII 2004, Budapest, March 31 – April 2, 2004, cited in *Ethics in the Public Service of the European Union Member States under the Irish Presidency* 2004, Ch. Demmke, D. Bossaert, EIPA, January to June 2004, p. 18.

Systemic causes of unethical behaviour in the Polish civil service include a deficient legislation, low wages (P. Heywood and J.-H. Meyer-Sahling argue the opposite in their study on the Polish civil service[422]), low professional status and the resultant low social position, decisions taken by individual officials in important individual matters, cronyism having general acquiescence, lack of effective and appropriate sanctions against officials acting unethically. Weakness of character and lack of personal integrity, both a matter of upbringing, characterise individuals predisposed to unethical conduct (personality causes).[423] The collected data shows that cases of corruption in the civil service are very rare, although minor unethical acts are quite common.

We can attempt an explanation of problems, dysfunctions and other serious ills in the civil service from at least three points of view: political, economic and socio-cultural. The aim is to describe the sources, the functioning mechanisms and the consequences of these wrongdoings not only for the civil service but also for the administrative institutions, the state and society. This is not to suggest that factors causing these problems occur individually, on the contrary, they interweave and multiply leading to violations of civil service integrity.

We can first look at the dysfunctions in the civil service from the *political point of view*. Here we find the main causes of the dysfunctions to be weakness of the democratic state and the alienation of the authorities as well as lack of political stability in the country, which translates into an increased sense of instability in public administration. If the status of government officials is not protected by clearly defined laws that set strict boundaries between politicians and officials, if the state does not guarantee permanent employment for public servants, if civil servants, especially those in senior positions, are changed with every change in the political makeup of the government then, unsure of their future, they succumb more easily to the enticement of undue benefit.

Civil servants are exposed to clientelism, which is contrary to the principle of egalitarianism and impartiality, and the 'patron-client relationship is an important and sometimes the main mechanism of arriving at political decisions'.[424]

The promotion or blocking of new laws or amendments to laws, the poor orientation of the government, citizens and persons employed in the civil service in the

---

422 See also P. Heywood and J-H. Meyer-Sahling, *Corruption Risks and the Management of the Ministerial Bureaucracy in Poland*, Sprawne Państwo, Ernst & Young Programme, Warszawa, 2008.

423 C. Trutkowski (ed.), 'Postawy członków korpusu służby cywilnej wobec kwestii etycznych. Raport z badań', study report, Warszawa, 2004.

424 J. Tarkowski, *Socjologia świata polityki. Patroni i klienci*, Warszawa, 1994, p. 105.

mechanisms of systemic change taking place in the administration are also sources of unethical behaviour. A regularity – observed in conditions of transition (but not only then) – is that the more intense the socio-economic transformation in the country, the more energy and time officials dedicate to the protection of their own interests. The aim of those seeking employment in public administration and the objectives of the administration itself often diverge. Rather than serve the public and the state, those seeking work in the civil service seek information and contacts in order to use them for the benefit of a political party that 'referred' them there. The dominant features are the close links and feedbacks occurring between political and economic groups – between the public and private sectors. Characteristic of this combination are excessive restrictions on the economy, the significant share of state entities in the economy, faultily interpreted principle of subsidiarity – the devolving of responsibility (duties) from a central authority to lower levels without the transfer or decentralisation of financial resources.

From an *economic point of view*, dysfunctions in the civil service can be explained by difficult economic conditions in the country. When the economy is in a recession or crisis or showing a persistent tendency to instability, risk of corruption increases and government officials, feeling threatened, find it easier to succumb to 'financial persuasion'. The experience of democratic states also shows that when the state raises taxes (or freezes tax thresholds) the most exposed to acts of corruption are employees of tax chambers and offices because it is with their help that citizens see a chance to avoid or to reduce the due amount of accrued tax. The process of privatisation, violation of public procurement rules (outsourcing of government contracts) also provide opportunities for abuse. Similar opportunities arise with the existence of off-budget and special funds, which are at the disposal of civil servants, so a large part of the budget remains outside the effective investigation or control of specialised units. The funds restrict the government's freedom of deploying financial resources to meet changes in priorities, thus limiting the efficient allocation of expenditure and making maintenance of financial discipline difficult. There are also significant losses in revenue due to income foregone and the waste of public funds as a result of the improper implementation of public procurement.

From the *socio-cultural point of view*, the most important cause of dysfunctions in the civil service is the poor moral condition of society. Public administration officials come from the same cultural circles as the rest of society. If members of a given society tolerate minor irregularities, if they themselves are taking part in them, if law is routinely broken in one area or another, we then end up with general acquiescence in acts of corruption, both individual and institutional. The relationship between the perceptions of corruption and the corrupt behaviour of an individual is widely described in scientific literature. If an individual perceives the world as increasingly corrupt, he/she feels quite certain that their corrupt actions, if not earning them outright approval of others, will definitely not draw them condemnation. From a sociological point of view, corruption 'develops and stabilises as a "by-product" of malfunctioning basic social structures'.[425] Some researchers are of the opinion that the phenomenon of corruption is supracultural in nature.[426]

Lack of public service culture is manifested in the way the state continues to be perceived as 'hostile' not only by those the state serves but also by those who work in its structures and benefit from it. There is moral relativism in the justification of one's wrongful conduct with the so-called objective reasons – such as the need to obtain the means for the treatment of a child, for material security in old age, to satisfy the needs of a demanding wife, or the assumption that 'everyone steals, so why shouldn't I?'

A factor that blurs the boundary between the public and private spheres may be *Familial culture (familiarism)*. This is the view of Aniela Dylus, who writes: 'in societies where family ties are very strong, government officials are inclined to favour their relatives'.[427] Some cultural factors support, while others suppress, corrupt practices. The attitude to these practices is decided by: historical tradition, the capital of public trust (for example, Poland is a country with a low degree of public trust), the degree of social acquiescence to corruption (in Poland there is no consent to corruption, but there is wide acceptance of minor ethical irregularities), informal ties, local and family culture as well as the organisational culture of enterprises.[428]

The inefficiency of governmental authorities is thought to be the cause of problems of the civil service at *administrative level*. The following play their part:

a) an overgrown state apparatus, the lack of clear procedures for the recruitment and promotion of government officials, inefficient administrative reform (the bigger the scope of reforms in the country and the faster their implementation,

---

425 A. Kojder, *Godność i siła prawa*. Warszawa 1995, p. 325; A. Dylus, 'Kulturowe uwarunkowania korupcji. Doświadczenia Polski', in A. Dylus, A. Rudowski and M. Zaborski (eds.), *Korupcja. Oblicza, uwarunkowania, przeciwdziałanie*, Ossolineum Wrocław-Warszawa-Kraków 2006, p. 108.

426 See W. Fehler, 'Kraje Unii Europejskiej w walce z korupcją', *Przegląd Europejski*, 2002, No. 1.

427 Dylus, op. cit, p. 114.

428 Ibid., pp. 109–117.

the more energy civil servants put into the preservation of existing structures and the safeguarding of their own interests);

b) an overblown system of certificates, approvals, permits and licenses that restrict trade;[429]

c) conflicting objectives of employees of an office and of the office itself. Persons employed in the office pursue their own private interests or the interests of companies they have secret ties with and remain employed in government offices only to reap profits from information they supply to those private companies;

d) the administration functioning in such a way as to become an engine of corruption (a point made by H. Egli and other German political scientists), forcing citizens to seek paid patronage and connections, resort to cronyism and bribery. Corruption-generating factors include: long queues (the more 'entrepreneurial' customers or those who are in a hurry will look for ways to skip the line), long waiting periods for administrative decisions (citizens seeking ways of speeding up resolutions will seek out extralegal methods), annulment of already issued decisions, termination of contracts with a view to their renegotiation, lack of clear criteria for promotion and reward of civil servants, delegation of representatives of the civil service corps to decision-making positions connected with the exercise of supervision (control) of superiors by the superiors themselves;

e) the discretionary system under which an official can be passed-over in promotions and prizes despite him/her being highly qualified, which may encourage him/her to accept undue favours. Low remuneration of civil servants is often cited as the cause of corruption.[430] This is most likely in situations where a low-paid civil servant decides in matters worth millions. Of course higher remuneration of civil servants alone will not solve the problem of corruption, however, as one of the elements in the fight against corruption – higher remuneration can indeed work for enhancing professionalism, effectiveness and transparency in the public service. Corruption is more likely where the functioning of institutions lacks transparency – in many cases state institutions are working without the required statutory or procedural regulations and their employees do not have clearly defined rights and duties. Other reasons are dilatoriness and inefficiency of various service departments in the state apparatus, such as customs services or the judiciary, and lack of orientation

429 M. Jarosz, *Władza, przywilej, korupcja*, PWN, Warszawa, 2004, p. 205.

430 I have written about this in Chapter 5.

in their own human potential – in other words – the syndrome of the wrong people in the wrong positions.[431] Mismanagement is very often justified both in the moral and legal sense (improperly performed privatisations being justified by the conditions prevailing during transition);

f) inadequate enforcement of personal accountability of officials who committed irregularities during their term in office. According to the Supreme Audit Office experts, for example, it is mismanagement that causes damage to public property that provides the only real trace of an irregularity – one that is possible to establish, prove and have it accounted for. Meanwhile in Poland, for example, it is very rare for harmful financial decisions or serious violations of the law to be punished. This breeds a sense of impunity which encourages violations of ethical standards. Areas particularly exposed to such temptations in the civil service are departments dealing with privatisation matters, or tax offices;

g) the lack of staff rotation in some departments that are vulnerable to corrupt practices (e.g. treasury chambers) is a highly corruption-generating situation;

h) the lack of transparency in public administration is another cause of wrongdoings. When citizens cannot control the activities of public administration through wide and open access to information, acts of corruption occur at every level of the decision-making process more often. The result of unequal access to information about certain areas of activity of public administration is that offices having the competence to handle specific issues do not always provide adequate information about those opportunities to all interested parties;

i) internal control in administration, when carried out poorly, chaotically, without compliance with procedures required by law, often without clearly specified reasons, cannot constitute an effective tool in combating corruption. The weakness of such control (for example, the weakness of the control of construction supervision services in Poland), including a lack of proper execution of its realisation, contributes to the increase in corrupt practices.

In short, the most serious causes of unethical behaviour in the civil service include:

- excessive powers in the hands of individual officials,[432]
- instability of employment,

---

431 M. Kostera, *Zarządzanie personelem,* Warszawa 1998, p. 9.

432 Z. Bielecki and M. Zajder, *Korupcja. Materiały pokonferencyjne,* postconference materials, Szczytno, 2004, p. 99.

- low remuneration, inadequate to qualifications and responsibility,
- injustice and discretion in the promotion of public officials,
- incompetence of superiors,
- discretionary decision-making; a situation in which the settlement of a specific case depends on the subjective assessment of the public official,[433]
- careless or unreliable record-keeping and reporting.

Vague criteria of remuneration are also to blame as they do not provide motivation to work and only give rise to a sense of injustice.

In a survey on the performance of public services conducted by CBOS, one of the public opinion polling centres, almost 59% of respondents gave the lowest scores to the way officials handled cases, citing connections and patronage to be the first and foremost requirement to get anything solved. Another negative feature cited was bribery – more than 40% of respondents believe that handing a gift or bribe speeds up the handling of cases. The final criticised aspect of public administration work was – according to less than 40% of Poles surveyed – that public servants show little commitment and hardly pay any attention do their customers.[434]

The evaluation of public servants and their work by citizens vary however from one opinion poll to another. In a February 1999 PBS study more than half of those surveyed judged the performance of duties by public servants as average, while a study in mid-December 2000 found 39% respondents regarding it as bad.[435] It turns out that contacts with authorities for most respondents narrow down to the tax authorities, and it is through this experience that they judge the entire administration. A similar survey was conducted by OBOP at the same time, but the results were differed. According to the OBOP survey, roughly half of respondents were convinced that public administration officials were prone to bribery. The Transparency International 2007 survey of 99 countries classifies Poland in 44th place with a downward trend (in 1998 – Poland was ranked 39th). The difference between the two studies is that in the PBS survey the questions concerned specific behaviours of officials, while the OBOP and Transparency International surveys asked general questions on the extent of corruption in the administration.

---

433 A. Z. Kamiński and B. Kamiński, *Korupcja rządów*, Warszawa, 2004, p. 28.

434 Opinions on the functioning of public administration in Poland. Results of a CBOS survey conducted for the Ministry of Interior, Warszawa, 2007.

435 R. Wróbel, 'Tłok za biurkiem', *Rzeczpospolita*, 22 Mar. 1999; S. Wysocki, 'Jak poprawić jakość działania administracji publicznej?', *Służba Cywilna* 2001, No. 2, pp. 25–51.

It is difficult to judge whose results are nearer to the truth. Taking and giving bribes is a criminal offence, so the answers may not have been that honest. The authors of the study however managed to determine the relationship between the status of the office and the position of an official in the government administration hierarchy and his/her vulnerability to corruption. They found that the higher the position in the official hierarchy and the higher the rank of the office, the greater was the corruption.

To sum up, the causes of ethical problems in the civil service can be described as legal (weakness of the law, bad law driving out good law, capture of the public sphere on the strength of applicable law), political (weakness of institutions of a democratic state, lack of transparency of actions, conflict of interest), economic (the desire for rapid, fraudulent enrichment) and social (social relativism, poor moral condition, nihilism).

## Unethical Behaviour in the Civil Service

Violations of ethical principles encompass various problems, wrongdoings and dysfunctions that can be observed in the civil service or threaten it to various degrees. They are: lack of professionalism, insolence and arrogance, irresponsibility, a Baroque (Byzantine) lifestyle, over-politicisation of the civil service, incompetence, dishonest lobbying, nepotism, cronyism and favouritism, sexual harassment, mobbing and corruption. Are we, as a result of the many irregularities, dealing in the civil service with what is termed 'lumpen-work'? If we are to accept Jerzy Stępień's interpretation of this concept to mean work which is the only source of income yet does not give satisfaction whatsoever nor sense of one's value as an employee or member of the community, then we are dealing with this degraded form of employment in the Polish civil service quite often. Although such work provides material security, it 'is not a source of professional satisfaction, often becoming the cause of disappointment and deep frustration.'[436]

Causes of problems in the Polish civil service should primarily be sought in its *over-politicisation,* which generates a number of illnesses or enhances those which, if there was no interference of political parties, would occur only sporadically and could easily be eliminated.[437]

---

436 Z. Galor and J. Stępień, 'Pojęcie i regionalne determinanty lumpen-pracy w gospodarce polskiej okresu transformacji', in S. Patrycki (ed.), *Strategia rozwoju społecznej gospodarki rynkowej w Polsce,* Lublin, 2002, pp. 59–62.

437 More on this dysfunction in Chapter 6.

One of the problems in the civil service is its *excessive professionalism or its lack*. A number of changes to legislation, political interference, lack of long-term stability, changing concepts of policymakers regarding the professionalisation of the civil service, high personnel turnover and its aging, and a number of other factors, are reasons for the problem of civil service professionalism remaining open. Policymakers do not take a clear stand on this issue. The role of professionalism in the civil service corps is appreciated in declarations and in most legal solutions, but in practice systemic solutions take precedence (an example of this is the Act of 24 August 2006 on the State Staffing Pool and its regulation concerning the exemption from the requirement of competitive recruitment to the civil service for employees of the Supreme Audit Office and territorial self-government units) and the pragmatics of the civil service, in accordance with which recruitment and staffing of senior posts is not determined by the candidate's skills and experience but political connections, patronage and cronyism. Undoubtedly, a civil service 'whose recruitment and promotion system is chiefly based on political patronage or cronyism is more likely to hamper professional integrity than a system based on merit'.[438] The trend to enhance the professionalism in the civil service helps to minimise political manipulation – the higher the professionalisation of the civil service, the greater is its reluctance to submit to pressures from political 'amateurs'.

An example of an irregularity which occurs in the Polish civil service is *insolence and arrogance* of officials or office. The insolence of office is its 'claim to dominance', resulting from the fact that, along with the distribution of office there is a distribution of many perks along with it such as honour and status, power and prerogative, wealth and comfort.[439] Sources of the insolence of civil servants (and the entire public administration in general) are the legal and political contexts, the low level of education in society and the lack of organisational culture in the office. This involves both the power – as Jan Boć writes – which the official is vested with due to his position and the lack of culture on his/her part as well as on the part of his/her superior who tolerates it.[440]

Paradoxically insolence and arrogance could have its source in professionalism which is one of the causes of aloofness or reserve of officials, equipped with the

---

438 OECD (1999), 'European Principles for Public Administration', *SIGMA Papers*, No. 27, OECD Publishing. < http://dx.doi.org/10.1787/5kml60zwdr7h-en >, p. 11.

439 M. Walzer, *Spheres of Justice: A Defense of Pluralism and Equality*, Basic Books, Inc., 1983, p. 155.

440 J. Boć, 'Administracja a obywatel', in A. Błaś, J. Boć and J. Jeżewski (eds.), *Administracja publiczna*, Kolonia Limited, 2003, pp. 291–292.

specialist knowledge, in their relations with customers-citizens who have no need for this kind of knowledge in their everyday lives. Expert knowledge becomes the property of the official, or the whole professional group, and tends to be strictly safeguarded. It is the asset they can use to negotiate a raise or bonus, continue reaping benefits by virtue of the position held, achieve promotion to higher rank in the professional hierarchy. Professionalism is becoming a way of 'drawing lines (…) of establishing power'. Specialists flaunt their knowledge in contact with those on the lower rung of the hierarchy ladder and with customers-citizens. Bureaucratic expansion and constant professionalisation complement each other, and people in positions of higher rank will always be trying to 'use their offices whenever they can to extend their power beyond what their qualifications warrant or their function requires'.[441] As long as those in office are not subordinate to citizens, and citizens do not participate in determining the essence of the functioning of public administration institutions, administration offices will not be considered a form of service, but 'another occasion for tyranny'.[442]

Insolence is an attribute not only of those currently holding important functions in public administration, politics or business, but also of those who have already ended their service.[443] Superiors too can often be *condescending towards their subordinates*. An arrogant superior assumes that subordinate staff have to execute his/her every command even when it is in violation of accepted cultural patterns, good custom or vacillates on the border of staff regulations and law. In these cases we are dealing with a superior who acts as if the office was his/her proverbial 'private playground' and the employed staff but average-trained servants whose future depends on his/her personal preferences and system of rewards and penalties he/she dispenses at his/her discretion. Such superiors are even more arrogant towards customers of the office. According to a 1999 PBS survey conducted among public administration customers, one in three respondents stressed the fact of officials in managerial positions being arrogant and condescending towards them.[444]

441 Walzer, op. cit., pp. 156–159.

442 Walzer, op. cit., p. 160.

443 Boć, 'Administracja a obywatel', op. cit., pp. 291–292.

444 The situation seems to be changing for the better for office customers – in 2005 only one in ten respondents confirmed such conduct of managerial staff. In 'Urzędnik państwowy w oczach obywatela. Badanie realizowane z klientami urzędów administracji państwowej. Porównanie wyników I i II fali', report from a PBS survey conducted for the Civil Service Office, Sopot, September 2005.

Unfortunately it does happen that *a public officer demonstrates superiority over a citizen*. Such arrogance derives from the assumption that he/she knows more and better than other citizens and is entitled to it by his/her function in the civil service. It is manifested in the patronising treatment of citizens, lack of impartiality in making decisions, disregard for individual or social interests in the decision-issuing process, insensitivity, attempts to make citizens dependent on the institution. Arrogance is also expressed in keeping customers-citizens waiting in long queues; the treatment of citizens in public institutions as if they were intruders; bureaucratic, medical or legal incompetency; burgeoning bureaucratic regulations; the use of bureaucratic, medical or law jargon in dealing with customers-citizens, or even refusal to pursue a case.

The arrogance of institutions is manifested in their violation of the principles of social justice by making a mockery of their very foundations, misleading citizens, openly breaking the law – with the certainty of total impunity. Its other manifestation is in the officially advertised competitions or recruitment to the civil service and then employment of political party nominees, persons 'referred' from the top or friends and family by way of reciprocity of mutual favours. As for the recruitment process itself, its preparation and conduct, the problem lies in waiting far too long before the publication of recruitment announcements, too long a time from announcement of the vacancy to it being filled, lack of training for freshly recruited and selected staff, overly complicated and time-consuming recruitment procedures, unnecessary selection procedures for 'replacements', the constant change of regulations. The insolence and the arrogance of public administration employees is particularly evident in the patronising treatment of stakeholders. And so 'the greatest irritant most people experience in their dealings with government is the arrogance of bureaucracy'.[445]

The arrogance of institutions is also manifested in the mismanagement of resources. One such example is the action of the Ministry of Labour and Social Policy which has set up a Web portal, for guess who – the homeless, at a cost of 49 million zlotys.[446] Similar cases of mismanagement can be found in other ministries, local government administration, health care, education institutions and public enterprises.

Customers experience arrogance and insolence in particular when dealing with *public enterprises with a monopoly on public services* such as the Ministry of

445 D. Osborne and T. Gaebler, *Reinventing government: How the entrepreneurial spirit is transforming the public sector*, Reading, MA: Addison-Wesley 1992, p. 167.

446 <http://finanse.wp.pl/kat,1013819,title,Portal-dla-bezdomnych-Emptia,wid,16494870,wiadomosc.html>, accessed 13 May 2014.

Health whose strategic objective is the improvement of people's health, and thus their quality of life, by such means as the shaping of healthy lifestyles; working for a healthy living, working and learning environment; reducing disparities in health and in the access to health services – all that it fails to do. Health care facilities where people have to wait their turn for hours in long queues and, in the case of specialists, need to make appointments a few months in advance – are confirmation of this.

Arrogance is an attitude that is also present in relations between one *public institution and another*. The National Health Fund (NFZ) shows arrogance towards hospitals when negotiating, in fact – forcing on them, contracts from a position of strength, thus demonstrating bureaucratic insensitivity.

The lack of clear external audit criteria and a poorly functioning or non-existent internal control, an obscure system of recruitment, selection, promotion and penalties for public administration employees and, finally, job instability contribute to the rise in arrogance and insolence mainly among mid-level managers but also among those in senior public positions in Poland.

The proliferation of competences among various institutions leads to an increasing sense of *irresponsibility* of those institutions and the persons representing them. On the one hand, there is the irresponsibility of civil servants and, on the other, that of society which tolerates it. In Poland, you can observe the phenomenon of individual and collective irresponsibility, which also affects the civil service corps. The result of this is a lack of accountability for progress of matters in hand and, especially, for the effects of their practical implementation. Failure to respond to voiced public opinion is proof of the civil servants feeling no sense of responsibility.[447] Vague rules, excess bureaucracy and social consent allow irresponsibility on the part of people performing functions in the public sphere. An example of the lack of accountability are the decisions of the National Health Fund which, in the name of falsely understood concern for public money, 'saves' large sums every year while helpless patients wait in endless queues for an appointment with a specialist. What is more, nurses have no wage increases and care of patients is below standards.[448]

When taxpayers' money is spent on lavish furnishings of offices, company cars and business trips, we must ask ourselves whether we are dealing with a

447 M. Machińska, ' Przeciwdziałanie korupcji i zorganizowanej przestępczości', Centre for Europe University of Warsaw, Council of Europe Information Centre, Warszawa 1999, Bulletin No. 3–4, pp. 118–124; Public opinion on the work of state officials, a PBS survey conducted for the Civil Service Office in 1999 and 2005, *<dsc.kprm.gov.pl>*.

448 The NFZ answers to the Ministry of Health.

*magnate (Byzantine) lifestyle* of civil servants and civil service employees. The media widely report on demonstrations of such ostentatious lifestyles which do not seem to change despite the changes in the political leadership. This is true of presidents of government agencies, heads of central offices, ministers or senior civil servants. Requests have no end for the latest items on the market and representatives of the public sector compete with managers of private companies.[449] The costs are borne by the taxpayer, who unfortunately has no way of controlling these expenditures.

Lavish offices go hand in hand with *title mania* which is flourishing in Polish public life. The titles of officials-politicians have replaced the lost titles of nobility, and their use, after the term in office had ended, has become a socially accepted fact.[450] Polish public opinion sees nothing wrong in title mania, and the belief that in a democratic society all people are equal and functions by appointment are not for a whole lifetime has not gained ground yet.

The theory of *incompetence* has been formulated by a Canadian educator Laurence J. Peter and assumes that a hierarchical and rigid system in an organisation serves to develop such a phenomenon. An example of a hierarchical organisation is the career model in the civil service. Any employee who works in an institution, managed for instance hierarchically, has a designated path of advancement.

---

449 A trendy Prada phone for PLN 4 800, best-quality leather armchair for PLN 3 800. and a satellite navigation car kit for PLN 1 500 – these are the items one of the presidents of an agency could not imagine working without. Apart from the expensive Prada phone, he requested the purchase of two other phones, an LCD TV, two computer monitors, a music centre, two reproductions of paintings and a leather Arizona Wittchen case, according to Newsweek.
<http://www.dziennik.pl/polityka/article150022/Fura_skora_i_komora_prezesa_rzadowej_agencji.html 8 02 2009>;
M. Kowalski and J. Gałęzewski, ' Wojewoda urządził sobie w urzędzie mieszkanie', *Gazeta.pl*, 29 June 2006. The Voivod Józef Ramlau decided to reside in the Voivodship Office for Bydgoszcz. He spent over PLN 3 000 of state funds to furnish his bedroom, had at his disposal a music centre, VCR, TV and air-conditioner. To secure a sense of privacy, he ordered the removal of security cameras on the first floor and the installation of a bathroom at the back of his office.

450 Public opinion is constantly bombarded in the media with interviews with prime ministers, ministers, directors regardless of whether they are holding a function or have long since ended their bureaucratic career. The once held official title emphasizes the guest's significance, the journalist feels satisfaction at having such an 'important' guest in his studio and the audience knows it is not listening to a 'nobody'. This way the yearning for social inequality, which – according to prof. J. Czapliński's research – over 50% of Poles express, is fulfilled.

In this model 'every employee tends to rise to his level of incompetence', which means that, in time, every post will be occupied by an employee who is incompetent to carry out his/her duties. The only people performing their work well are those who cannot be promoted and so have not yet reached their level of incompetence, or those who cannot be promoted because they are already at the highest level of the organisation.[451] In big bureaucratic structures 'the refusal to change positions often is a form of suicide (…). It shows that a person does not have initiative, but even worse, that he is not "cooperative"'.[452] And Jan Boć aptly sums up the issue of incompetence with regard to the situation in Polish public administration: 'The level of incompetence cannot be reached by those who are incompetent from the very beginning.'[453]

The conclusion for the civil service from this theory is that in a situation where the only people who perform their work well are not those who have reached the limit of their incompetence but those who, after having reached their competence limit, are not given new tasks and responsibilities, it is better at some level of the organisational hierarchy to reward than to promote them. In the process of employee assessment it is necessary to take into account not only his/her current performance but his/her potential skills in other areas. Promotion in an organisation should not lead to exceeding an employee's abilities as this will result in personal injury and disruption in the functioning of the institution. It seems worthy of consideration to adopt promotion and pay rise systems as well as staffing of posts through competition instead of automatic promotion.

The acceptance of the proposition that members of the civil service corps are incompetent can however lead to the use of public funds for *outsourcing tasks of public administration*. Outsourcing of tasks is practiced by many democratic state administrations but, unfortunately, it can at times lead to bad practices. The Supreme Audit Office (NIK) has for example (in the information for 1999 and the first half of 2000) evaluated as 'inappropriate and wasteful outsourcing of advisory and expert services to people lacking documented qualifications to execute them, namely students'. In around 10% of the examined contracts the providers were students and their principal employer was the Prime Minister's Chancellery. We read in the NIK report that 'students were entrusted with, among others, the preparation of legal and substantive analyses of documents to be deliberated

451 L. J. Peter and R. Hull, *The Peter Principle: Why Things Always Go Wrong*, New York: William Morrow and Company 1969, p. 8.; Boć, "Administracja a obywatel', op.cit., pp. 295–296.

452 R. Sennet, *The Fall of Public Man*, Cambridge University Press 1977, pp. 329–330.

453 Boć, 'Administracja a obywatel', op. cit, p. 296.

upon by the Council of Ministers; legal opinions on various issues, including compliance of certain laws and regulations with the objectives of constitutional reform or the screening procedure pursuant to the act on the protection of classified information and its application to judges; economic analyses, including those of draft legislation amending the "Energy Act" and the draft of Polish energy policy objectives till 2020'. The audited entities justified outsourcing the services to external entities claiming that 'the employees of the audited entities did not have the required qualifications nor legislative practice, despite the fact that in accordance with the Civil Service Act and the Act of 16 September 1982 on Employees of State Institutions (Dz.U. [Journal of Laws], No. 31, item 214 as amended) every employee should have the qualifications necessary to perform the required tasks, yet the tasks falling within the scope of that employee's responsibilities were outsourced to students, even less qualified and lacking professional experience, for which they received payment not much different from that paid to other outside service providers for a similar job (from PLN 1,500 to PLN 7,000 per service)'.[454] According to NIK controllers, 'the tasks outsourced did not always require specific qualifications or additional formal training, or there were no substantive reasons at all on the part of the organisational entities to outsource and finance specific jobs, such as drafting reports for the entities, departmental action plans, training schedules and cost estimates, work that had already been once commissioned, services on behalf of and for other entities than the payer, legal services for entities, opinions and analyses that should have been done by the employees of the entity, as they are within the scope of their work and there were no reasons to exempt these employees from performing the duties assigned to them'.[455]

It appears from the control findings that in many cases the nature of the outsourced tasks did not require knowledge or experience beyond the competence of entities, so the financing of the outsourced tasks, which were assigned to the staff of these units, was an unnecessary expense. The representative of the Ministry of Labour and Social Policy argued in defence of outsourcing of services that 'work performed by outside experts supported the work at the ministry, and the use of commission contracts, which do not require payment of social security contributions, lowered administrative costs; the tasks required of these entities exceeded their staff potential (insufficient staffing); lack of employees with

454 'Informacja o wynikach kontroli prawidłowości korzystania z usług doradczych i eksperckich przez organy administracji rządowej', audit report on outsourcing practices, Departament Kontroli Doraźnych, NIK, Warszawa, October 2001, pp. 36–39.

455 Ibid.

appropriate qualifications and experience, for example: "abilities of employees were insufficient to fully and in time implement the tasks..."; legal cells operating in the structures of organisational entities (in this case the Ministry of Foreign Affairs) refused to issue the relevant opinions; the tasks needed to be implemented in accordance with the Annual Action Plan'.[456]

Another serious issue that needs to be dealt with by the civil service is *sex discrimination*. As observed by Marie-France Hirigoyen in her *Le harcèlement moral : la violence perverse au quotidian*, the Scandinavian countries or Germany demonstrate a real concern for equal opportunities for both sexes; an atmosphere of male chauvinism prevails in Latin countries; while in Italy, Spain and Latin America it is the belief that the professional activity of women is the source of unemployment for men. A popular stereotype, as noticed by R. J. Edelmann in his *Interpersonal Conflicts at Work*, is that men are more objective and independent while women are too submissive and emotional, and so the characteristics of males predestine men to occupy managerial positions. Despite increased numbers of professionally active women, managerial positions are for the most part held by men.

Despite the fact that in Poland the representation of women is proportionally higher in the civil service than in the economy as a whole (which stems from the fact that the civil service allows better work/life balance through such means as part-time work, greater stability, etc.), proportionately more women in the civil service are generally employed in posts that require relatively lower skill levels. The situation in the Polish civil service indicates an evolution in the role and place of women in the office. In 2009 women accounted for 69% of civil service corps members.[457] In 2002, for the first time, the number of women nominated to civil servant rank, after having passed the qualification procedure, was higher than the number of male civil servants. Nevertheless, the disproportion remains between the number of men and women holding higher positions in the civil service. For example, in 2003, of the 54 directors-general only 14 were women,[458] while as on 20 April 2012, of the 64 directors-general around half were women. However, the employment index for women is falling in institutions and offices that offer higher salaries (this applies to ministries and central authorities) and

456 Ibid., pp. 24–34.

457 'Ogólna diagnoza sytuacji w zakresie zarządzania zasobami ludzkimi w służbie cywilnej', 23 March 2010, *Przegląd Służby Cywilnej*, Departament Służby Cywilnej Kancelarii Prezesa Rady Ministrów, 2010, No. 2.

458 J. Arcimowicz, 'Rządzące czy rządzone? Kobiety urzędniczki służby cywilnej', in *Służba Cywilna,* 2006, No. 15, p. 48.

rising where lower wages are offered, such as regional, voivodship offices.[459] The employment structure is reminiscent of the classic pyramid model in which the higher the managerial level – the fewer the women. The reasons for such a small representation of women in senior positions in the civil service the women themselves see in politically motivated cadre changes as well as in the lack of clarity and transparency in the competition procedures.[460]

One of the most important issues that contemporary political systems struggle with is *conflict of interest* between groups of interest (understood to mean the representation of narrow, individual interests) and public administration (understood to mean an impartial, honest and apolitical representative of the state). Of particular significance in the analysis of the relationship between government and interest groups is the category of 'non-negotiable policies' (R. Herbut). The development and implementation of these policies frees the government from having to negotiate with powerful interest groups and thus to surrender by the government of part of its sovereignty in favour of groups which have no democratic legitimacy.

Among the laws adopted in relation to this interface between public administration and private interests in Poland is the Lobbying Act which formally came into force in 2005.[461] In accordance with the Act, lobbying means any action carried out by legally admissible methods designed to influence public authorities during the legislative process. The Act sets out the principles of transparency in lobbying legislative decisions, rules to follow by professional lobbyists, forms of monitoring lobbying and register-keeping rules of entities engaged in such activities.[462] The law is criticised for imprecise rules as far as monitoring of the transparency of lobbying is concerned. Lobbying in the civil service may be twofold: members of the civil service corps may be targets of attempts to pressure or influence them by individuals, interest groups, politicians from the various

459 Ibid., p. 49.

460 Ibid., pp. 63–64.

461 Ustawa z dnia 7 lipca 2005 r. o działalności lobbingowej w procesie stanowienia prawa, [Act on Lobbing Activity in the Legislative Process of 7 July 2005], Dz. U. No. 169, item 1414.

462 According to a 2008 survey conducted among Polish parliamentarians, attempts to influence their decisions were made not so much by lobbyist as by local authorities (often – according to 53% of respondents), by trade unions (45%), by non-governmental organisations (40%) and by sector interest groups (36%). Also considered to be lobbying groups are journalists who organise media campaigns and the Church (often – 10%, rarely – 35%).

political parties, or they themselves may attempt to influence decisions at the drafting stage of projects, during their consultations within and among the respective ministries.

Lobbying is considered, by part of the scientific community and by Polish public opinion, as another dysfunction in the sphere of public administration. The common understanding of the term lobbyist is a dishonest man, a swindler, someone trying with unethical means to influence decisions made by public officials, politicians or businessmen. Unfortunately, the provisions of the Lobbying Act are too narrow and incomplete. The definition of lobbying does not include most of the actions taken in practice, because it only applies to professional lobbying activities and thus excludes those who do it in an unpaid capacity but who make up the majority. The effect of this provision, from a legal standpoint, is that competition between the various groups of lobbyists is unfair as it divides lobbyists into those covered by the law and those who are outside its reach or can circumvent it. Moreover, a large part of the lobbying activity is not covered by the law's regulations and in consequence requires the introduction of additional regulations concerning lobbying at the level of ministries and, in addition, exposes officials of ministerial departments to complex lobbying tactics. There are no provisions introducing the principle of authorisation of amendments to drafted legislation or administrative decisions, and no functioning rule that requires establishing the degree of personal involvement in the preparation of administrative decisions.

Lobbying, as we know, fosters political corruption when there are no clear regulations regarding relationships between lobbyists, officials or politicians. A corruption-generating area is, for example, lobbying in the armed forces. The most common lobbying activity in the military is finding people performing important functions there, who are willing to act as informal collaborators of lobbying corporations.[463] Despite the Lobbying Act, the number of people registered in the various ministries and engaged in lobbying is minimal. In the years 2006–2009 a total of 67 entities were registered as officially lobbying in the various ministries, which does not constitute sufficient grounds to state that lobbying in Poland is seen as an efficient tool of the development and activity of a civil society.

There are more problems that the civil service and the whole of public administration, and the public sphere as a whole, have to face; these include *nepotism,*

463 According to the Ministry of National Defence, they had no lobbing entities registered in 2006–2008; no data is available for 2009, < http://www.bip.mon.gov.pl/33.html>, 20 Jan. 2010.

*cronyism and favouritism* that are fairly simple to define on a theoretical level but more difficult to identify in practice. These phenomena are indisputably negative in terms of public service principles yet often underestimated and unnoticed. Favouritism is defined as a relationship arrangement in which the favourites are in positions of influence; cronyism – as the mutual promotion of people based on family relations, friendship, common, not always honest, interests; and nepotism[464] – the abuse of one's position by favouring or patronising relatives.[465]

Nepotism as we know is always looking for a variety of excuses: 'And what's wrong with that?', 'That's just hearsay and libel', 'Where is it prohibited?', 'I don't see a conflict of interest', 'It's a politically motivated attack', 'That's life', 'The political system is blocking us', 'Something has to be done, or it will be the end of the coalition.' Although the problem of nepotism is regulated by law, much remains unregulated, such as the issue of persons in non-marital partnerships who support each other for promotions and in decisions in the official hierarchy and those who can work in the same office or institution because they are not in direct line of reporting. According to a CBOS survey, 82% of respondents believed that senior government officials and politicians employed their relatives, colleagues and friends in offices, companies, banks and other institutions, and 75% believed that arranging government procurement and other contracts for relatives, colleagues, friends running private companies was a common practice. As much as 74% of respondents believed that politicians and bureaucrats gave in to pressure from businesses, companies, professional or social groups when concluding contracts, deciding on government procurement, etc.[466]

Hiring people based on family ties, connections or common interest is in contradiction to the basic purpose for which the civil service was established, which is to serve the public. The principle of equality before the law is thus also violated

464 'An extensively covered case of nepotism in the 1990s was that of a former Gorzów Voivod Wacław Niewiarowski who during his term as minister of trade and industry in the government of Hanna Suchocka was at the same time on the supervisory board of Cenzin. This company financed activities of the TAAK company, which took over from Stilon in Gorzów one of its buildings, a defunct canteen, and turned it into a supermarket. The state company specializing in arms trade invested in a supermarket in Gorzów, because the president of TAAK was minister Niewiarowski's son-in-law', <http://www.dziennik.pl/magazyndziennika/article345257/Kazdy_ma_jakas_kon kubine_nepotyzm_po_polsku.html>

465 See also, for e.g., M. Surkont, *Łapownictwo,* Sopot, p. 25.

466 The CBOS survey was carried out in the period 2–8 April 2009 on a representative randomly selected sample of 1094 Poles.

(Article 60 of the 1997 Constitution of the Republic of Poland). What is more, often the result is that incompetent people occupy positions in the office, and this affects the efficiency of the office, the public's perception of the office's work, etc. The adverse effects of such decisions may be felt not only within public administration but also beyond as a result of their social impact (e.g. financial costs resulting from decisions by incompetent, but family related employees, or unfavourable and suboptimal choices in public tenders). It is probably society that is hardest hit by the effects of this phenomenon. A high level of nepotism destroys citizen trust in public institutions. A mistrustful citizen convinced of widespread dishonesty is not only a more difficult customer but also one who begins to circumvent or break the law using similar practices. Nepotism and cronyism collide with the principle of justice which consolidates society and forms the foundations of a democratic state. Justice so understood concerns citizen equality before the law and equality of their treatment by public authorities. A citizen aware of nepotism in an office may feel discriminated against (both as a customer and as a candidate for employment there) and can lose trust in the impartiality of decisions taken by public service representatives. What is more, such attitudes can lead to more serious problems such as corruption. The indirect effect can be the loss of respect by citizens for public institutions and loss of interest in public affairs or identification with the state as the common good.

A phenomenon that has not avoided the Polish civil service is *sexual harassment*, which has become recognisable to the public relatively late, i.e. not until the 1990s, as a result of the ongoing debate on the issue in the developed countries. Contemporary problems with sexual harassment in Poland, despite legal regulations, have not been resolved and are still often effectively swept under the carpet, ignored or ridiculed.

The concept of sexual harassment is not easy to define because, just as mobbing, *it is burdened with a large dose of subjectivity*. This is clearly demonstrated by how the affected person reacts; for some it is a tasteless joke, a flirtation, 'an excess' or 'a stupidity' while for others an act degrading and violating their personal dignity.

According to a CBOS survey, sexual harassment in Poland is more often experienced by women than men. A greater percentage of women than men admit to being subjected to repeated cases of harassment. The problem is more often mentioned by people living in medium to large cities than in small towns or villages. People with a higher or secondary education, in liberal professions or white-collar workers show greater awareness of the issue.[467] The survey does not provide reliable data as the phenomenon of sexual harassment is often ignored, disregarded in statistics or ridiculed.[468]

Publicised cases of sexual harassment in Poland[469] also seem to confirm the idea that sexual harassment is an expression of status and dominance in relation

---

467 CBOS on harrasment, <www gazeta.pl>.

468 M. Środa [Polish philosopher, professor of ethics and feminist author] writes: 'the Feminoteka Foundation decided to check how the State Labour Inspectorate (PIP) deals with cases of sexual harassment brought before them. Persons monitoring the issue made phone calls to all PIP offices in Poland claiming to be victims of harassment and describing behaviour that could have occurred anywhere. 'My boss pats my bottom!', 'My boss orders me to wear short skirts', 'My boss embraces me, gives me hugs and tells me dirty jokes', 'I keep hearing comments about my appearance and its sexual aspects', 'Pornographic pictures adorn my boss's office' – was what they said on the phone and asked for help and advice. Only in 16 of the 60 PIP branches someone picked up the phone. At 44 branches the victim of sexual harassment would not have a chance not only to get help but even talk about his/her problem. As a matter of fact, this would be the case not only with the problem of sexual harassment but also with any other case of breaches of Labour Law (bad health and safety conditions at work, violations of contract of employment, forced work after hours, etc.). It turned out that at offices to which they successfully got through, officials could be divided into three groups. The 'ignorant' ones who have no idea what sexual harassment is, which means that they are not familiar with the Labour Code. The 'jokers', who completely disregard the problem by turning it into a joke ('I, too, sometimes embrace/ hug female friends', 'Don't you like compliments?') and 'sceptics', who claim that such is the nature of the world and there is no way of changing it ('If someone is a scoundrel, there is no way that we can change him into an angel', 'I believe you, but I just cannot imagine how I could help'). By not answering phone calls and with officials such as the 'ignorant', 'jokers' and 'sceptics', the State Labour Inspectorate rightly prides itself on the fact that there is no discrimination on grounds of sex in Poland because complaints of harassment and mobbing account for only 4% of total complaints. Due to this evaluation, we have one of the lowest levels of harassment in Europe.', <http://wyborcza.pl/1,75515,5957543,Mezczyzni_w_Polsce_szczyca_sie_molestowaniem_seksualnym.html>; J. P., 'Seks służbowo', *Polityka* 2008, No. 46.

469 An example of sexual harassment (publicised by the press) was the case of female officials of the Voivodship Office in *Łódź*, who complained to the daily 'Gazeta Wyborcza' about the sleazy SMS messages from their boss. One was dismissed from work under the pretext of her post being slashed, while her harasser continued working in the Voivodship Office in Łódź. 'Piekarski [the boss] focused on two unmarried women from the department he was heading. He began with 'hot kisses', then moved on to

to subordinates, as was the case with one member of parliament who kept putting his hands on the buttocks of the interpreter accompanying him in public claiming that it was a gesture of friendship (researchers explain this gesture as symbolic of taking possession).[470] A study conducted at the Ministry of Labour and Social Policy has shown that one in five female employees at that ministry feels 'persistently humiliated or degraded by her superiors or colleagues at work', and four women admitted to receiving inappropriate propositions of a sexual nature.[471]

When explaining relations between both sexes, it is said that for centuries Polish women functioned only in the private sphere and appeared in the public sphere only as candidates for wives or as sexual objects. Although in the 20th century women increasingly took up paid jobs, they nevertheless, by cultural custom, continued to be seen as private individuals. An expression of this is the patronising attitude towards women in the workplace – the use of diminutives, excessive protectiveness, seemingly innocent familiarities and telling sexist jokes. Such behaviour of a private nature, but considered natural by men, is the reason why the boundary between patronising conduct and sexual harassment is by many overlooked.[472]

---

concrete proposals – one of the women reported and showed her phone with the SMS message: 'Hello. Will non-committal sex satisfy you?' was one of Piekarski's messages to Ms. Małgorzata. – He then became more offensive – asked if he could lick my body, dreamed about my 'muszelka' [literally 'shell', a term for female genitalia]. It was disgusting. I felt humiliated and uncomfortable – another harassed woman related. The women repeatedly asked their boss to stop. He nevertheless continued to send his SMS messages for nearly a year. In an interview with the daily 'Gazeta Wyborcza' Piekarski admitted [to sending the messages], but insisted that it 'was just a game at the office of who would send a bawdier SMS message.' He then asked us not to write about it, because he had already made amends and confessed to his wife. The day after our publication Piekarski was dismissed from the position of director of the department. He was also expelled from the Łódź branch of PiS [Law and Justice Party]. He was also to face disciplinary action. But as it turned out the 'proceedings' were never initiated and the ex-director, who ever since is known at the office as the 'shell', is still working there as a senior voivodship inspector. M. Kwintkiewicz, M. Masłowski, 'Straciła pracę, bo ujawniła obleśne SMS-y swojego szefa', *Gazeta Wyborcza*, 14 Feb. 2007.

470 J. Podgórska, 'Koszty szczypania i sapania', *Polityka* 2005, No. 2, p. 34.

471 Source <http://gazetapraca.pl/gazetapraca/1,90444,6210509,Mobbing_w_ministerstwie.html>, accessed 14 March 2010.

472 Podgórska, op. cit., p. 33.

In Polish law the problem of sexual harassment was defined with the amendment of the Labour Code in 2003,[473] where under Section $18^{3a}$ (6) it is stated that 'discrimination on grounds of sex also means any unwanted conduct of a sexual nature or related to the sex of an employee, the purpose or effect of which is violation of the dignity or humiliation or degradation of a person; this conduct may consist of physical, verbal or non-verbal elements (sexual harassment).[474] Later, modified provisions of the Labour Code under Section 94(2b) impose on employers the obligation to counteract any forms of discrimination in the working environment and to strive to make the workplace non-discriminatory in employment, especially on grounds of sex, age, disability, race, ethnic origin, religion, creed or sexual orientation.

The provisions of the Penal Code provide the means of fighting cases of sexual harassment.[475] Under Section 197 PC, a penalty of up to 10 years imprisonment awaits anyone who with force, threat or deception makes another person succumb to sexual contacts. Under Section 199, a penalty of up to 3 years imprisonment awaits anyone who by abusing superior-subordinate dependence or by taking advantage of a person being in a critical situation, makes that person submit to sexual intercourse or to other sexual acts.[476]

As in the case of mobbing, employees brought up on commonly held opinions, on the one hand, and law enforcement authorities such as the police, courts or the public prosecutor's office, on the other hand, often dismiss as harmless such forms of harassment as jokes, pinching bottoms, erotic phones or messages with sexual overtones; the problem arises only in the case of rape or attempted rape. In many social circles unwanted courtship or sexual harassment is not condemned or considered dangerous, and family abuse or marital rape is regarded as a private family matter that should not be interfered with. Complaints of sexual

---

473 Ustawa z 14 listopada 2003 r. o zmianie ustawy – Kodeks pracy oraz o zmianie niektórych innych ustaw, [Labour Code Amendment Act of 14 Nov. 2003], Dz. U. No. 213, item 2081.

474 Ibid.

475 The first Polish case of this type to serve as precedent was held before the magistrate court in Katowice in May 1937. It was brought by private prosecution by an auxiliary office staff worker Miss R. against Mr K., a higher official of Wspólnota Interesów [a large mining/smelting concern], who made her ambiguous and increasingly insistent proposals, until finally dismissing her from work. The court adjourned the case without setting the next trial date. J. Podgórska, 'Koszty szczypania i sapania', *Polityka* 2005, No. 2.

476 Ustawa z dnia 6 czerwca 1997 r. Kodeks karny, [Act of 6 June 1997 – Penal Code], Dz.U. 1997 No. 88, item 553 as amended.

harassment encounter a lot of resistance both on the part of society (taboo) and law enforcement bodies. The first cases of harassment to be won were the result of collective legal action, which increased their credibility, as was the case in which the director of the emergency ward in Włocławek was charged by nurses with sexual harassment (he was given a suspended sentence and was dismissed from work) or in the case brought against the director of Teatr Współczesny in Wrocław by the theatre actresses (the court found that harassment had taken place but departed from imposing a penalty). There are no separate studies of this phenomenon conducted in the civil service. The number of cases of harassment in the civil service is based on random data (for example, from the Ministry of Labour and Social Policy[477]). There are no estimates of the direct costs of this phenomenon for the civil service, nor the indirect costs for society as a whole.

An example of mental harassment is *mobbing*, the intention of which is to destabilise another person and completely subdue him/her. The phenomenon of mobbing occurs most often in public administration, educational institutions, the military and the police. Workplace bullying is also present in the health and social service sectors. In the EU Member States, mobbing affects on average 10% of women and 7% of men. A higher risk of mobbing occurs in the public sector: 14% in public administration[478] and uniformed services, 12% in the area of education and health care.[479] In Poland it is estimated that about 30% of those employed had contact with some form of mobbing. A survey conducted by CBOS in 2002 showed that perpetrators of harassment were as a rule the superiors. Only 6% of respondents confessed to having experienced mobbing by colleagues or other people at their workplace.[480] According to information provided by the

---

477 The person who initiated the survey was dismissed from work.

478 'A former archivist at a voivodship office accuses her superior of mobbing. Her friends confirm her allegations. The office, the court and the State Labour Inspectorate do not want to look into the charges. "Training in Łeba – an event with alcohol, I refuse to participate, Jolka and Ewa also refuse – the beginning of the conflict" – this is how Katarzyna's, a former archivist in the Voivodship Office, account begins in which she wrote down all cases of mental harassment she had experienced from her superior. Dates, facts, witnesses, all together 19 points – brawls and insults/verbal abuse (dumb heads, idiots, waste material), knocking on the toilet door when Katarzyna is there too long, commenting on her outfits, gossip'. In M. Wąs, 'Oskarżenie o mobbing w Urzędzie Wojewódzkim', *Gazeta.pl*, 8 Dec. 2002.

479 H. Bochniarz, 'Mobbing w miejscu pracy'. Conference on mobbing and its impact on employees and employers, Ministry of Justice, Warszawa 2005.

480 <http://www.kobieta.gov.pl/?2,18,343>

Institute of Psychosomatics, nearly half a million Poles experience harassment in the workplace.[481]

In Poland the factors that facilitate the development of mobbing cases are unemployment, low social and legal awareness and a defective work organisation system.[482] The situation recurring frequently is one in which it is the victims who have to switch their jobs, are bullied or dismissed from work altogether while the perpetrators keep their jobs. Such cases rarely come up in court and when they do the ruling is usually not favourable to the victimised person.[483]

These factors translate into a lack of understanding of the nature of mobbing, and as a result the public reacts only to drastic cases which end in attempted suicide or suicide. Only such cases draw the interest of journalists of gossip magazines or other media that should provide current information but instead take part in the race for sensation. In popular opinion some forms of conduct are considered normal on the part of superiors and the blame is put on the persecuted person who is accused of 'a lack of understanding for the boss's moods', 'failure to adapt to the requirements of the present day' and, finally, of complete 'incompetence' and 'making a mountain out of a molehill'. The person who is forced to leave their job as a result of mobbing has the opinion of a 'weakling', 'failure', 'neurotic case' or, at best, a 'misfit.'

The most common form of mobbing in Poland, according to CBOS research and indicated by persons subjected to harassment in the workplace, is the creation of an unfriendly or even hostile atmosphere with insulting or unpleasant comments, all sorts of penalties, restrictions and repression such as: demanding to stay after hours without pay, limiting possibilities of taking or of choosing a

481 Polish Press Agency, 23 July 2009.

482 A. Baranowska and I. Miecik, 'Uwaga mobbing!', *Polityka* 2004, No. 3, pp. 20–21.

483 In 2005, a year after Section $94^3$ of the Labour Code went into force, a total of 159 claims of harassment were initiated before district courts and 68 before regional courts. However, in the years 2006–2008 there has been an upward trend in the number of labour actions related to the issues in question. In 2006, there were 403 such cases in the district courts (in 2007–506, in 2008–536) and in the regional courts – 35 (in 2007–173, in 2008–155). In the years 2005–2008, the largest percentage of cases concerned prevention of further harassment (Section $94^3$(2) LC), next were for damages for harm suffered (Section $94^3$(3) LC) and the least number of claims was for compensation for termination of employment as a result of harassment (article $94^3$ (4) LC). The data contained in this document indicate that women slightly outnumbered men in the cases mentioned. Non-binding inquiry No. 11878 to the Minister of Labour and Social Policy concerning harassment, <http://www.podatki.biz/artykuly/14_9185.htm>

convenient time of holiday leave, forcing to break regulations, imposing exorbitant tasks on employees without adequate assessment of the chances of them being implemented, threatening with dismissal, unjustified criticism, falsifying data on performance and degrading employees even in the presence of clients.[484]

Poland is the fourth European country to introduce regulations aimed at combating harassment in the workplace. Section 94 of the Labour Code, which entered into force on 1 January 2004, defines harassment or mobbing as any action or behaviour regarding an employee or directed against him/her, which consists of persistent and prolonged harassment and bullying of the employee that results in the employee feeling inapt for the job, humiliated or ridiculed, isolated or eliminated from his/her team of associates.[485]

The provisions on mobbing apply to the formal employer or any person acting on behalf of the employer as well as any employee.[486] Mobbing in the civil service may be performed by a person in high office,[487] a mid-level official with seniority of service or a relatively young person but enjoying support due to informal networks (political affiliation, family, fellow ties).[488]

---

484 CBOS 2002 survey.

485 14 Nov. 2003 Labour Code Amendment Act, op. cit; M. Nałęcz, *Kodeks pracy. Komentarz*, Warszawa 2004.

486 M. Chakowski, *Mobbing – aspekty prawne*, Warszawa 2005, pp. 65–66.

487 The press reports about cases of mobbing in the Ministry of Labour: 'Lost their jobs in the ministry: Head of the Department of Migration Janusz Grzyb, Head of the Department for Women, Family and Counteracting Discrimination Berenika Anders and the Director of International Cooperation Paweł Wilczek. (…) the real problem of officials at the ministry is not necessarily the minister's weakness for drinks, but rather the stress they experience when she strides out barefoot from her office to her staff, waiting for a meeting with her, and throws off hand, "Nice working with you", leaving them in consternation, unable to tell whether they've been complimented on a good job or have just being sacked. (…) they remember when the minister expressed dissatisfaction with the work of her Deputy Minister Agnieszka Chłoń-Domińczak, and the Undersecretary Czesława Ostrowska, a close associate of Minister Jolanta Fedak, spoke in her defense. "Be quiet, sweetie"- clipped Minister Fedak.' <http://www.polityka.pl/kraj/ludzie/298483,1,fedak-jolanta.read>

488 Harassment or mobbing issues are rarely recorded, unless the injured person chooses to go to court. The press reports: 'Matters took the most dramatic turn in the Ministry of Finance. Ministry authorities received complaints from six employees that they were being humiliated by their superiors. Five people were so desperate as to sue the ministry. Individual processes are also underway against the Ministry of Interior and the Ministry of Sport. The Ministry for the Economy avoided being taken to court when the harassment of one of its employees was confirmed by a special team set up

The Labour Code imposes on the employer the obligation: to prevent mobbing by averting the occurrence of psychological violence in the workplace, to help victims of mobbing and to eliminate such practices, to raise awareness among staff and provide appropriate training for the managerial staff, to include in the rules of work the banning of mobbing and the duty to inform of any such instances, and to implement procedures that allow an employee harassed by the employer to bypass official channels to report the occurrence of such by indicating the person he/she may apply to.[489] Unfortunately, in many cases, the provision remains a dead letter.

There are methods and forms of mobbing prevention such as an appropriate approach to candidates during the recruitment process, a policy of equal treatment, a staff monitoring system and monitoring of undesirable conduct in the social sphere. An important element of the preventive measures against harassment is the creation of a system of continual flow of information within an information-sharing triangle: employees – superiors – human resources unit. An increasingly important role in the fight against mobbing is played by non-governmental organisations, such as the National Anti-Mobbing Association established in 2002 in Wrocław (with offices in Kraków, Łódź and Gdańsk). Harassment can be countered by both the superior and the potential victim. In the case of the superior, it is he/she who is assumed to be responsible, as he/she is the direct superior of the perpetrator and is responsible for the introduction

---

to combat such practices. The teams that deal with complaints of officials claiming harassment by their superiors also met in the Ministry of the Environment and the Ministry of Education (they found no irregularities, and the concerned decided not to assert their rights in court)', <http://www.newsweek.pl/artykuly/sekcje/polska/w-ministerstwach-szykanuja-pracownikow,51210,1, accessed 13 March 2010; 'Seven of them are employed in the Ministry of the Economy. "The case was considered in March by a team appointed by the director-general," says Mariusz Kozłowski from the Ministry's Press Office. (…) The Ministry admits only that measures have been taken to prevent similar incidents from happening in the future. Cases of harassment on the part of their superiors have also been reported in other ministries. We've established that in 2008 ill treatment was claimed by two employees of the Health Ministry and an official from the Ministry of Regional Development, who was in constant disagreement with his departmental director who supervised his work. Both cases are still in progress'.
<http://www.newsweek.pl/artykuly/sekcje/z_ostatniej_chwili/newsweek--mobbing-na-szczycie-wladzy,6103,1>, accessed 10 March 2010.

489 'Praca nie może być terrorem', *Rzeczpospolita*, Dodatek Prawo Pracy, 30 March 2005, No. 456.

of preventive measures. It is not allowable for a manager to passively watch mobbing in action. Superiors are required to immediately react in instances of moral harassment, help in solving problems rather than avoid getting involved them.

There is in the civil service a growing phenomenon of *letaprivacy*, or the treatment of the state by civil servants as 'anybody's property'; its assets there for the taking in an official manner using legal mechanisms created by the state.[490] The essence of the letaprivacy phenomenon is the fact that, by legalising certain forms of interest or the use of laws and regulations in force, civil servants, in collaboration with private business, benefit from public property. By this we mean the use of legislation or legal loopholes for personal gain. In this situation we are dealing with the braking of the principle of equality before the law and taking advantage of this fact for personal gain.

The letaprivacy phenomenon can occur on several levels. First, it very often affects the *process of economic transformation, especially privatisation.*[491] The process of privatisation, prepared without regard for the legal infrastructure and long-term ownership transformation programme, created 'favourable and convenient conditions for criminal activity'.[492] During this particular period, there was an increased tendency to create new legislation, to circumvent the law, to exploit available loopholes in the law and to interpret law to personal advantage by those with formal or informal influence on that very law. Privatisation decisions in Poland were dictated by particular groups and party bureaucrats to suit their interests. At the beginning of the 1990s the effect of the application of free-market solutions led to the capture of public resources by managers and politicians from the PRL [Polish People's Republic] era strategically placed in the very core of the economic decision-taking system.[493] An example of this was

490 Boć, 'Administracja a obywatel', op. cit., pp. 291–292.

491 For example, the Regional Prosecutor's Office in Białystok accused the former Treasury Minister Andrzej Chronowski and former Deputy Minister of the Ministry Jakub T. of causing significant losses in state assets in the privatisation of the Białystok Power Plant SA. The case concerns the agreement of 15 February 2001 with the French company Societe Nationale d'Electricite et de Thermique (SNET), under which the Treasury sold its 45 percent share in the power plant for almost EUR 49 million, and the damages to the State Treasury from the sale exceeded EUR 6.5 million, or the equivalent of PLN 24.5 million. The two former government officials heard charges of having caused significant damage to state assets, <http://www.gazetaprawna.pl/wiadomosci/artykuly/261548,byly_minister_skarbu_oskarzony_w_sprawie_prywatyzacji_ec_bialystok.html>, accessed 20 Nov. 2009.

492 M. Jarosz (ed.), *Manowce polskiej prywatyzacji,* Warszawa, 2001, p. 89.

493 Ibid., p. 38.

the 2000–2005 privatisation of the Polish steelworks that in the report of the Supreme Audit Office was assessed negatively in the part concerning the financial terms of the privatisation contract, disadvantageous to the State Treasury because of the low valuation of the share price. What is more, the government signed an agreement selling the company for even less than the undervalued shares amounted to.[494]

Secondly, it *can mean the creation of legislation to the advantage of a specific person or group of people.*[495] The legislation refers to a very narrow group of people – mostly to entrepreneurs, sporadically directly to politicians – and provides them with material benefits or improves their situation in some other way. Even a report of the World Bank carries information on how much it costs to arrange the adoption of 'legislation to order' in Poland. A typical example of this kind of phenomenon is the so-called gelatine affair. Kazimierz G. took over the gelatine factory in Puławy as a result of its privatisation in the early 1990s. The public prosecutor's investigation into fraud at the joint stock company Żelatyna S.A. took over 10 years and was twice discontinued.[496] The gelatine affair that shook the AWS-UW coalition began near the end of 1997 when the Veterinary Department of the Ministry of Agriculture received a letter signed by Hanna Piotrowska-Twardokęs, a Polish LOT airlines stewardess, concerned about the raging 'mad cow disease' in Western Europe. The stewardess specifically asked whether 'it was possible to test the imported gelatine for prion strain contents that cause spongy encephalitis in cattle, which in the case of consumption of this gelatine by humans would result in a very serious disease'. On 4 December 1997, the Director of the Veterinary Department Henryk Maciołek – as it happened, the last day of his work for the department – consulted the State Veterinary Institute for their opinion. The Institute replied that 'there was no effective detection method for the presence of prions in gelatine'. On this basis, Director Maciołek drafted his opinion that gelatine should not be imported from areas affected by the disease, and on 19 December 1997 the Polish government introduced a total ban on the import of gelatine (including that of pig origin, although pigs were not affected by the disease), thus providing a legal solution that was beneficial

494 37th meeting of the Sejm on 16 March 2007. Government information regarding results of the NIK audit concerning the privatisation of Polskie Huty Stali S.A in 2000–2005, transcript, <www. prywatyzacja+raporty+NIKandhl=plandnum=10andbtnG>

495 In 2004 in Poland, over two thirds of respondents (69%) believed that in Poland money could buy the adoption of a parliamentary act or a change of law. M. Wenzel, 'Korupcja, nepotyzm, nieuczciwy lobbing', *Katalog Komunikatów CBOS,* 2004, N0. 3049.

496 'Żelatynowy król oskarżony', *TVN,* UWAGA!, 6 May 2005.

to the national monopolist Kazimierz Grabek.[497] It turned out in the end that Hanna Piotrowska-Twardokęs never wrote to the ministry asking about gelatine and the 'mad cow disease', and that her signature was forged.[498]

Thirdly, it is a matter of the *capture of the organisational part of the state* and then reaping legitimate revenue and profits from this. For example, seats on management and supervisory boards of state-owned enterprises (SOEs) are often filled by civil servants. This is contrary to corporate governance principles in respect to companies with state shareholdings and other national legal resources as well as to OECD Principles of Corporate Governance where it is stated that 'the ownership entity should avoid electing an excessive number of board members from the state administration'. The aim is 'depriving the government from the possibility to directly intervene in the SOE's business or management and at limiting the state responsibility for decisions taken by SOE boards'.[499] Meanwhile, a NIK audit report on corporate governance by the Ministry of the Economy in companies with state majority ownership in the years 2004–2008, with particular focus on the supervision in coal mining companies, showed that nominations to supervisory boards went as a rule to members of the civil service corps; the practice led to the owner exercising effective influence on members of supervisory boards, additionally accomplished through the existence of an employment relationship with them, but which aroused doubts of NIK controllers in terms of conflict of interest issues.[500]

---

497 <http://www.halat.pl/ekologia01.html>, Nov. 2009.

498 Zbigniew Nowak, president of Nova International in Łódź, which produces food mixes containing gelatine, told reporters what the affair was all about and on 22 February 1998 informed the Warsaw Prosecutor's Office that a crime had been committed. The crime was the falsification of a letter and overstepping of powers by Director Maciołek. On 5 November 1998, the Regional Prosecutor's Office in Warsaw sent the case files: notice of offence with annexes and record from the interview of the witness Zbigniew Nowak, to the District Public Prosecutor's Office Warszawa-Śródmieście, and has not moved a pace forward since, although we now have the end of September 2000', L. Kraskowski, 'Nie widać końca afery żelatynowej', *Rzeczpospolita* 10 Oct. 2000, <http://rceczpospolita.pl/Pl-iso/gazeta/wydanie_001010/kraj/kraj_a_8.html>.

499 OECD Guidelines on Corporate Governance of State-Owned Enterprises, OECD 2005, p. 25.

500 Post audit report by NIK Vice President Stanisław Jarosz to Deputy Prime Minister Waldemar Pawlak on corporate governance by the Ministry of the Economy in companies with state majority ownership in the years 2004–2008, with particular focus on the supervision in coal mining companies. www.prywatyzacja, NIK reports, filetype: pdf.

The *use of bank cards*, for purposes other than those intended for and even with the consent of the departments responsible for their settlement, also falls under the third category. The report by Julia Pitera, a minister in the government of Prime Minister Donald Tusk, showed that within a two year period nearly 1.4 million zlotys were spent by government administration employees using company credit cards. Formally no limits were exceeded on the cards. It however turned out that government employees used company credit cards to finance private expenses despite the lack of any authorisation. It was reprehensible that two ministries even authorized their employees to make private purchases using company credit cards. In most ministries part of the transactions made by members of the management were unreasoned expenses, their business nature very unlikely or disqualified, and yet the finance departments of those ministries accepted these expenses. In the vast majority of cases no action was taken to recover them. Employees of the ministries used a total of 223 credit cards. Monthly limits granted to the card users ranged from a thousand to fifty thousand zlotys. Company cards were used to pay for hotel services – 38% of the total, next the catering services – accounting for 26% of the total, and purchases of fuel and company car services – 17% of the expenses.[501] A particular form of acquiring company funds was through cash withdrawals using company credit cards. Cash expenditure was settled without requiring the submission of proof of purchase, and refunds of card transactions (even over a month after the transaction date) were made without any explanation as to why the cards had been used. There is a presumption that they were 'loans' to the company card holders for their private purchases.[502]

The phenomenon of letaprivacy includes taking high allowance and severance payments or in wider terms – use of public assets, interpreting the law to one's advantage, due to holding a high position in the hierarchy. It is connected

501 Government administration employees used company credit cards to finance private expenditure, <http://www.money.pl/archiwum/wiadomosci_agencyjne/iar/artykul/pracownicy;administracji;rzadowej;wykorzystywali;sluzbowe;karty;kredytowe;do;finansowania;prywatnych;wydatkow,241,0,346609.html>.
Among the bank card transactions was, for example, the purchase of cod for PLN 8.16, cufflinks for PLN 619.65, cosmetics for PLN 776, woollen blanket for PLN 1200, jewellery for PLN 2 379, ties for PLN 300, cosmetics for: PLN 776, 520 PLN, 290 PLN; shopping in EMPiK stores for: PLN 359, PLN 305, shopping at 'Almidecor' for PLN 360 and PLN 218. These expenses were, for example, made by Tomasz Nowakowski, Undersecretary of State in the Ministry of Regional Development, and accounted for 18% of total payments with that company card.

502 <http://wiadomosci.onet.pl/1762121,11,item.html>.

with grey-area corruption or morally objectionable behaviour which defies clear legal judgment. It includes bribery which occurs during procurement transactions, contracts and other government benefits, concessions, court judgments, as well as customs duty and tax evasion. Similarly, social forms which are difficult to eliminate such as taking advantage of one's official position for personal or family gain also bear the mark of letaprivacy. Examples are many: the use of company cars for private purposes, use of office phones for private conversations, stealing of office supplies such as paper or toner to use for private purposes, charging private phones at work, accepting small gifts such as pens, notebooks and calendars from private companies. Officials see nothing offensive or disturbing in hanging up calendars of private companies in public buildings. They do not see a conflict of interest, although public buildings should display only items provided by the official employer (the state). Otherwise the presumption is that the company logo on the poster or calendar displayed in a prominent position in a public office indicates that company's privileged position in comparison to other similar companies. There seems to be a correlation between the identification with a government administration institution the civil service representative is working for and the level of performance and work efficiency. It seems that letaprivacy is complementary to corruption as it accentuates phenomena that in cases of corruption are dismissed as not of primary importance or even ignored as secondary.

The problem of *corruption in the civil service* can be analysed on many levels: beginning with the definition of the concept of corruption in the civil service, through the examination of areas where it occurs, and ending with the indication of sources of corruption, taking into account the various aspects of its development, especially the political and economic relations in the country and the values civil servants are guided by. When examining the corruption phenomenon, consideration should be given to the organisation of the civil service and an analysis made of potential sources of corruption in the way public administration functions. Corruption is a testament to the irregularities in the management of the civil service and in a broader context – of state institutions. I share the opinion that the chief goal of the state is not the elimination of corruption but the improvement of the general mechanisms a state functions by, the rule of law, fairness and efficiency. And as Susan Rose-Ackerman wrote, 'Enforcement and monitoring are needed, but they will have little long-term impact if the basic conditions that encourage payoffs are not reduced'.[503]

503 S. Rose-Ackerman, *Corruption and Government: Causes, Consequences, and Reform*, Cambridge University Press 1999, p. 6.

The oldest record on corruption in Poland can be found in the Chronicles by Gallus Anonymous: 'Meanwhile, Sieciech, having returned to Poland (…) tempted slyly the more important among them, the Silesian nobles, with promises and gifts and slowly enticed them to his side'.[504]

Corruption understood as abuse of public office for private gain and the fight against it is a matter of common interest of many states and international institutions. They cooperate with each other in order to develop common lines of action to contain corruption. In accordance with EU law, 'the deliberate action of an official, who, directly or through an intermediary, requests or receives advantages of any kind whatsoever, for himself or for a third party, or accepts a promise of such an advantage, to act or refrain from acting in accordance with his duty or in the exercise of his functions in breach of his official duties shall constitute passive corruption'[505] in the public sector.

Active corruption in the public sector is 'the deliberate action of whosoever promises or gives, directly or through an intermediary, an advantage of any kind whatsoever to an official, for himself or for a third party, for him to act or refrain from acting in accordance with his duty or in the exercise of his functions in breach of his official duties.'

In terms of political science, corruption is defined as any failure to comply with the obligations arising from the position, function or office held if the purpose of this failure is to achieve undue personal gain. One of the manifestations of political corruption is the system of patronage (political spoils), the practice of taking public positions in order to obtain the means that serve political party purposes. These means are jobs in public administration and the transfer of public funds to a political party through various foundations, associations, research institutes (even if in name only), mutual assistance funds or commercial companies. Countries where public service is highly politicised are more prone to corruption and vulnerable to the loss of specialist personnel and the continuity of institutional memory than those with an independent, apolitical and a stable civil service.

Space – wrote Jadwiga Staniszkis – nominally 'public' (media, agencies, financial institutions, major foundations) is gradually taking on the features of an 'institutionalising policy' – institutions and public positions become 'the spoils of the connected few' and 'the different sectors of power are captured by individual

---

504 Jarosz, *Władza*, op.cit., p. 234.

505 EU Convention of 26 May 1997 on the fight against corruption involving officials of the European Communities or officials of Member States of the European Union. Official Journal of the European Communities No. C 195, No. 40, 25 June 1997.

groups/parties competing with each other'.[506] Political corruption reflects the political system in which it occurs and falls into the category of 'white collar' crime, people who are educated and holding exposed positions. Kleptocracy 'refers to a ruler or a top official whose primary goal is personal enrichment and who possesses the power to further this aim while holding public office'. Corrupt rulers 'influence not only the size of government, but also the mixture of taxes and spending priorities' (Rose-Ackerman, *Corruption and Government*).

Corruption means the use of public resources for the funding of election campaigns and the party apparatus, the exercise by a party of formally undue control over an area of the functioning of the state or sphere of public life and the misuse of power given by virtue of the public or quasi-public position held.[507]

A perfect example of political spoils in Poland are state-owned companies and their supervisory boards that take on the role of 'mechanisms of political corruption, in which the primary goals are those of the party-group: staffing the boards with their people' and 'the companies provide the economic base for the political parties in power: a source of assets and capital that can be transferred to private companies controlled by the parties, as well as a number of posts (on management and supervisory boards) for political clients'.[508] The fate of the largest state-owned companies (M. Jarosz) is determined in the offices of political leaders.[509]

Corruption in institutions consists of pay-offs and bribery, in which the perpetrator or the subject of perpetration is the person holding office, considered to be under national law a person performing a public function or acting in an official capacity.[510] 'Political corruption occurs when individual agents – government officials – put their own private pecuniary interests ahead of those of their principals'.[511]

---

506 J. Staniszkis, 'Wolność bez odpowiedzialności czyli rozmowa z duchami', in *Zwierzę niepolityczne*, Komorów, 2003, pp. 300–305; *Rzeczpospolita,* 6 Nov. 1999, No. 208.

507 Machińska, ' Przeciwdziałanie korupcji', op.cit.

508 M. Jarosz, 'Okazja czyni złodzieja, czyli proces transformacji i prywatyzacji w Polsce', in A. Dylus, A. Rudowski and M. Zaborski (eds.), *Korupcja. Oblicza, uwarunkowania, przeciwdziałanie*, Ossolineum Wrocław-Warszawa-Kraków, 2006, pp. 65–66.

509 Jarosz, *Władza,* op.cit., pp. 242–248.

510 O. Górniok and B. Mozga, 'Pojęcie korupcji', in *Zagrożenie korupcją w świetle badań kontrolnych Najwyższej Izby Kontroli*, Warszawa, 2000, p. 4.

511 Francis Fukuyama, *State-Building: Governance and World Order in the 21st Century*. Cornell University Press, New York, 2004, p. 49.

Corruption has a destructive effect on many areas of life and society with irreversible consequences for the economy and public awareness. The costs of corruption include:

- Macro-fiscal costs: lost revenues (from tax, customs duty and privatisation) and excessively high expenditure through, for example, corruption loadings on state contracts.[512] Corruption can undermine public finances and thus slow down economic growth. The biggest danger then is the growing deficit that causes the rise of interest rates and increases public debt and the ensuing burdens; full-size corruption – says Leszek Balcerowicz – deters foreign investors.[513] Falling investments and economic growth are in part the results of overregulation and improperly conducted public procurement procedures. According to international data, the higher the incidence of corruption, the lower the rate of investment and economic growth. 'Compromises' adopted in the area of economic and social infrastructure often become sources of risk to public safety; the pressure increases to raise government expenditure, which can then be further used for purposes other than those declared. Such a situation occurs when salaries of public officials are kept at relatively low levels while other administration costs increase. As a result the inefficiently functioning public sector forces taxpayers to incur further costs for the same service but performed by the private sector.[514] Corruption restricts the strategic dimension of state activity with short-term goals becoming more important than long-term ones. Corruption destroys free competition as it largely relies on limiting free access to information and a monopoly on the decision-making process, which preclude free competition; this hits smaller companies in particular, especially domestic companies, which are not only deprived of support from public authorities but are arbitrarily excluded from competition.[515] In the private sector bribes not only raise the running cost of businesses by about 5–10% but also reinforce corruptive practices and their costs with each successive transaction – the effect of a drop in investor interest.
- Social costs: the burden to the public and to the poor in particular. This is due to bribe-extraction in the delivery of services, poor access to services and

---

512 World Bank Report, 'Corruption in Poland: Review of Priority Areas and Proposals for Action', World Bank, p. 2.

513 G. Kopińska, 'Geneza powstania programu "Przeciw Korupcji"', <www.przeciw-korupcji.org.pl>

514 T. G. Grosse, 'Działania antykorupcyjne w państwach członkowskich OECD', Florence 2000, p. 11.

515 Ibid., p. 12.

their poor quality. Although bribes paid by the lowest wage earners are not high, they represent a major part of their income. Damages from construction disasters are incurred because corrupt engineers, supervisors and inspectors accept undue benefits in exchange for the approval or omission of certain planning-technical elements. Taking of bribes leads to building constructions that become a threat to the health and lives of people and have devastating effects on the environment.[516] This, too, leads to the loss of confidence in public institutions. Corruption undermines the sheer foundations of the rule of law, tax compliance, respect for public order and safety, and ultimately – the legitimacy of a democratic state. Corruption fosters the development of organised crime which is trying to take over areas of legitimate activity in order to have influence on political and administrative decision-making processes. And last, but not least, corruption raises sharply the costs of goods and services, increases country debt, leads to the lowering of quality standards; the result is that decisions are made with a preference for capital-intensive techniques, because it is more profitable for one businessman or another instead of the human factor, or the labour-intensive technique, which would have been more appropriate to development in a less-developed country.[517]

On the basis of an analysis carried out by NIK controllers, irregularities that could have their source in corrupt behaviour can be divided into dysfunctional areas, which include:

---

516 The effects of this type of corruption are construction disasters such as the collapse of water parks in Moscow, homes in Turkey or the Atlanta tragedy. The 2005 Transparency International report shows how destructive corruption can be for the environment. One example is the Bakun dam reservoir in Sarawak, Malaysia – the building permit was given to a friend of the governor of Sarawak, a wood manufacturer, and in the meantime, the local government is still looking for buyers of the electricity produced by the plant. The construction involves the planned destruction of 700 sq.km of tropical rainforests. Another example is the Yacyreta Hydroelectric project on the border between Argentina and Paraguay – the costs of the energy produced by it are so high that they must be subsidised by the government in order to find buyers for it. In addition, it threatens the ecological balance of the Ibera marshes. Still another is the Bataan nuclear power plant in the Philippines – built near a major earthquake fault, it risks damage and contamination. 'Global Corruption Report', Transparency International, Berlin 2005, <www.globalcorruptionreport.org/>

517 Frisch Dieter, The Effects of Corruption on Development, paper presented to the Africa Leadership Forum on Corruption, Democracy and Human Rights in Africa, Cotonou, Benin, 19–21 September 1994.

- lack of clear and transparent criteria regarding the exercise of administrative tasks,
- failure to apply the principles of openness and transparency in administration, and in decision-making procedures in particular,
- failure to apply the principle of responsibility and full accountability of officials,
- a weak civil service that frustrates building a stable public administration, independent of political turmoil.

Without a doubt, 'the corruption of the system of governance leads to its depreciation in the eyes of voters and citizens'.[518]

Opinion polls show that as many as two-thirds of Poles are of the opinion that officials often take bribes, and half of the respondents believe that senior officials use their positions to obtain private benefits. There is a widespread consensus that public administration, the highest state authorities and the justice administration top the list of the most corrupt institutions in the country, ahead of the health services, the police and political parties.

Assessments of the level of corruption in Poland vary. In the Corruption Perception Index by Transparency International Poland has not been improving its ranking as well as some other former socialist countries. There are however opinions (for example that of M. Jarosz) that the level of corruption in Poland is rather low. These opinions are supported by research, such as that of Nations in Transit, which shows that in Central and Eastern Europe, Poland, Estonia and Slovenia are the countries with the lowest corruption indicators.[519] The 2008 public opinion poll showed that fighting corruption was among the priorities that citizens expected of their government.

Many corrupt activities in Poland remain outside criminal liability. These include bribery of public officials abroad by private and legal persons.[520] In general opinion, Poland is a weak, 'soft' country ineffectively fulfilling its functions, prone to corruption and easily deceived.[521]

---

518 Jarosz, 'Okazja czyni złodzieja', op. cit., p. 63.

519 Ibid., pp. 60–61.

520 W. Krajewski, 'Etyka w służbie publicznej. Uregulowania prawne dotyczące etyki w służbie publicznej w Polsce', *Służba Cywilna*, 2000/2001, No. 1, p. 119.

521 More in J. Kochanowicz, 'Znękany Lewiatan. Państwo wobec gospodarki w Polsce schyłku lat dziewięćdziesiątych w świetle badań porównawczych', in J. Kochanowicz et al., *Ustrojowa wizja gospodarki polskiej*, IRiSS Warszawa, 1997.

NIK investigations show lack of effective systemic solutions aimed at containing corruption in the public service. The Anti-Corruption Act of 1997 exists only in formal terms – in the opinion of experts – and its prohibitions are easy to circumvent. For example, statements submitted by officials of having no private relationships with private business, pursuant to the Act's relevant provisions, are in practice very rarely checked and verified, as shown by NIK audits. Despite the fact that the law has some moral significance, as it places certain requirements on public officials, it is, in the evaluation of NIK, 'more of a symbolic than a practical anti-corruption instrument'.

## Instruments to Tackle Unethical Behaviour in the Civil Service

Instruments intended to reduce wrongdoings in the civil service include:

a) legal instruments,
b) institutional solutions,
c) standards of administrative services delivered to citizens (Citizen Card or the Diversity Charter),
d) access of citizens to information on the activities of public administration,
e) codes of ethics,
f) complaints,
g) training,
h) efficient control, and
i) practical examples of combating dysfunctions.

The majority of European countries are in favour of applying a combination of several instruments to tackle the various wrongdoings in the civil service. Governments are convinced that legal instruments are vital in the fight against unethical behaviour, but in the opinion of many of them (nine) punitive measures are not always the most efficient of them. Effective tools combating unethical behaviour in public offices are: training (22 states), commitment by political leadership (19 states) and working conditions, including fair salaries (16 states).[522] Other instruments are: appropriate selection and recruitment procedures, objective criteria for promotion, rotation of positions and jobs, a clear description of tasks, a clear division of competence, social security of employees. An efficiently, reliably and honestly working administration is the basis for the functioning of a democratic state.

---

522 *Ethics in the Public Service of the European Union Member States, under the Irish Presidency* 2004, Ch. Demmke, D. Bossaert, EIPA, January to June 2004, p. 7.

a) Legal instruments

Legislators in various countries, authorities and supranational institutions see corruption as the major problem and the weakness of administration. As a result, the adopted international acts and laws enacted by various countries in the world pay particular attention to this problem. Participants of the Conference Against Corruption held in Lima in 1997, among them ministers and experts from different countries (including representatives from Poland), concluded that improvement of the effectiveness of regulations and available means in containing corruption will contribute to:

- making acceptance of gifts by officials illegal, and to abolishing the requirement to prove that an official who received an illegal gift actually gave favours in return;
- providing a system for the declaration of assets by persons holding public positions of trust (and their families), and placing on them the obligation to justify increases out of line with legitimate sources of income;
- introducing periodic or random monitoring of the assets and lifestyles of significant decision-makers in the public sector (and their families and associates), where appropriate by an independent agency;
- laws which effectively empower the freezing, seizure and confiscation of the illicitly acquired wealth of officials found guilty of corruption, wherever it may be and by whomsoever it may be held;
- providing appropriate protection for witnesses (and their families) and protecting whistle-blowers;
- providing a system for the recording of gifts received by officials;
- ensuring that officials at all levels cannot hide behind immunities but are fully subject to corruption laws; and
- debarring convicted criminals from standing for political office and appointment to positions of public trust.

In Poland, there is a need for a well educated, professional civil service, a clear rewards system, effective mechanisms of public and financial management, including monitoring of public finances and minimising political interference in public procurement processes and appointment to positions.

Another important element should be the verification of management structures in ministries and agencies. A simple transfer of structures (the World Bank) modelled on the private sector creates an unnecessarily large number of well-paid supervisory positions that serve the multiplication of political contacts and networks. At the same time as the number of new jobs increases, the structure becomes less and less clear, there is a lack of clear policy direction and the responsibility for their implementation becomes blurred between the parent ministry and its agencies.

A guarantee of the impartiality of administrative proceedings in Poland is the institution of exclusion pursuant to Article 24 of the Code of Administrative Procedure, which is a legal instrument safeguarding against a conflict of interest, 'or abuse of a public function for private purposes', and exclusion is the 'narrow concept of impartiality that assumes independence of issued administrative decisions from the entity issuing them'.[523]

b) Institutional solutions

Institutional forms of combating unethical behaviour in Poland comprise the Central Anti-Corruption Bureau (CBA) and the Internal Security Agency (ABW).

c) Standards of administrative services

Another example of improved empowerment of citizens as recipients and consumers of public benefits and services could be the standardisation of those services. Unfortunately in Poland the standardisation of services delivered by the civil service is in its infancy and applies only to matters governed by law, such as the waiting time of citizen for a response.

d) Citizen access to information on the activities of public administration

An instrument which supports the fight against wrongdoings in the civil service is the access of citizens to information about the activities of public administration.

The adoption of the law on access to information in Poland was preceded by long discussions that date back to the early 1990s. Their considerations found their expression in the 1997 Constitution of the Republic of Poland. Article 54 of the Constitution grants every citizen the right to receive and impart information. Preventive censorship of the media and licensing of the press are prohibited. Accordingly, every citizen has the right to information that public authorities have a duty to provide irrespective of who applies for it, with the exception of information classified for reasons of national security.[524] Article 61 of the Constitution provides that citizens have the right to obtain information on the activities of

523 P. J. Suwaj, *Gwarancje bezstronności organów administracji publicznej w postępowaniu administracyjnym,* Kolonia Limited 2004, p. 147.

524 M. Mucha, *Obowiązki administracji publicznej w sferze dostępu do informacji,* Wrocław, 2002, p. 54.

public authorities, persons performing public functions as well as economic and professional self-government bodies and other persons and bodies in connection with their performance of duties prescribed in the area of public administration and management of communal assets or property of the State Treasury (Article 61 of the Constitution).

O the other hand, Article 74.3 of the Polish Constitution, which states that everyone has the right to information on the quality of the environment and its protection, cannot be applied directly but subject to statutory limitations as stipulated under Article 81. Thus the scope of this right is conceived narrowly as to exclude foreigners and stateless persons, which is incompatible with international law and is not a democratic solution. This regulation is also contrary to Article 54, which states that everyone has the right to acquire and disseminate information.[525] On the basis of the Polish Constitution, the provisions on the right of access to information can be applied directly, which indicates the rank the legislator gave this matter.

The Act on Access to Public Information was not passed until 6 September 2001 and went into force on 1 January 2002.[526] In some cases a moratorium was introduced of two to three years, so that it is being fully implemented as of 1 January 2006. Access to information regarding internal and foreign policy, including the intentions of legislative and executive authorities, drafts of normative acts, programmes on realisation of public tasks, the methods and consequences of their realisation were deferred for 24 months from the coming into effect of the Act. The ban on disclosure of said information during the same period applied to entities representing state legal persons or legal persons of local authorities.

The adoption of the Act on Access to Public Information in Poland was to be the next step towards the creation of a civil society, on the strength of the constitutional principle of transparency in public life.[527] The regulations of the Polish Act do not specify any restrictions on the base of citizenship and state that 'each person' is entitled to the right of access to public information. The acceptance in the second article of 'each person' as the entitled entity therefore applies also, as stipulated in the Constitution, to foreigners as well as legal persons, unincorporated bodies, social organisations, and as some authors believe, also to foreign institutions.

---

525 M. Jaśkowska, *Dostęp do informacji publicznych,* Toruń 2002, p. 16.

526 Ustawa z dnia 6 września 2001 r. o dostępie do informacji publicznej, [Access to Information Act of 6 Sep. 2001], Dz.U, 2001 No. 112, item 1198 as amended.

527 J. Jędrośka and M. Stoczkiewicz, 'Ustawa o dostępie do informacji publicznej a regulacje szczególne', *Państwo i Prawo,* June 2003, p. 89.

Access to requested information should be provided without undue delay, but not later than 14 days from the date the petition is submitted. There are exceptions to this rule which state that if the entity cannot provide access to the requested information within the set time limit, it must notify of the reasons for the delay and of the date by which it will make the information available, but not later than two months from the date the petition was submitted (Article 13.2). If the entity has to incur additional costs connected with making the information available in the form requested in the petition or the need to transform the information into a form indicated in the petition, the entity is entitled to charge the petitioner a fee to cover the incurred costs and, within a period of 14 days from the date the petition was submitted, notify the petitioner of the fee amount. The information is then provided after the expiry of 14 days of notifying the petitioner of the said fee. Once the entity notifies the petitioner in writing of the reasons for its inability to provide the information in the form requested, indicating at the same time the form in which it can be made available immediately – the initiative then belongs to the petitioner, and if the petitioner fails to submit the petition for the information to be provided in the form indicated, the procedure for access to information is discontinued.

The information that can be made available immediately should be made available in oral or written form without a written petition. Public information should also be provided displayed in public places.

The right to public information in Poland, in accordance with the Act on Access to Information, is subject to limitations:

(a) pursuant to regulations on the protection of confidential information and information protected by law;
(b) in relation to the privacy of a natural person or the secret of an entrepreneur. This limitation does not apply to information on persons performing public functions, connected with performing these functions, and when the natural person or entrepreneur forgo their right to such protection. Access to public information cannot be limited for the protection of the interests of the parties in matters resolved before the state authorities, in particular in the administrative, criminal or civil proceedings, if the proceedings concern the public authorities.[528]

The Polish legislator chose not to set up a separate institution to enforce the law. In the discussion on the merits of setting up such a body some say that an additional institution would only increase bureaucracy and strain the state budget,

528 6 Sep. 2001 Access to Information Act, op. cit., Art. 5.

while others are of the opinion that considering the inefficiency of the present justice system – the adopted rules for contesting refusals to provide information may in effect prove unworkable.

The implementation of the right of access of citizens to information about the activities of public administration faces many difficulties. First, people in Poland have little knowledge about the right of access to information, its extent and scope. Second, officials, who regard the right as yet another incomprehensible (annoying) duty, delay making the information available, fail to consider the right as a tool that builds a civil society, apply additional charges as a barrier to access, and there are instances of giving in to political pressure and denying access to information to the persons concerned altogether. Third, there is a problem with the verification of the accuracy of the information provided by the officials. Fourth, the deluge of information causes a problem for its recipients to assemble, understand, and analyse, and it is rejected by them in its entirety.[529]

Access to documents in the possession of public administration and the resulting openness and transparency constitutes one of the major issues in the process of building the foundations of citizen trust in the state.

e) Codes of ethics

A tangible example of combating wrongdoings in the civil service was the 2002 Polish Civil Service Code of Ethics[530] (described earlier in the Chapter 5), which was superseded by the Order of the Prime Minister of 6 October 2011 on the Guidelines for the Civil Service on Compliance With Rules and on the Ethics of the Civil Service Corps.[531] The Order not only raises the awareness among civil servants and civil service employees of their role in society, but is also designed to protect the citizen against unreliability and unfairness on the part of public administration. This order bridges the gap between the standards of law and professional ethics. The fact of compiling all ethical rules in a single document facilitates their interpretation and prevents conflicts between superiors and subordinates. The importance of the Order should not be overestimated as practice verifies behaviour of officials, nevertheless it provides a model to aspire to.

---

529 Transparency International Polska, Warszawa 2006.

530 Zarządzenie Prezesa Rady Ministrów *w sprawie nadania kodeksu etyki służby cywilnej* z dnia 11 października 2002 r. nr 114, [Order 114 of the Prime Minister of 11 October 2002 on Provision of a Civil Service Code of Ethics], M. P., No. 46, item 683.

531 Zarządzenie Prezesa Rady Ministrów z dnia 6 października 2011 roku *w sprawie wytycznych w zakresie przestrzegania zasad służby cywilnej oraz w sprawie zasad etyki korpusu służby cywilnej,* M.P. No. 93, item. 953.

f) Complaints

Everyone is entitled to submit petitions, proposals and complaints in the public interest, their own interest or any other person's – with their consent, in accordance with Article 63 of the Constitution of the Republic of Poland of 2 April 1997. Complaints may be submitted to public authorities as well as to organisations and social institutions in connection with their performance of duties prescribed in the area of public administration. The procedure for considering petitions, proposals and complaints is specified in the Act of 14 June 1960 – the Code of Administrative Procedure (Part VIII: Complaints and Proposals). Pursuant to Article 226 of the Code, the Council of Ministers issued the Regulation of 8 January 2002 regarding the Receipt and Processing of Complaints and Proposals.[532, 533]

g) Training

Civil service training plays a very important role in the fight against unethical behaviour in the service. The objective of training is to develop the skills of working in a group, coordination of work in the office and administration, acquaint-

532 Rozporządzenie Rady Ministrów z dnia 8 stycznia 2002 r. *w sprawie organizacji przyjmowania i rozpatrywania skarg i wniosków*, Dz. U. z 2002 r. No. 5, item 46.

533 Reports of the Supreme Audit Office from audits in government administration institutions revealed, among other things, slowness of those institutions in dealing with complaints, leaving complaints unprocessed without justification, unreliable, delayed or lacking in-depth investigations of complaints, irregularities in recording complaints. The report also disclosed handling of complaints by persons the complaints directly concerned and the limitation of seeing citizens in matters relating to complaints to the hours of work of the office. (Information on audit results regarding the preparation and implementation of the project 'Development and modernization of the Warsaw – Okęcie International Airport – Terminal 2', Ref. No. 157/2003/I/02/010/KKT; Information on audit results regarding the institutional efficiency of the General Directorate of National Roads and Motorways in terms of achieving objectives laid down by law Ref. No. 147/2008/P/07/069/KKT; Information on audit results regarding the supervision of large-scale pig farms Ref. No. 135/2007/P06106/KSR; Information on audit results regarding the provision of electricity services Ref. No. 24/2003/P02057/KGP; Information on audit results regarding police response in the Masovian Voivodeship to reports of crime and missing persons Ref. No. 179/2005/P/05/154/LWA; Information on audit results regarding the organisation and financing of activity therapy workshops – with participation in the financing of the State Fund for the Rehabilitation of People With Disabilities Ref. No. 128/2005/P/04/139/LBY), in 'Informacja o wynikach kontroli funkcjonowania systemu przyjmowania i rozpatrywania skarg w wybranych naczelnych organach administracji rządowej', Department of Public Administration, NIK, Warszawa, March 2009.

ance with uniform, high standards of work and preparation for the European partnership.[534] The training schedule of the Polish civil service has such priorities as the development of the civil service ethos and the implementation of uniform human resources management standards in the administration.[535] The training includes such topics as civil service ethos, management psychology,[536] rules of appropriate contacts with the public, standards of effective and efficient administration.[537] Training in the past, addressed to the directors-general, dealt with the changes in public administration management, prevention of anomie[538] and development of the civil service ethos, a system of motivation in the Polish civil service and quality management in Polish government administration, among others.[539] Participation in the training courses is considered as part of civil servants' duties. The courses develop not only professional skills of civil servants but also their thinking in terms of a state run by professionals; highly qualified specialists are becoming 'a source of new ideas and new forms of governance'.[540]

h) Efficient control

Consistent enforcement of accountability of officials in the form of disciplinary responsibility[541] (disciplinary responsibility applies to the conduct of civil service corps members during and after work), regulatory, criminal, material responsibility (the employee's responsibility for damage caused to the employer and to

534 *Zasady naboru i uczestnictwa w szkoleniach centralnych na rok 2001,* Civil Service Office, Department for Training and Development of the Civil Service, Warszawa 2000.

535 Sprawozdanie Szefa Służby Cywilnej o stanie służby cywilnej i o realizacji zadań tej służby na rok 2000, HCS report, Warszawa 2001, Civil Service Office (typescript).

536 In 2000, including the training of trainers and studies in strategic management for directors-general, 1237 members of the civil service corps completed their training. In 2001–1286 persons.

537 Sprawozdanie Szefa Służby Cywilnej, 2001, op. cit.; Sprawozdanie Szefa Służby Cywilnej o stanie służby cywilnej i o realizacji zadań tej służby na rok 2001. Warszawa 2002, Civil Service Office (typescript).

538 Anomie – the state of society resulting from the breakdown of generally accepted standards of conduct; the situation in which moral standards, patterns of behaviour are vague, contradictory or inapplicable; disorientation, alienation.

539 Sprawozdanie Szefa Służby Cywilnej, 2002, op. cit.

540 G. Guy Peters, *The Politics of Bureaucracy*, London: Routledge, 2001.

541 Rozporządzenie Prezesa Rady Ministrów z dnia 9 kwietnia 2009 r. *w sprawie postępowania wyjaśniającego i postępowania dyscyplinarnego w służbie cywilnej,* [Regulation of the Prime Minister of 9 April 2009 on the investigation and disciplinary procedure in the civil service], Dz. U. No. 60, item 493.

company property entrusted to him/her) and liability for breach of discipline regarding public finances.

One of the control measures of civil service integrity is disciplinary responsibility of civil service members for abuse of powers or breach of duties. Performing one's tasks in an unreliable way should always be associated with having to bear disciplinary responsibility.

Disciplinary proceedings were introduced by the Act on the State Civil Service of 17 February 1922 mentioned earlier. A civil servant could be expelled from the service following the decision of a disciplinary board.

A detailed organisation of disciplinary authorities and disciplinary proceedings was set down under the Act on the Organisation of Disciplinary Authorities and Disciplinary Proceedings Against State Officials dated 17 February 1922.[542] Disciplinary penalties were imposed by the disciplinary board. In 1932, the President of the Second Polish Republic issued the regulation that led to the setting up of disciplinary boards and created the position of disciplinary prosecutor and defence counsel.[543]

Disciplinary penalties imposed on officials at the time consisted of a reprimand or deduction of 1 to 3 years from years of service. In disciplinary matters regarding civil service corps members, disciplinary committees were set up: of first instance – the office disciplinary board, its members appointed by the director-general of office, and of second instance – the High Disciplinary Board, its members appointed from among the civil servants by the Prime Minister at the request of the Head of the Civil Service.[544]

The subject of disciplinary proceedings (legal status as on 30 March 2010) is any breach of duty by civil service corps members. The penalisation of disciplinary misconduct ceases after 4 years from the time of its commitment.[545] Unfortunately, the legislator failed to directly specify acts subject to disciplinary responsibility and the duties set down in the Act are of a general nature. Consequently, it is up to the director-general to assess whether or not an act or a failure

---

542 *O organizacji władz dyscyplinarnych i postępowaniu dyscyplinarnym przeciwko funkcjonariuszom państwowym* z 17 lutego 1922 roku, Dz. U. No. 21 item 165.

543 M. Jełowicki, *Instytucje prawa urzędniczego,* Warszawa 1986, p. 22.

544 Ustawa z dnia 17 lutego 1922 r. *o państwowej służbie cywilnej*, [State Civil Service Act of 17 Feb. 1922], Art. 72 et seq.

545 Under the Civil Service Act of 24 Aug. 2006 duration of disciplinary proceedings is limited to two years from their commencement.

to act by a civil service corps member is an infringement of the obligations of a civil service corps member.[546]

Disciplinary penalties are varied. Those that apply to civil servants are: a warning, reprimand, denial of promotion to a higher service rank for a period of two years, a decrease in basic salary – by a maximum of 25% – for a period of up to 6 months, a downgrading in civil service rank, expulsion from the civil service.[547] Possible penalties that can be applied to civil service employees are: a warning, reprimand, a decrease in basic salary – by a maximum of 25% – for a period of up to 6 months, a downgrading in civil service rank, expulsion from work in the office.[548] In accordance with the Act of 21November 2008, the list of penalties is exhaustive, based on the following principles: incompatibility (only one penalty can be imposed on the corps member once his/her guilt is proven), appropriateness (the punishment must be commensurate with the guilt) and scaling (from the most lenient to the most severe penalty).[549]

i) Practical examples of combating dysfunctions

There are also some practical examples of combating unethical behaviour, collected from the experience of various countries. These include:

- Blacklisting – registering dishonest contractors who undermine principles of business ethics, previously cooperating with institutions where members of the civil service corps are working, and defaulting on contracts in the past.
- Civil measures – reserved for those applying for a contract and who themselves have suffered due to corrupt practices. They provide the possibility of action against those who give bribes and thus cause losses to those who do not. Such civil action allows victims to take over the initiative without having to wait for the initiation of appropriate administrative investigative procedures.
- 'Whistle-blowers' – employees working in enterprises, where corrupt practices are widespread, inform relevant authorities or the public about committed offences and are provided legal protection against reprisals in their workplace or being dismissed from work, altogether.

546 W. Drobny, M. Mazuryk and P. Zuzankiewicz, *Ustawa o służbie cywilnej*, commentary, Warszawa 2010, p. 447.

547 Civil Service Act of 21 Nov. 2008, Art. 114.1.

548 Ibid., Art. 114.2.

549 Drobny, Mazuryk and Zuzankiewicz, op. cit., pp. 450–451.

- Anti-corruption commitments, or written statements, in which all applicants for a contract agree to refrain from fraudulent acts in order to secure the contract. Violation of the commitment entails legal penalties and sanctions.[550]
- 'Mystery shopping /client' – control regime of persons and organisational structures under the name of 'Mystery Shopping' (MS), which involves the monitoring and assessment of organisational procedures by using 'fronts' who pretend to be customers in an office or organisational unit of city authorities, institutions, public institutions, self-government entities and check on the quality of services and conditions of their delivery. Their task involves testing different types of administrative acts and services (e.g. examination of tendering procedures, the aim of which is to assess implementation of principles of transparency, equality and competitiveness in public procurement procedures), assessing access to information, customer service standards and contact standards followed in customer-office/office-customer relations through internet pages.
- Local civil groups – watchdog organisations monitoring local authorities, providing advice on anticorruption, access to information on the activities of public administration, civic education and social action, such as: 'Transparent Poland'.
- The use of new information technologies, for example, through electronic auctions, access of citizens to information on the activities of public administration on-line.

To counter the dysfunctions, either clear rules have to be adopted to prevent politicians from aptly compensating a narrow group of their supporters at the expense of public resources or, using an administrative decision, political positions have to be separated from positions in the administration. At the same time, recruitment and promotion of officials should be based solely on objective criteria of merit, and clear rules should be established for making public decisions on the basis of impartiality and the good of all citizens.[551]

The 'simplest' solution to the problems described in this chapter which also concern the civil service is, first of all, a review of legislation so as to eliminate legal arrangements that contribute to the spread of the various problems and wrongdoings described above; secondly, public education; and thirdly, consistent prosecution and punishment of those found guilty.

---

550 For example, five South Korean firms were banned from taking part in international tenders for a period of 5 years for violation of the agreement.

551 T. G. Grosse, op. cit., p. 19.

And finally, the conclusion of Michał Kulesza who argues that moral standards cannot be enforced by law, democratic mechanisms or under pressure from the media: 'you either have them or you don't, because it's an element of class – the class of a person, of an official, of a politician (…). If we can make the hypothesis that the level of public morality in Poland is low, it means that (…) it is very difficult to start out from this level as it requires extremely tough, repressive measures; but, due to the advancement of our civilisation, now is not the time for repression.'[552]

552 M. Kulesza: 'Reforma samorządu terytorialnego. Bariery antykorupcyjne', in A. Dylus, A. Rudowski and M. Zaborski (eds.), *Korupcja. Oblicza, uwarunkowania, przeciwdziałanie*, Ossolineum Wrocław, Warszawa, Kraków 2006, p. 38.

# Conclusion

The development of the civil service in Poland has been overcome by obstacles and challenges for a long time. The ongoing debates concerning its operation and the choice of a model to emulate are indicative of the importance politicians, the media and public opinion attach to the civil service. Many opinion-making circles in Poland take the view that it is impossible to build democratic standards in this country without the civil service.

However, the civil service has failed to consolidate in Poland. Despite its historical traditions, there has not been a single political party to date which would favour its development. The political debates the civil service stokes invariably prove to be emotional and sterile; they abound in political bartering – the main actors are usually amateurs incapable of contributing quality solutions.

The conditions under which the Polish civil service has operated can be analysed in a historical and systemic context. The historical perspective reveals the cause of some of the difficulties affecting the civil service, for example, the fact that Poles harbour an ambivalent attitude towards the state is most often attributed to the 18th century partitions and the time of People's Poland – neither of which was conducive to building confidence in state authorities and public administration. The Third Republic which followed did little to improve the distrust and reluctance stirred by state power and its officials. In contrast, systemic changes, the growing importance of knowledge and information technology, modernisation and Poland's EU membership have undoubtedly exerted a favourable impact on civil service development.

Other problems plaguing the Polish civil service are generated by the way the civil service is organised and by ethical issues. Although treated as minor complications by policy-makers, many of them affect the way the civil service functions and is perceived by members of the public, amongst them are: incompetence, arrogance, mobbing, sexual harassment, conflict of interest, nepotism, cronyism and sex discrimination.

The biggest barrier to growth of the Polish civil service, however, is its excessive politicisation. Political pressure leads to the instrumental treatment of the civil service and the spoils system, a practice in which the political party winning the election rewards its active supporters with government jobs. Political interference in the workings of the civil service has a degenerative influence, adversely affecting the quality and image of the service, its performance and social prestige.

The never-ending reforms of the civil service pressed for by subsequent governments seem to originate from political calculations and politicians' inability to understand the nature of a law-governed democratic state. More often than not, unaware of the standards binding in the modern civil service, politicians seek to implement their political priorities 'despite' or 'bypassing' the civil servants. In political debates they emphasise their government's achievements while depreciating the role of civil servants. The latter become frustrated with the lack of recognition which, coupled with the scarcity of positive role-models and means of work and career planning, represents another impediment to the improvement of the civil service. On top of this, the civil service must make do with a low budget for training, insufficient knowledge of new HR management methods and frequent restructuring – which all hamper its development.

Some of the difficulties the civil service faces in Poland are related to the operation of political cabinets in individual ministries of the government administration. In a misguided move, political cabinets were removed from the ambit of the Civil Service Act thus undermining the stability of employment of cabinet members, opening them to the considerable risk from the conflict of interest and corruption. The particular susceptibility of cabinet members to unlawful or unethical behaviour results from fears about their future in case a minister or another government member is dismissed. The relationship between those employed in political cabinets and civil service corps members is a very complex one. Although both parties cooperate in drafting policies, cabinet members (if it only lies in their self-interest) are in a position to exert pressure on civil servants – uncertain of their fate and overly dependent on political decision-makers.

A standardization of the services provided by Polish public administration seems too heavy a task to implement for politicians and civil servants alike, although in the UK and the Netherlands citizens have had their Citizens Charter since the early 1990s. However, the discussion on this subject in Poland has largely been inconclusive and made no dents in the indifference surrounding the subject. One of the reasons seems to be the fact that the Charter lists the basic principles guiding public service and promises to deliver goods which the Polish state is as yet unable to provide. The main items in this broad category include: defining and making public the standards of service to be expected by the citizens; publishing information on the practice of applying these standards; taking into account citizens' opinions in setting these standards; giving the citizens a choice wherever possible; adopting a kind and helpful attitude towards citizens;

ensuring easy to follow complaints and recourse mechanisms; and providing the most effective delivery of public services. Finally, in the political sense, the Citizen's Charter represents a change of attitude on the part of the government towards the citizens – an understanding that they are both taxpayers and recipients of services provided by the state.

# Bibliography


Konstytucja Rzeczypospolitej Polskiej z dnia 2 kwietnia 1997 r. (Dz. U. Nr 78, poz. 483).

Ustawa z dnia 17 lutego 1922 roku *O organizacji władz dyscyplinarnych i postępowaniu dyscyplinarnym przeciwko funkcjonariuszom państwowym* (Dz. U. Nr 21 poz. 165).

Ustawa z dnia 17 lutego 1922 r. *o państwowej służbie cywilnej* (Dz. U. R. P. Nr 21, poz. 164 ze zm.).

Ustawa z dnia 28 lipca 1922 r. *w przedmiocie zmian w ustawie z dnia 17 lutego 1922r. o państwowej służbie cywilnej.* (Dz. U. 1925 nr 129 poz. 920).

Ustawa z dnia 21 marca 1924 r. *w przedmiocie zmian niektórych postanowień ustawy o państwowej służbie cywilnej.* (Dz. U. 1924 nr 29 poz. 286).

Ustawa z dnia 31 marca 1925 r. *o zmianie niektórych postanowień ustawy o państwowej służbie cywilnej.* (Dz. U. 1925 nr 43 poz. 294).

Ustawa z dnia 22 grudnia 1925 r. *zmieniająca niektóre postanowienia ustawy z dnia 17 lutego 1922 r. o państwowej służbie cywilnej.* (Dz. U. 1925 nr 129 poz. 920).

Ustawa z dnia 4 marca 1939 r. *o zmianie ustawy o państwowej służbie cywilnej.* (Dz. U. 1939 nr 18 poz. 107).

Ustawa z dnia 16 września 1982 r. *o pracownikach urzędów państwowych* (Dz. U. Nr 31, poz. 214 z istotnymi zmianami w 1994 r. Dz. U. 1994, nr 136, poz. 704).

Ustawa z dnia 14 czerwca 1991 r. *o Krajowej Szkole Administracji Publicznej (*Dz. U. z 1991 r. Nr 63, poz. 266 ze zm.).

Ustawa z dnia 2 grudnia 1994 r. *o zmianie ustawy o pracownikach urzędów państwowych z dnia 16 września 1982 r.* (Dz. U. Nr 136, poz. 704).

Ustawa z dnia 5 lipca 1996 r. *o służbie cywilnej (*Dz. U. Nr 89, poz. 402; z 1997 r. Nr 106, poz. 679; z 1998 r. Nr 58, poz. 366 i Nr 162, poz. 1126).

Ustawa z dnia 26 czerwca 1974 r. (Kodeks pracy Dz. U. z 1998 r., Nr 21, poz. 94 ze zm.).

Ustawa z dnia 18 grudnia 1998 r. *o służbie cywilnej* (Dz. U. z 1999 r. Nr 49, poz. 483 ze zm.).

Ustawa z dnia 6 września 2001 r. *o dostępie do informacji publicznej.* (Dz. U. nr 112 poz. 1198 ze zm.).

Ustawa z dnia 24 sierpnia 2006 r. *o służbie cywilnej* (Dz. U. z 2006 r. Nr 170, poz. 1218 ze zm.).

Ustawa z dnia 24 sierpnia 2006 r. *o państwowym zasobie kadrowym i wysokich stanowiskach państwowych* (Dz. U. z 2006 Nr 170, poz. 1217 ze zm.).

Ustawa z dnia 11 maja 2007 o zmianie ustawy *o państwowym zasobie kadrowym i wysokich stanowiskach państwowych oraz o zmianie niektórych innych ustaw.* (Dz. U. Nr 123, poz. 847).

Ustawa z dnia 21 listopada 2008 r. *o służbie cywilnej*. (Dz. U. Nr 227 poz. 505).

Ustawa z dnia 27 sierpnia 2009 r. *o finansach publicznych* (Dz. U Nr 157, poz. 1240).

Ustawa z dnia 5 sierpnia 2010 r. *o ochronie informacji niejawnych,* (Dz. U., Nr 182, poz. 1128).

Rozporządzenie Rady Ministrów z dnia 16 stycznia 1925 r. *o służbie przygotowawczej i egzaminie kandydatów na stanowiska II kategorji w państwowej służbie administracyjnej*. (Dz. U. Nr 16, poz. 103.

Rozporządzenie Rady Ministrów z dnia 19 grudnia 1933 r. o ustanowieniu tabeli stanowisk we władzach, urzędach, zakładach i instytucjach państwowych. Dz. U. 1993, Nr 102, poz. 780.Rozporządzenie Prezydenta Rzeczypospolitej z 28 października 1933 roku *o uposażeniu funkcjonariuszy państwowych.* (Dz. U. Nr 86, poz. 663).Rozporządzenie Prezesa Rady Ministrów z dnia 9 kwietnia 2009 r. *w sprawie wynagrodzenia członków Wyższej Komisji Dyscyplinarnej Służby Cywilnej, komisji dyscyplinarnych oraz rzeczników dyscyplinarnych i ich zastępców.* (Dz. U. Nr 60, poz. 492).

Rozporządzenie Prezesa Rady Ministrów z dnia 9 kwietnia 2009 r. *w sprawie wynagrodzenia członków Rady Służby Cywilnej.* (Dz. U. Nr 60, poz. 491).

Rozporządzenie Prezesa Rady Ministrów z dnia 9 kwietnia 2009 r. *w sprawie postępowania wyjaśniającego i postępowania dyscyplinarnego w służbie cywilnej.* (Dz. U. Nr 60, poz. 493).

Rozporządzenie Prezesa Rady Ministrów z dnia 23 kwietnia 2009 r. *w sprawie rodzajów dokumentów potwierdzających znajomość języka polskiego przez osoby nieposiadające obywatelstwa polskiego, ubiegającego się o zatrudnienie w służbie cywilnej.* (Dz. U. Nr 64, poz. 539).

Rozporządzenie Prezesa Rady Ministrów z dnia 8 maja 2009 r. *w sprawie warunków i sposobu przeprowadzania ocen okresowych członków korpusu służby cywilnej* (Dz. U. nr 74, poz. 633).

Rozporządzenie Prezesa Rady Ministrów z dnia 9 maja 2009 r. *w sprawie świadczeń przysługujących urzędnikowi służby cywilnej przeniesionemu do pracy w innej miejscowości.* (Dz. U. Nr 93, poz. 763).

Rozporządzenie Prezesa Rady Ministrów z dnia 8 czerwca 2009 r. *w sprawie świadczeń przysługujących urzędnikowi służby cywilnej przeniesionemu do pracy w innej miejscowości.* (Dz. U. Nr 93, poz. 763).

Rozporządzenie Prezesa Rady Ministrów z dnia 15 czerwca 2009 r. *w sprawie szczegółowych warunków i sposobu dokonywania pierwszej oceny w służbie cywilnej.* Dz. U. Nr 94 poz. 77 Rozporządzenie Prezesa Rady Ministrów z dnia 16 grudnia 2009 r. *w sprawie sposobu przeprowadzania postępowania kwalifikacyjnego w służbie cywilnej* (Dz. U. nr 218, poz. 1695).

Wyrok Trybunału Konstytucyjnego z dnia 28 kwietnia 1999 r. sygn. Akt K 3/99 (Monitor Polski z dnia 6 maja 1999 r., Nr 16, poz. 227).

Wyrok Trybunału Konstytucyjnego z dnia 10 kwietnia 2002 r., sygn. Akt K. 26/00 (Dz. U. Nr 56, poz. 517).

Wyrok Trybunału Konstytucyjnego z dnia 12 grudnia 2002 r. Sygn. Akt K. 9/02. (Dz. U. Nr 238, poz. 2025).Wyrok Trybunału Konstytucyjnego z dnia 16 czerwca 2003 r. Sygn. Akt K 52/02. (Dz. U. Nr 110, poz. 1059).

Statut Krajowej Szkoły Administracji Publicznej nadany Rozporządzeniem Prezesa Rady Ministrów z dnia 7 października 1999 r. (Dz. U. nr 82, poz. 920 ze zm.).

Rekomendacja Komitetu Ministrów Rady Europy z dnia 11 maja 2000 r. w sprawie kodeksu postępowania urzędników w służbie publicznej. Nr R/2000/10.

Zalecenie nr R (2000) 6 przez Komitet Ministrów dla państw członkowskich on the status of public officials in Europe w sprawie statusu funkcjonariuszy publicznych w Europie. *(Adopted by the Committee of Ministers on 24 February 2000* Przyjęte przez Komitet Ministrów w dniu 24 lutego 2000 at the 699 th meeting of the Ministers' Deputies) na 699 th posiedzeniu Komitetu Delegatów Ministrów.

Zalecenie nr Rec(2007)7 Komitetu Ministrów Rady Europy dla państw członkowskich w sprawie dobrej administracji.

Traktat ustanawiający Konstytucję dla Europy, Dz. U. C 310 z 16 grudnia 2004. Traktat Unii Europejskiej, Dz. U. z 2004 r., Nr 90, poz. 864/30.

Konwencja UE z 26 maja 1997 r. dotyczącą zwalczania korupcji wśród urzędników Wspólnot Europejskich lub urzędników państw członkowskich Unii Europejskiej. Dz. Urz. WE nr C 195, 07.06.25.

Wspólne działanie nr 98/742/JHA z 22 grudnia 1998, przyjęte przez Radę Unii Europejskiej na mocy Traktatu o Unii Europejskiej, w sprawie korupcji w sektorze prywatnym. Dz. Urz. WE nr L 358, 98.12.31.

Decyzja Rady z 25 maja 1999 dotycząca zasad i warunków dochodzeń wewnętrznych w odniesieniu do przeciwdziałania nadużyciom finansowym, korupcji i wszelkim nielegalnym działaniom godzącym w interesy Wspólnoty. 1999/394/WE.

Decyzja Komisji dotycząca zasad i warunków dochodzeń wewnętrznych w odniesieniu do przeciwdziałania nadużyciom finansowym, korupcji i wszelkim nielegalnym działaniom godzącym w interesy Wspólnoty. Notyfikowana jako dokument nr SEC (1999) 802.

Recommendation No. R(2000) 13 of the Committee of Ministers to member states on a European policy on access to archives. https://wcd.coe.int; Rekomendacja No. R (2000) 13 w sprawie europejskiej polityki dostępu do archiwów Komitetu Ministrów państw członkowskich w sprawie europejskiej polityki dostępu do archiwów z dnia 13 lipca 2000 r.

*Charter of Fundamental Rights of the European Union.* Official Journal of the European Communities. 18.12. 2000/C 364/01.

Zarządzenie nr 70 Prezesa Rady Ministrów z dnia 6 października 2011 roku *w sprawie wytycznych w zakresie przestrzegania zasad służby cywilnej oraz w sprawie zasad etyki korpusu służby cywilnej*, MP Nr 93, poz. 953.

Zarządzenie nr 16 Ministra Spraw Zagranicznych z dnia 31 lipca 2009 r. w sprawie służbowych kart płatniczych używanych w Ministerstwie Spraw Zagranicznych, placówkach zagranicznych oraz w Zarządzie Obsługi. http://www.infor.pl/dzienniki-urzedowe/ministra-spraw-zagranicznych,rok,2009,nr,4/poz,49,zarzadzenie-nr-16-ministra-spraw-zagranicznych.

Załącznik do Zarządzenia Nr 3 Szefa Służby Cywilnej z 30 maja 2012 r. *w sprawie standardów zarządzania zasobami ludzkimi w służbie cywilnej.*

Komunikat Nr 23 Ministra Finansów z dnia 16 grudnia 2009 r. Dz. U. Min. Fin. Nr 15, poz. 84.

*Administracja i polityka. Proces decyzyjny w administracji publicznej* pod red. Ludwika Habudy. Wrocław 2000.

*Administracja publiczna. Wyzwania w dobie integracji europejskiej*, pod red. J. Czputowicza, Warszawa 2008.

*Administracja publiczna.* pod red. A. Błaś, J. Boć, J. Jeżewski Kolonia Limited 2003.

Antoszewski A., *Grupy interesu w systemie politycznym.* W: *Grupy interesu. Teorie i działanie*, pod red. Z. Machelskiego i L. Rubisza, Toruń 2003.

*Barlett T. K., Gender and law: theory, doctrine and commentary.* New York 1998.

*Bauman Z., Szanse etyki w zglobalizowanym świecie.* Kraków 2007.

*Bechowska-Gebhardt A., Stalewski T., Patologia zarządzania personelem.* Warszawa 2004.

*Biurokracja*, pod red. J. Łukaszewicza, Rzeszów 2007.

*Biurokracja. Fenomen władzy politycznej w strukturach administracyjnych*, pod red. K. Zuby, Toruń 2007.

*Bogucka I., Pietrzykowski T., Etyka w administracji publicznej*, Warszawa 2009.

*Bossaert D., Demmke Ch., Służba cywilna w państwach akcesyjnych. Tendencje i wpływ procesów integracyjnych*, Łódź 2003.

*Bugdol M., Zarządzanie jakością w urzędach administracji publicznej*, Warszawa 2008.

*Brunetko K., Służba cywilna w III RP: punkty krytyczne*, Warszawa 2003, www.batory.org.pl/korupcja.

*Chakowski M., Mobbing – aspekty prawne*. Warszawa 2005.

*Cieślak Z., Jagielski J., Rączka K., Komentarz do ustawy o służbie cywilnej*, Warszawa 1998.

*Classics of Administrative Ethics*, ed. W. Bruce, University of Illinois At Springfield 2001.

*Czuchnowski W., Polityka prorodzinna po polsku. Sami swoi na państwowym*. Gazeta Wyborcza z 30 lipca 2012 r.

*Czuchnowski W., Urzędy, park, TBS-y*, Gazeta Wyborcza 31 lipca 2012 r.,

*Demmke Ch., Civil Services Between Tradition and Reform*, EIPA, Maastricht 2004.

*Demmke Ch., Are Civil Servants Different Because They Are Civil Servants? Who Are The Civil Servants- And How?*, European Institute of Public Administration, Maastricht 2005.

*Długosz D., Kadry w administracji publicznej*, w: *Administracja publiczna*, pod red. J. Hausnera, Warszawa 2008.

*Długosz D., Neutralność polityczna służby cywilnej*, w: *Służba cywilna – wybrane zagadnienia*, Biuro Informacji i Dokumentacji Senackiej Kancelarii Senatu. Warszawa, listopad 2000.

*Dobrowolski Z., Korupcja w życiu publicznym*. Zielona Góra 2001.

*Drobny W., Mazuryk M., Zuzankiewicz P., Ustawa o służbie cywilnej. Komentarz*, Warszawa 2010.

*Drobny W., Mazuryk M., Zuzankiewicz P., ABC służby cywilnej*, Warszawa 2010.

*Drucker P., Praktyka zarządzania*, tłum. T. Basiuk, Z. Broniarek, J. Gołębiewski, Warszawa 1992.

*Dylus A., Kulturowe uwarunkowania korupcji. Doświadczenia Polski*. W: *Korupcja. Oblicza, uwarunkowania, przeciwdziałanie*, pod red. A. Dylus, A. Rudowski, M. Zaborski, Ossolineum Wrocław, Warszawa, Kraków 2006.

*Etos urzędnika*, pod red. D. Bąka, Warszawa 2007.

*Etyka w służbie cywilnej*, Warszawa 1995.

*Fitzgerald F. L., Sexual harassment: the definition and measurement of a construct"* w: *Ivory power: sexual harassment on campus.* ed. M. A. Paludi, University of New York Press, Albany 1990.

*Fukuyama F., Budowanie państwa. Władza i ład międzynarodowy w XXI wieku.* Poznań 2005.

*Galor Z., Stępień J., Pojęcie i regionalne determinanty lumpen-pracy w gospodarce polskiej okresu transformacji.* W: *Strategia rozwoju społecznej gospodarki rynkowej w Polsce.* Pod red. S. Patrycki, Lublin 2002.

*Grosse G. T., Działania antykorupcyjne w państwach członkowskich OECD.* Florencja 2000.

*Hausner J., Zarządzanie publiczne,* Warszawa 2008.

*Herbut R., Przesłanki procesu reformowania administracji publicznej,* w: *Administracja i polityka. Administracja publiczna w procesie przemian,* Pod red. A. Ferensa, I. Macek, Wrocław 2002.

*Heywood A., Politologia.* Warszawa 2006.

*Heywood P., Meyer-Sahling J- H., Występowanie stref korupcji w zarządzaniu polską administracją rządową,* Warszawa 2008.

*Hirygoyen F. M., Molestowanie moralne.* tłum. J. Cackowska-Demirian, Poznań 2002.

*Huberts L., Kaptein M., Lasthuizen K., Leadership and Integrity Violations at Work: A Study on the Perceived Impact of Leadership Behaviour on Integrity Violations within the Dutch Police Force,* Paper for IRSPM VIII 2004, Budapest, March 31 - April 2, 2004, w: *Ethics in the Public Service of the European Union Member States under the Irish Presidency* 2004, Ch. Demmke, D. Bossaert, EIPA, January to June 2004.

*Itrich-Drabarek J., Uwarunkowania, standardy i kierunki zmian służby cywilnej w Polsce na tle europejskim,* Warszawa 2010.

*Itrich-Drabarek J., The Legal Foundations and the Quality and Ethical Standard of the Polish Civil Servic,* in: *Civil service in Poland,* ed. J. Itrich-Drabarek, K. Mroczka, Ł. Świetlikowski, Warszawa 2012.

*Itrich-Drabarek J., The civil service in Central and Eastern Europe*, *Służba cywilna w Europie-Środkowo-Wschodniej*, wydawnictwo dwujęzyczne, Warszawa 2013.

*Izdebski H., Kulesza M., Administracja publiczna – zagadnienia ogólne,* Warszawa 2000.

*Jackiewicz A., Prawo do dobrej administracji jako standard europejski,* Toruń 2008.

*Jagielski J., Kontrola administracji publicznej,* Warszawa 2007.

*Jagielski J., Rączka K., Komentarz do ustawy o służbie cywilnej,* Warszawa 2001.

*Jagielski J., Rączka K., Ustawa o służbie cywilnej, Komentarz,* Warszawa 2010.

*Jaśkowska M., Dostęp do informacji publicznych,* Toruń 2002.

*Jełowicki M., Instytucje prawa urzędniczego.* Warszawa 1986.

*Kamiński T., Etos służby – obowiązek czy heroizm?* w: *Wartości społeczne w służbie publicznej,* pod red. L. Dziewięckiej-Bokun, J. Kędzior, Toruń 2009.

*Kmiecik-Baran K., Mobbing – zagrożenie współczesnego miejsca pracy,* Gdańsk 2004.

*Kojder A., Korupcja – mechanizmy i strategie przeciwdziałania.* Warszawa 1992.

*Kojder A., Godność i siła prawa.* Warszawa 1995.

*Kratz J. H., Mobbing. Rozpoznawanie, reagowanie, zapobieganie.* Gliwice 2007.

*Kudrycka B., Dylematy urzędników administracji publicznej,* Białystok 1995.

*Kudrycka B., Neutralność polityczna urzędników,* Warszawa 1998.

*Kudrycka B., Kodeks etyki służby cywilnej na tle reform administracji publicznej,* w: *Stosunki pracy w służbie cywilnej,* Białystok 2001.

*Kudrycka B., Rozwój kadr administracji publicznej,* Białystok 2001.

*Kulesza M., Reforma administracji publicznej w Polsce – materiały szkoleniowe,* KPRM, Warszawa, I-II 1999.

*Kulesza M., Reforma samorządu terytorialnego. Bariery antykorupcyjne.* W: *Korupcja. Oblicza, uwarunkowania, przeciwdziałanie,* pod red. A. Dylus, A. Rudowski, M. Zaborski, Ossolineum Wrocław, Warszawa, Kraków 2006.

*Małajny R., Neutralność a bezstronność światopoglądowa państwa,* w: *Bezstronność, religijna, światopoglądowa i filozoficzna władz Rzeczypospolitej polskiej,* pod red. T. Zieliński, Warszawa 2009.

*Manowce polskiej prywatyzacji.* pod red. M. Jarosz, Warszawa 2001.

*Marciniak J., Przeciwdziałanie dyskryminacji w zatrudnieniu. Jak w praktyce zwalczać mobbing i inne formy dyskryminacji.* Ostrołęka 2004.

*Masłyk-Musiał E., Społeczeństwo i organizacje: socjologia organizacji i zarządzania,* Lublin 1999.

*Mączak A., Rządzący i rządzeni.* Warszawa 1986.

*Mills C., Elita władzy.* Warszawa 1961.

*Moralność i profesjonalizm. Spór o pozycję etyk zawodowych,* pod red. W. Galewicz, Kraków 2010.

*Myśliwiec G., Elementy etyki gospodarowania.* Warszawa 1996.

*Odpowiedzialność urzędnika administracji publicznej*, pod red. J. Borkowska, Warszawa 2009.

*O sprawności i niesprawności organizacji*, pod red. J. Kurnala, Warszawa 1972.

*Osborne D., Gaebler T., Rządzić inaczej. Jak duch przedsiębiorczości przenika i przekształca administrację publiczną*. Przeł. A. Jankowski, Poznań 2005.

*Page C. E., Political Authority and Bureaucratic Power. A Comparative Analysis*. Prentice Hall 1992.

*Pastwa J., Służba cywilna – pytania i odpowiedzi*. Warszawa 1999.

*Peter J. L., Hull R., Zasada Petera. Dlaczego wszystko idzie na opak*. Warszawa 1975.

*Peters G., Administracja publiczna w systemie politycznym*. Warszawa 1999.

*Peters G., Pierre J., Politicization of the Civil Service in Comparative Perspective*. Routledge 2004.

*Pilipiec S., Szreniawski P., Socjologia administracji*, Lublin 2008.

*Pope J., Rzetelność życia publicznego. Metody zapobiegania korupcji*. Warszawa 1999.

*Postawy członków korpusu służby cywilnej wobec kwestii etycznych. Raport z badań*, opr. C. Trutkowski, Warszawa 2004.

*Pracownicy administracji w PRL*, pod red. J. Łętowski, Ossolineum 1984.

*Prawo administracyjne – część ustrojowa*, praca zbiorowa pod red. Z. Niewiadomskiego, Warszawa 2002.

*Prawo urzędnicze*, pod red. Liszcz T., Borek-Buchajczyk R., Perdeus W., Lublin 2005.

*Proces decyzyjny w administracji publicznej*. pod red. L. Habudy, Wrocław 2000.

*Profesjonalizm w administracji publicznej*. Pod red. A. Dębickiej, M. Dmochowskiego, B. Kudryckiej, Białystok 2004.

*Public management reforms in Central and Eastern Europe*, ed. G. Bouckaert, Bratislava 2008.

*Przybyszewski R., Administracja publiczna wobec przemian społeczno-ekonomicznych epoki informacyjne*, Toruń 2009.

*Rau Z., Przestępczość zorganizowana w Polsce i jej zwalczanie*. Kraków 2002.

*Rose – Ackerman S., Korupcja i rządy*. Warszawa 2001.

*Rydlewski G., Służba cywilna w Polsce na tle innych rozwiązań ustrojowych*, Warszawa 2001.

*Rydlewski G., Polityka i administracja w rządach państw członkowskich Unii Europejskiej*, Warszawa 2006.

*Rydlewski G., Systemy administracji publicznej w państwach członkowskich Unii Europejskiej*. Warszawa 2007.

*Sennet R.,: Upadek człowieka publicznego*. Warszawa 2009.

*Sitkowska K., Służba cywilna w nowym ustawodawstwie*. Toruń 1998.

*Sinkowska L., Status prawny członka korpusu służby cywilnej*. Toruń 2002.

*Skrzydło W., Konstytucja Rzeczypospolitej Polskiej. Komentarz*, Warszawa 2007.

*Służba cywilna a etyka w życiu publicznym*. Pod red. J. Jacki, Warszawa 1996.

*Smyk G., Korpus urzędników cywilnych w guberniach Królestwa Polskiego w latach 1867–1915*, Lublin 2004.

*Sobiecki E., Status urzędnika administracji publicznej*. Lublin 2003.

*Staniszkis J., Zwierzę niepolityczne*. Komorów 2003.

*Stelina J., Prawo urzędnicze*. Warszawa 2009.

*Stypiński J., O zawodzie urzędnika*. Warszawa 1928.

*Such H. M., Wojciechowicz J., Dybuła M., Korupcja w Polsce*. Bank Światowy, Warszawa 1999.

*Suwaj J. P., Gwarancje bezstronności organów administracji publicznej w postępowaniu administracyjnym*. Kolonia Limited 2004.

*Szewczyk K.: Zatrudnienie w służbie cywilnej*. Bydgoszcz-Katowice 2006.

*Szczerski K., Porządki biurokratyczne*, Kraków 2004.

*Śledzińska-Simon A., Prawa polityczne urzędników*, Warszawa 2010.

*Środa M., Wstęp* do wydania polskiego książki Susan Rose-Ackerman: *Korupcja i rządy*. Warszawa 2001.

*Świątkiewicz J., Europejski Kodeks Dobrej Administracji*. Warszawa 2002.

*Świątkowski A., Komentarz do pragmatyki urzędniczej*, Warszawa 1988.

*Tarchalski K., Korupcja i przywilej. Zarys teorii i praktyki*. Warszawa 2000.

*Ura E., Prawo urzędnicze*. Warszawa 2010.

*Ura E., Służba cywilna w Polsce*. w: *Polska lat dziewięćdziesiątych, przemiany państwa i prawa*. Lublin 1998.

*Ura E., Wyższe stanowiska w służbie publicznej*. w: *Prawo, Administracja, Policja. Księga Pamiątkowa W. Bednarka*, Olsztyn 2006.

*Urzędnik w administracji publicznej*, pod red. B. Sprengiel, A. Strzelecki, Włocławek 2005.

*Uslaner E., The moral foundations of Trust*. Cambridge 2002.

*M. Walzer: Sfery sprawiedliwości. Obrona pluralizmu i równości*. Warszawa 2007.

*Wartościowanie pracy w służbie cywilnej*, pod red. T. Rostkowski, W. Zieliński, Kraków 2008.

Weber M., *Gospodarka i społeczeństwo. Zarys socjologii rozumiejącej.* przeł. D. Lachowska, Warszawa 2002.

Weber M., *Polityka jako zawód i powołanie*, przeł. A. Kopacki, P. Dybel, Warszawa–Kraków 1998.

*Władza, przywilej, korupcja*, pod red. M. Jarosz, Warszawa 2004.

*Zagadnienia prawne stosunków pracy w administracji państwowej*, pod red. W. Piotrowskiego, Poznań 1981.Zieleniewski Z.: *Prawo urzędnicze*. Kraków 1937.

Zieliński E., *Administracja rządowa w Polsce*. Warszawa 2001.

Arcimowicz J., *Kobiety w służbie państwa – rzecz o korpusie służby cywilnej w Polsce*. Societas/Communitas 2008, nr 2(6).

Bida A.: *Po co komu służba cywilna?* Rzeczpospolita 1998, nr 55.

Bogucka D., *Komisja kwalifikacyjna na starcie*. Biuletyn Służby Cywilnej 1997, nr 1.

Bogucka D., *Czy lubimy urzędników?* Biuletyn Służby Cywilnej 1997, nr 1.

Brunetko B., *Bezpańskie dziecko*. Tygodnik Powszechny, 2 sierpień 2003, nr 31.

Buchacz T., Wysocki S.: *Zarządzanie jakością w administracji – europejskie wzorce, polskie doświadczenia*. Służba Cywilna 2002/2003, nr 5.

Cieślak W., Stelina J., *Definicja mobbingu oraz obowiązek przeciwdziałania temu zjawisku*. Państwo i Prawo 2004, nr 12.

Czaputowicz J., *Implikacje integracji z Unią Europejską dla polskiej służby cywilnej (europeizacja administracji publicznej)*. Służba Cywilna, 2000/2001, Nr 1.

Czaputowicz J., *Służba cywilna w Polsce – między polityzacją a profesjonalizacją*. Służba Cywilna 2004/2005, nr 9.

Czaputowicz J., *Służba cywilna a prawo do dobrej administracji*, Biuletyn Informacyjny Rady Europy 2003, nr 4.

Dąbrowski M., *Zatrudnienia i wynagrodzenia w korpusie służby cywilnej w 2011r*. Przegląd Służby Cywilnej, Maj-czerwiec 2012, nr 3.

*Definicje molestowania seksualnego*. Gazeta Wyborcza – dodatek Praca i Kariera, 2002–04–25.

Długosz D., *Służba cywilna – jaki system dla Polski*. Res Publica Nowa, Warszawa czerwiec 1998.

Długosz D., *Neutralność polityczna służby cywilnej*. W: *Służba cywilna – wybrane zagadnienia*. Opr. I. Szymanowska-Woźniak, Biuro Informacji i Dokumentacji Senackiej Kancelarii Senatu, Warszawa 2000.

*Dmochowski M., Dębicka A., Strategie antykorupcyjne jako integralny element procesu kształcenia kadr administracji publicznej.* Służba Cywilna, 2003/2004, nr 7.

*Dubowik A., Organizacja i struktura służby cywilnej w świetle ustawy z 2008 r.*, Praca i Zabezpieczenie Społeczne 2009, nr 6.

*Działocha K., Łukaszczyk A.: Nowa ustawa o służbie cywilnej.* Państwo i Prawo, listopad 2006, z. 11.

*E-urząd,* Gazeta Wyborcza z 17 listopada 2003.

*Fehler W., Kraje Unii Europejskiej w walce z korupcją.* Przegląd Europejski 2002, nr 1.

*Filipowicz W., Bolączki służby cywilnej.* w: Paragrafy i Kaptury, Warszawa 7 lipca 2004.

*Filipowicz W., Leczenie trądu nowotworem - recenzja raportu „Służba cywilna w III RP: punkty krytyczne.* Warszawa 25 czerwca 2003 r.

*Ruano de la Fuente J. M., Nowe technologie informatyczne w administracji publicznej.* Służba Cywilna, zima 2005/2006, nr 13.

*Garbacik A., Ustawa o państwowym zasobie kadrowym*, Służba Pracownicza 2006, nr 11.

*Garbacik A., Ocena kwalifikacji urzędników*, Służba Pracownicza 2007, nr 7.

*Gintowt-Jankowicz M., Krajowa Szkoła Administracji Publicznej. Cele, działalność, zamierzenia.* Biuletyn Służby Cywilnej 1997, nr 1.

*Gintowt-Jankowicz M., Rola wyższej kadry administracji publicznej - wyzwania XXI wieku.* Służba Cywilna jesień - zima 2001/2002, nr 3.

*R. Goździk: Odszkodowanie, zadośćuczynienie za mobbing w miejscu pracy.* Przegląd Sądowy 2004, nr 5.

*Góra J., Polska chora na administrację.* Gazeta Prawna, 9 marca 2004 r., nr 48.Góra J.: *Bój o widełki.* Gazeta Prawna, 28 kwietnia 2004, nr 83.

*Góra J., W służbie politykom.* Gazeta Prawna 6 kwietnia 2006.

*Góra J., Urzędnicy powoływani przez polityków.* Gazeta Prawna 7 sierpnia 2006.

*Góra J., Wyższe stanowiska będą włączone do służby cywilnej.* Gazeta Prawna 28 grudnia 2007, nr 251.

*Góra J., Powrót służby cywilnej i jej szefa.* Gazeta Prawna z 25 lutego 2008 r.

*Góra J., Służba cywilna ma służyć państwu.* Gazeta Prawna z 25 lutego 2008.

*Górski A., Ustawa o służbie cywilnej z 18 grudnia 1998 r. w świetle aktów prawnych o państwowej służbie cywilnej z lat 1918–1922.* Służba Cywilna 2000/2001, nr 1.

*Górski A., Civil servans czy politicus servance – w okresie międzywojennym i obecnie.* Służba Cywilna 2001/2002, nr 3.

*Grosse T. G., Służba cywilna w Polsce i możliwości jej rozwoju.* Służba Cywilna 2001, nr 2.

*Grosse T. G., Aspekty metodyki szkolenia w służbie cywilnej.* Biuletyn Służby Cywilnej, 1997, nr 4.

*Gulczyńska H., Urzędnicy a obywatele – profesjonalizm i podmiotowość. Zmiana zasad oraz wzajemnych relacji.* Biuletyn Służby Cywilnej, 1998, nr 10.

*Hausner J., Od idealnej biurokracji do zarządzania publicznego.* w: M. Marody: *Wymiary życia społecznego. Polska na przełomie XX i XXI wieku.* Warszawa 2002.

*Hausner J., Korpus służby cywilnej – uwarunkowania społeczne i polityczne.* Służba Cywilna wiosna-lato 2004, nr 8.

*Hołyst B., Patologia w miejscu pracy: lobbing i molestowanie seksualne.* Prokuratura i Prawo, 2004, nr 1.

*H.J. Kratz: Mobbing. Rozpoznawanie, reagowanie, zapobieganie.* Gliwice 2007.

*Itrich-Drabarek J., Ścieżki kariery urzędników Unii Europejskiej i Polski.* Przegląd Europejski, 2008, nr 1.

*Itrich-Drabarek J., Poland's Civil Service at the Local Government Level: Facts and Myths.* The Polish Yearbook of the Civil Service, 2005.

*Itrich-Drabarek J., Proces kształtowania się służby cywilnej w III Rzeczypospolitej.* Zeszyty Politologiczne, Białystok 2005.

*Itrich-Drabarek J., Samorządowa służba cywilna w Polsce – fakty i mity*"; Służba Cywilna Nr 9; jesień zima 2004/2005.

*J. Itrich-Drabarek: Korupcja w Polsce w świetle raportów Banku Światowego i Najwyższej Izby Kontroli.* Służba Cywilna 2000/2001, nr 1.

*Itrich-Drabarek J., Apolityczność jako czynnik profesjonalizacji administracji publicznej*", w: „*Profesjonalizm w administracji publicznej*". Pod red. A. Dębickiej, M. Dmochowskiego, B. Kudryckiej. Białystok 2004.

*Itrich-Drabarek J., Status i ochrona praw pracowników służby cywilnej w Polsce i na świecie*", w: Zeszyty Politologiczne Białystok 2001, nr 3.

*Itrich-Drabarek J., Służba cywilna w Polsce w świetle ustawy z roku 1998*" – Zeszyty Politologiczne, Białystok, XI 2000, z. 2.

*Itrich-Drabarek J.*, Drabarek K., „*Standardy kontroli w Europie*". W: *Rola projektów europejskich w rozwoju regionalnym i lokalnym.* Materiały pokonferencyjne SGGW. Warszawa 2004.

*Izdebski H., Administracja publiczna – zagadnienia ogólne i terminologiczne.* Biuletyn Służby Cywilnej, 1997, nr 3.

*Jabłoński A. W., Tendencje przemian administracji publicznej na Zachodzie.* W: *Administracja i polityka. Wprowadzenie,* pod red. A. Ferens, I. Macek, Wrocław 1999.

*Jabłoński M., Prawo dostępu do służby publicznej.* w: *Prawa i wolności obywatelskie w konstytucji RP.* Warszawa 2002.

*Jakubowska E., Odpowiedzialność zawodowa w administracji.* Biuletyn Służby Cywilnej, Warszawa 1998, nr 10.

*Jak zrobić służbę cywilną, żeby jej nie było.* Gazeta Wyborcza 2 kwietnia 2006.

*Jasiński F., Powołanie Europejskiej Szkoły Administracji.* Służba Cywilna, jesień 2005, nr 12.

*Jędrośka J., Stoczkiewicz M., Ustawa o dostępie do informacji publicznej a regulacje szczególne,* „Państwo i Prawo", czerwiec 2003.

*Jurkiewicz M., Nowelizacja kodeksu pracy. Mobbing zakazany. W Unii Europejskiej od lat, a u nas w przyszłym roku.* Gazeta Prawna 2003, nr 239.

*Kałucki J., Przyspieszone awanse dla urzędników.* Rzeczpospolita 19 września 2007.

*Kałużna H., Kałużny S., Urzędnik w służbie publicznej,* Gazeta Samorządu i Administracji 2002, nr 1.

*Kieżun W., Czterej jeźdźcy apokalipsy polskiej biurokracji.* Kultura 2000, nr 3.

*Kiciński K.: Kultura służby cywilnej,* w *Prace ISNS,* Warszawa 2000.

*Kołakowska D., Nie chcą służby.* Rzeczpospolita 2003, nr 226.

*Kołakowska D., Kadry w polityczne ręce.* Rzeczpospolita, 5 listopada 2003, nr 258, A3.

*Konzal P., Skiba Z., Politycy zamiast prawników.* Rzeczpospolita z 6 luty 2006.

*Kopyt B., Waszkiewicz B., Administracja p.o.* Rzeczpospolita 2002, nr 288.

*Kornaś J., Apolityczność służby cywilnej w Polsce.* Biuletyn Służby Cywilnej 1998, nr 2.

*Kosewski M., Kiedy urzędnicy naruszają wartości moralne i kiedy można to ograniczać,* Służba Cywilna 2001, nr 3.

*Kudrycka B., Podstawy kodeksów etycznych służby cywilnej w Polsce.* Państwo i Prawo 1997, nr 2.

*Kudrycka B., Profesjonalizm a ochrona politycznej neutralności służby cywilnej urzędników.* Samorząd Terytorialny 1998, nr 3.

*Kudrycka B., Zmiany w pozycji i statusie urzędników administracji publicznej. Nowe wyzwania i trendy.* Służba Cywilna 2002, nr 4.

*Kolasińska M., Oceny okresowe urzędników służby cywilnej.* Biuletyn Służby Cywilnej, 1999, Nr 3.

*Kulesza M, Barbasiewicz A., Funkcje gabinetów politycznych.* Służba Cywilna 2000/2001, nr 1.

*Kulesza M., Karuzela z urzędnikami.* Gazeta Wyborcza, 25 października 2006.

*Kurzynoga M., Stefański K., Służba przygotowawcza w ustawie o służbie cywilnej.* Praca i Zabezpieczenie Społeczne 2006, nr 5.

*Liszcz T., Nabór do służby cywilnej po nowelizacji ustawy.* Kontrola Państwowa, 2006, nr 1.

*Łętowski J., Niektóre problemy służby państwowej w świetle aktualnych rozwiązań prawnych.* Państwo i Prawo 1975, nr 8–9.

*Łyś G., Dobry fachowiec, ale apolityczny.* Rzeczpospolita 15 września 2006.

*Malec J., Studia z dziejów administracji nowożytnej.* Acta Academiae Modrevianae, Kraków 2003.

*Matys M., Brama dla swoich.* Gazeta Wyborcza 2002–06–13.

*Mazur S., Biurokracja jako dylemat.* Zarządzanie Publiczne 2007, nr 2.

*Michalik M., Uwagi w sprawie „kodeksów" etyki zawodowej,* Etyka 1966 nr 1.

*Miśkiewicz A., Służba cywilna według nowych zasad,* Służba Pracownicza, 2009, nr 1.

*Mniej kolesiostwa w resortach.* Rzeczpospolita 2004, nr 213.

*Mołdawa T., Konstytucyjny system wartości a jakość administracji publicznej – wybrane problemy.* w: *Praworządność-sprawność-rozwój lokalny a samorząd terytorialny,* Warszawa 2004, Zeszyty Naukowe CSSTiRL, nr 8.

*Mroczka K., Zarządzanie wiedzą jako element systemu zarządzania zasobami ludzkimi,* Mazowiecki Urząd Wojewódzki w Warszawie, Warszawa 2012.

*P. Miklis: Sexual harassment w administracji federalnej USA.* Biuletyn Służby Cywilnej, Warszawa 1998, nr 7–8.

*Najnigier S., Administracja czy biznes?* Służba Cywilna, 2001, nr 2.

*„Nie" ręcznemu mianowaniu,* Trybuna, 2 luty 2007.

*Nowak Z., Korpus urzędniczy w hibernacji.* Rzeczpospolita 14 listopad 1994.

*Nowotny S., Rada Służby Cywilnej.* Biuletyn Służby Cywilnej 1997, nr 1.

*Paradowska J., Korpus w rozkładzie.* Polityka 2002, nr 42.

*Paradowska J., Rząd urzędów* Polityka 1999, nr 3.

*Paradowska J., Służba czy drużba.* Polityka 1998, nr 11.

*Pastwa J., Nowe rozwiązania w służbie cywilnej.* Biuletyn Służby Cywilnej 1998, nr 7–8.

*Pastwa kontra Wagner.* Gazeta Wyborcza z 17 listopada 2003 r.

*PiS upolitycznia i centralizuje służbę cywilną. Rozmowa z Markiem Rockim*, Gazeta Wyborcza, 26 lipca 2006.

*Płoskonka J., Korupcja – zagrożenia i metody jej zwalczania. Empiryczne badania nad poziomem korupcji.* Służba Cywilna 2003, nr 6.

*PodgórskaJ., Koszty szczypania i sapania.* Polityka 2005, nr 2.

*Praca nie może być terrorem.* Dodatek Prawo Pracy, Rzeczpospolita 30.03.2005, nr 456.

*Praczyk G., Jesteś doktorem, zostać dyrektorem.* Rzeczpospolita, 5 kwietnia 2007.

*Praczyk G., Administracja według PiS.* Rzeczpospolita 22–23 lipca 2006.

*Rabska T., Zdanie odrębne do „Opinii Rady Służby Cywilnej o projekcie ustawy o służbie cywilnej".* Biuletyn Służby Cywilnej, Warszawa 1998, nr 9.

*Radwan A., 180 tysięcy złotych kosztuje wykształcenie urzędnika.* Gazeta Prawna z 4 sierpnia 2009.

*Rabska T., Zdanie odrębne do „Opinii Rady Służby Cywilnej o projekcie ustawy o służbie cywilnej".* Biuletyn Służby Cywilnej, Warszawa 1998, nr 9.

*Rexed K., Służba cywilna a modernizacja sposobu sprawowania władzy.* Służba Cywilna 2004/2005, nr 9.

*Rocki M., Polityka zamiast neutralności*, Rzeczpospolita z 23 VII 2006.

*Rohr J., Professionalism, legitymacy, and the constitution*, Public Administration Quarterly, Winter 1985, Vol. 8.

*Rozmowa z Marią Gintowt-Jankowicz*, Tygodnik Powszechny, 25 września 2005.

*Rybak A., Karuzela urzędników.* Newsweek 2002, nr 2.

*Rydlewski R., Problemy europeizacji administracji publicznej.* Służba Cywilna 2004/2005, nr 9.

*Rządy odchodzą, urzędnicy zostają.* Rzeczpospolita 20 grudnia 2001.

*Sadłowska K., Za mało profesjonalistów.* Rzeczpospolita 2000, nr 280.

*Sanetra W., Służba cywilna a prawo pracy.* Prawo Pracy 1996, nr 10.

*Sanetra W., O nawiązaniu i ustaniu stosunku pracy w służbie cywilnej.* Przegląd Sądowy 1997, nr 2.

*Sanetra W., Nawiązanie stosunku pracy w służbie cywilnej.* Prawo Pracy 1997, nr 3.

*P. Sawecki: Nierentowne Bizancjum*, Angora, 5 X 2008, nr 40.

*Sempruch Z., Jaki sprawdzian musi przejść urzędnik przed mianowaniem.* Rzeczpospolita 5 luty 2007.

*Siewierski J., Administracja publiczna jako podstawowy element sektora publicznego III Rzeczypospolitej.* Służba Cywilna 2004, nr 8.

*Skoczyński J., Status prawny urzędnika służby cywilnej. Cz. I.* Praca i Zabezpieczenie Społeczne 1996, nr 11.

*Skoczyński J., Status prawny urzędnika służby cywilnej. Cz. II.* Praca i Zabezpieczenie Społeczne 1996, nr 12.

*Służby państwowe pod lupą prawa,* rozmowa z Laurencem Engelem i Antonim Garaponem. Nowa Res Publica 1998, nr 6.

*Snarski P., Druga strona KSAP.* Przegląd 15 lipca 2002.

*Sobczak K., Krok do przodu, dwa w tył.* Rzeczpospolita 20 styczeń 2004.

*Sobczak K., Politycy nie chcą służby cywilnej.* Rzeczpospolita 12 maja 2006.

*Sobków D., Status urzędnika oraz zasady naboru do służby cywilnej w V Republice Francuskiej.* Biuletyn Służby Cywilnej 1997, nr 2.

*Stanisławska E., Zarządzanie przez cele. Doświadczenia Mazowieckiego Urzędu Wojewódzkiego,* Warszawa 2012.

*Starski P., O KSAP raz jeszcze,* Przegląd 12 sierpnia 2002.

*Stawowiak Z., Stanowisko do Raportu z przeprowadzonej analizy i oceny tworzenia służby cywilnej.* Biuletyn Służby Cywilnej, sierpień 1996-wrzesień 1997, nr 5.

*Stefański K., Kryteria rekrutacji pracowników służby cywilnej.* Praca i Zabezpieczenie Społeczne 2001, nr 4.

*Suwaj R., O przecenianej roli kodeksów etycznych, Administracja Publiczna, Studia Krajowe i Międzynarodowe,* 2007, nr 2.

*Szachułowicz J., Uwagi do „Raportu z przeprowadzonej analizy i oceny tworzenia służby cywilnej" sierpień 1996-wrzesień 1997.* Biuletyn Służby Cywilnej Warszawa 1998, nr 5.

*Szachułowicz J., Perspektywy służby cywilnej.* Biuletyn Służby Cywilnej, 1997, nr 1.

*Szaniawski P.,* Kwiatek B.: *Rządy biur.* Newsweek Polska 2004, nr 16.

*Szarkowska K., Odpowiedzialność dyscyplinarna członków korpusu służby cywilnej.* Służba Cywilna wiosna-lato 2004, nr 8.

*Szwalbe S., Obywatele o urzędnikach i urzędach.* Służba Cywilna, 2000/2001, nr 1.

*Śledzińska A.M., Konstytucyjne prawo wolności słowa i stowarzyszeń urzędników służby cywilnej.* Służba Cywilna, lato 2005, nr 11.

*Śledzińska A. M., Polskie obywatelstwo jako warunek dostępu do służby cywilnej. Analiza kompatybilności ustawy o służbie cywilnej z Art. 39 ust. 4 Traktatu ustanawiającego Wspólnotę Europejską,* Służba Cywilna, wiosna 2006, nr 14.

*Tomaszewska A., Informacja nt. raportu końcowego dotyczącego ewaluacji wybranych działań szkoleniowych realizowanych w ramach projektu „Wdrożenie strategii szkoleniowej",* „Przegląd Służby Cywilnej", 2012, Nr 1.

*Torbus A., Kto wymyślił służbę cywilną?* Biuletyn Służby Cywilnej, 1998, nr 3.

*Torbus A., Organizacja urzędów administracji rządowej (w aspekcie funkcji i zadań dyrektora generalnego - artykuł dyskusyjny.* Biuletyn Służby Cywilnej, 1998, nr 1.

*Uhlig D., Czy oni w ogóle znają ten rosyjski.* Gazeta Wyborcza, 2 grudzień 2005, Nr 280.

*Uhlig D., Raczej służba niż cywilna.* Gazeta Wyborcza, 2004-01-01, http://wyborcza.pl/.

*Ura E., Urzędnik w świetle zasad Europejskiego Kodeksu Dobrej Administracji,* Zeszyty Naukowe Politechniki Rzeszowskiej (Zarządzanie i marketing), 2008, nr 248, z.12.

*Ura E., Ewolucja służby cywilnej (wybrane zagadnienia).* Zeszyty Naukowe Politechniki Rzeszowskiej (Zarządzanie i marketing), 2007, nr 245, z.11.

*Urzędnik jest jak trawa - z dr Marią Gintowt-Jankowicz, dyrektorem Krajowej Szkoły Administracji Publicznej rozmawiają Witold Bereś i Krzysztof Burnetko.* Tygodnik Powszechny 2000, nr 14.

*Urzędnicy, przepisy, decyzje* - dodatek Rzeczpospolitej z 22 marca 1999.

*Western A., Droga do kariery nad Wisłą.* Rzeczpospolita 2000, nr 290.

*W stronę zmian,* rozmowa z Janem Pastwą, Biuletyn Służby Cywilnej 1998, nr 4.

*Walenciak R., Cywilna czy partyjna.* Przegląd Tygodniowy, 1998, nr 14.

*Walencik I., Poprawić tak, żeby zepsuć.* Rzeczpospolita 2004, nr 16.

*Walencik I., Wysoki urzędnik z zasobu kadrowego niższy ze służby cywilnej.* Rzeczpospolita 16 październik 2006.

*Wdowiak D.,* Bugdol M.: *Wdrażanie systemów jakości w urzędach administracji publicznej.* Ekonomika i Organizacja Przedsiębiorstwa, 2002, nr 5.

*Winczorek P., Służba cywilna i system łupów.* Rzeczpospolita 6 września 1995.

*Winczorek P., Opinie o sprawie dostępu do informacji do kancelarii Sejmu,* Przegląd Sejmowy 2003, nr 1.

*Wniosek Prezydenta RP do Trybunału Konstytucyjnego.* Biuletyn Służby Cywilnej 1999, nr 1.

*Wojnarska-Krajewska E., Wybrane zagadnienia dotyczące służby cywilnej w krajach członkowskich Unii Europejskiej,* Zeszyty Prawnicze Biura Analiz Sejmowych Kancelarii Sejmu 3(11) VII-IX 2006.

*Wojtuch M., Biurokracja większa, ale nowoczesna i perfekcyjna.* Gazeta Prawna 2003, 02.10. nr 192.

*Wójcik M., Inna służba.* Nasz Dziennik, 24 lipca 2006.

*Wróbel R., Urzędnicy trzeciej tysiąclatki.* Rzeczpospolita 1994, nr 209.

*Wróbel R., Zwycięzca bierze wszystko.* Rzeczpospolita 6 września 1995.

*Wróbel R., Tłok za biurkiem.* Rzeczpospolita z 22 marca 1999 r.

*Wydra T., Wynagrodzenia w służbie publicznej*, Służba Cywilna, lato 2005, nr 11.

*Wysocki S., Jak poprawić jakość działania administracji publicznej?*, Służba Cywilna 2001, nr 2.

*Zamieszanie w służbie cywilnej.* Rzeczpospolita 22 luty 1997.

*Znamierowski Cz., Elita i demokracja.* Warszawa 1991.

*Zybala A., Państwo transformacyjne: politycy i urzędnicy*, Służba Cywilna, wiosna 2006, nr 14.

*Żakowski J., Podróż z krańca świata.* Polityka 2007, nr 34.

*Żarczyński M., Ocena urzędników w Polsce.* W: *Służba cywilna w doświadczeniu zachodnich demokracji.* Warszawa 1996.

*Żarowski J., Jak zrobić karierę w służbie cywilnej.* Gazeta Prawna 14 kwietnia 2004, nr 73.

*Żarowski J., Obowiązki zatrudnionych w służbie cywilnej. Urzędnik specyficznym pracownikiem.* Gazeta Prawna 19 marca 2003, nr 55.

*Żarowski J., Jak wynagradzana jest służba cywilna.* Gazeta Prawna 8 grudnia 2004, nr 239.

*M. Żukowski: Mobbing w prawie pracy.* Edukacja Prawnicza, 2004, nr 3.

*Administration and the Civil Service in the EU 27 Member States*, Ministère du Budged, des Comptes Public et de la Fonction Publique. Francja 2008.

*Audyt organizacyjny i wdrożenie usprawnień zarządczych*, Deloitte, Warszawa 2012.

*Badanie wpływu informatyzacji na działanie urzędów administracji publicznej w Polsce w 2011 roku*, MSWiA, Warszawa sierpień 2011.

*Działocha K., Opinia o zgodności z Konstytucją RP poselskich projektów ustaw o służbie cywilnej i państwowym zasobie kadrowym, obsadzaniu wysokich stanowisk oraz o zmianie niektórych ustaw*, Biuro Analiz Sejmowych, 8 lipca 2006.

*Efektywne metody zarządzania w administracji publicznej*, J. Zaleski, C. Kociński, A. Sołecki, B. Turowski, S. Wysocki, J. Duda, W. Skiba, A. Szarycz, P. Tomaszewski, Instytut Spraw Publicznych, Warszawa 2000.

*Europejskie zasady dla administracji publicznej.* Dokumenty SIGMY: nr 27, SIGMA-OECD, http://www. ocd.org/puma/sigmaweb.

*Funkcjonowanie służby cywilnej w ramach obowiązujących regulacji prawnych, Informacja o wynikach kontroli*, NIK, Warszawa, marzec 2012.

*Informacja o wynikach kontroli prawidłowości korzystania z usług doradczych i eksperckich przez organy administracji rządowej*. Departament Kontroli Doraźnych, NIK, Warszawa, październik 2001.

*Informacja o wynikach kontroli organizacji i funkcjonowania służby cywilnej*. Departament Administracji Publicznej, Najwyższa Izba Kontroli, Warszawa, kwiecień 2005.

*Informacja o wynikach kontroli funkcjonowania systemu przyjmowania i rozpatrywania skarg w wybranych naczelnych organach administracji rządowej*. Departament Administracji Publicznej. NIK, Warszawa, marzec 2009.

*Izdebski H., Opinia o przedmiocie zgodności z konstytucją projektów ustaw o służbie cywilnej (druk 552) oraz projektu ustawy o państwowym zasobie kadrowym, obsadzaniu wysokich stanowisk państwowych oraz o zmianie niektórych ustaw (druki sejmowe nr 553 i 553-A)*, Warszawa 2006.

*Karta Praw Podstawowych Unii Europejskiej*, Dziennik Urzędowy Unii Europejskiej, 2007/C303/01.

*Kłos B., Przeciwdziałanie mobbingowi w krajach członkowskich Unii Europejskiej*. Biuro Studiów i Ekspertyz Kancelarii Sejmu RP, Warszawa 2002, nr 941.

*Kodeks Etyki Służby Cywilnej*. Załącznik do Zarządzenia nr 114 Prezesa Rady Ministrów z dnia 11 października 2002 r. Zarządzenie nr 114 Prezesa RadyMinistrów z dnia 11 października 2002 r. *w sprawie ustanowienia kodeksu etyki służby cywilnej* Monitor Polski Nr 46, poz. 683.

*Korupcja w Polsce. Przegląd obszarów priorytetowych i propozycji przeciwdziałania zjawisku*. Bank Światowy, Oddział w Warszawie, Warszawa, listopad 1999.

*Kulesza M.,, Opinia na temat systemu funkcjonowania służby cywilnej w obszarach projektowanych ustaw* (druki nr 552, 553 i 553-A). Biuro Analiz Sejmowych, Warszawa 24 lipca 2006 r.

*Materiał źródłowy z badania służby cywilnej*, Badanie (wywiady) wykonane pod kierunkiem dr Jolanty Itrich-Drabarek, mgr Łukasza Małeckiego-Tepichta. Warszawa, lipiec 2009.

*Nabór do korpusu służby cywilnej. Poradnik dobrej praktyki*. Warszawa, kwiecień 2006.

*Nowak-Far A., Opinia w sprawie zgodności z prawem Wspólnoty Europejskiej poselskich projektów ustaw:* o *służbie cywilnej oraz o państwowym zasobie kadrowym, obsadzaniu wysokich stanowisk państwowych oraz o zmianie niektórych ustaw(druk nr 552, 553 i 553-A)*. Warszawa 2006.

*Nowy system organizacji służby publicznej*. KPRM, Warszawa 2009.

*Obowiązki urzędników i innych pracowników Parlamentu Europejskiego* – Przewodnik Kodeks Postępowania przyjęty przez Prezydium dnia 7 lipca 2008 r.

*OECD, (GOV/PGC/PEM (2008) 2), The Senior Civil Service in National Governments of OECD Countries;* Paris, 31 January 2008.

*Ogólna diagnoza sytuacji w zakresie zarządzania zasobami ludzkimi w służbie cywilnej.* 23 marca 2010, Przegląd Służby Cywilnej, Departament Służby Cywilnej Kancelarii Prezesa Rady Ministrów, 2010, nr 2.

*Olejniczak K.*, Domaradzka A., Krzewski A., Lendzion B., Widła Ł., *Polskie ministerstwa jako organizacje uczące się,* Raporty i Analizy EUROREG 2010, nr 1.

*Opinia Rady Służby Cywilnej o projekcie ustawy o służbie cywilnej.* Biuletyn Służby Cywilnej 1998, nr 9.

*Państwowa służba publiczna* (red.) K. Zonn-Pastemak, Materiały Reformy Administracji Publicznej, Dział IV, *Pracownicy administracji*, Warszawa 1993.

*Pawłowski J., Wydział Kadr Służby Cywilnej. Urząd Służby Cywilnej* Warszawa 2003.

*Perzanowska M., Zarządzanie etyczne (ethical management) jako czynnik efektywnego zarządzania państwem (z uwzględnieniem Banku Światowego, Transparency International),* www.ceo.org.pl/binary/file.action?d.

*Postawy członków korpusu służby cywilnej wobec kwestii etycznych. Raport z badań*, opr. C. Trutkowski, Warszawa 2004.

*Proces naboru do służby cywilnej – równe szanse. Podstawowe zasady i procedury.* Kancelaria Prezesa Rady Ministrów, Warszawa 2009.

*Przepisy normujące stosunek państwowej służby cywilnej*, Zarząd Główny Stowarzyszenia Urzędników Państwowych, Warszawa 1925.

*Raport z przeprowadzonej analizy i oceny tworzenia służby cywilnej (sierpień 1996 - wrzesień 1997).* Biuletyn Służby Cywilnej Warszawa 1998, nr 4.

*Raport z badania dotyczącego monitorowania procesu naboru w służbie cywilnej przeprowadzonego na losowej próbie urzędów, obejmującego okres od 1 stycznia do 30 czerwca 2007 r.*, opr. A. Sidor, J. Pawłowski, KPRM, Warszawa 2008.

*Rekomendacje Szefa Służby Cywilnej dotyczące przeprowadzania naboru na wyższe stanowiska w służbie cywilnej.* Warszawa czerwiec 2009.

*Rydlewski G.*, Opinia politologiczno-prawna dot. Poselskich projektów ustaw: *– o służbie cywilnej (druk nr 552) oraz o – państwowym zasobie kadrowym, obsadzaniu wysokich stanowisk państwowych oraz o zmianie niektórych ustaw(druk nr 553 i 553-A).* Warszawa 2006.

*Siedem kroków do Karty Obywatela zawierającej Standardy Usług.* Kancelaria Prezesa Rady Ministrów, Warszawa 2008.

*Strategia zarządzania zasobami ludzkimi w służbie cywilnej 2011–2020.* KPRM Warszawa 2011.

*Społeczny wizerunek służby cywilnej. Analiza dyskursu publicznego: Analiza znaczeń kulturowych, Analiza opozycji, Analiza kodów w ramach projektu:* Strategia Zarządzania Zasobami Ludzkimi w Służbie Cywilnej, Warszawa, 2011.

*Społeczeństwo informacyjne w liczbach 2009.* Departament Społeczeństwa Informacyjnego, Ministerstwo Spraw Wewnętrznych i Administracji, Warszawa 2009.

*Sprawozdanie Szefa Służby Cywilnej o stanie służby cywilnej i realizacji zadań tej służby za rok 1998.* Urząd Służby Cywilnej Warszawa 1999.

*Sprawozdanie Szefa Służby Cywilnej o stanie służby cywilnej i realizacji zadań tej służby za rok 2000.* Urząd Służby Cywilnej Warszawa 2004.

*Sprawozdanie Szefa Służby Cywilnej o stanie służby cywilnej i realizacji zadań tej służby w 2011 roku,* Warszawa marzec 2012.

*Stanowisko Rady Służby Cywilnej w sprawie realizacji ustawy o służbie cywilnej.* Biuletyn Służby Cywilnej Warszawa 1998, nr 7–8.

*Strategia szkoleniowa służby cywilnej na lata 2004–2007.* Biuletyn Służby Cywilnej 2004, nr 12.

*Stres P., Thijs N., Stoffels A., Geldof S., Pięć lat CAF 2006: od odrastania do dojrzałości - co dalej? Badanie zastosowania, wspierania i przyszłości Wspólnej Metody Oceny.* Warszawa 2011.

*Szczerski K., Ekspertyza prakseologiczno-organizacyjna do druku nr 552 - poselski projekt ustawy o służbie cywilnej, druku nr 553 poselski projekt o państwowym zasobie kadrowym, obsadzaniu wysokich stanowisk państwowych oraz o zmianie niektórych ustaw (druki sejmowe nr 553 i 553-A),* Warszawa 2006.

*Uchwała Rady Służby Cywilnej z 18 września 1998 r. w sprawie decyzji Prezesa Rady Ministrów z 3 lipca 1998 r. odwołującej członków Komisji Kwalifikacyjnej do Służby Cywilnej.* W: Biuletyn Służby Cywilnej, Warszawa 1998, nr 11/12.

*Ura E., Opinia dotycząca projektu ustawy o służbie cywilnej i ustawy o państwowym zasobie kadrowym, obsadzaniu wysokich stanowisk państwowych oraz o zmianie niektórych ustaw oraz autopoprawki do projektu ustawy o państwowym zasobie kadrowym, obsadzaniu wysokich stanowisk państwowych oraz o zmianie niektórych ustaw.* Biuro Analiz Sejmowych 14 czerwca 2006.

*Urzędnik państwowy w oczach obywatela.* Raport z badań sondażowych przeprowadzonych na zlecenie USC, przez PBS. Warszawa 1999.

*Urzędnik państwowy w oczach obywatela. Badanie realizowane z klientami urzędów administracji państwowej. Porównanie wyników I i II fali.* Raport z badania PBS dla Urzędu Służby Cywilnej, Sopot wrzesień 2005.

*Uzasadnienie do projektu ustawy o służbie cywilnej z 1998 r.* Rada Ministrów, Druk sejmowy nr 450, 25 czerwiec 1998 r.

*Uzasadnienie do projektu ustawy o zmianie ustawy o pracownikach samorządowych, ustawy o Najwyższej Izbie Kontroli oraz ustawy o służbie cywilnej*. Rada Ministrów, Druk sejmowy nr 233, 6 stycznia 2006 r.

*Uzasadnienie do projektu ustawy o państwowym zasobie kadrowym, obsadzaniu wysokich stanowisk państwowych oraz zmianie niektórych ustaw*. Grupa posłów na Sejm V kadencji, Druk sejmowy nr 553, 29 marca 2006 r.

*Uzasadnienie do projektu ustawy o służbie cywilnej*. Grupa posłów na Sejm V kadencji, Druk sejmowy nr 552, 29 marzec 2006.

*Wenzel M., Korupcja, nepotyzm, nieuczciwy lobbing*. Katalog Komunikatów CBOS, 2004, nr 3049.

*Wspólna Metoda Oceny. Doskonalenie organizacji poprzez samoocenę*. Tłum. I. Sikorska, KPRM, Warszawa 2008.

*Wspólne wnioski EUPAN i TUNED dot. poprawy zaufania do administracji rządowych szczebla centralnego poprzez efektywny dialog społeczny*. EU, Praga 18 czerwiec 2009.

*Wytyczne OECD dotyczące nadzoru korporacyjnego w przedsiębiorstwach publicznych*. OECD 2005.

*Wykaz zagadnień do sprawdzianu wiedzy*. Załączniki do Rozporządzenia Prezesa Rady Ministrów z dnia 28 września 1999 r. Załącznik nr 1. Dz. U. Nr 79, poz. 894, 1999.

*Wytyczne OECD dotyczące nadzoru korporacyjnego w przedsiębiorstwach publicznych*. OECD 2005.

*Zagrożenie korupcją w świetle badań kontrolnych Najwyższej Izby Kontroli*, Warszawa 2000.

*Zarządzanie wiedzą w społeczeństwie uczącym się*, OECD, Radom 2000.

*Zestaw kompetencji dla stanowisk w służbie cywilnej. Stanowiska dla średniego szczebla, zarządzania, koordynujące, samodzielne, specjalistyczne i wspomagające. Wzmocnienie zdolności administracyjnych*. Projekt bliźniaczy PHARE, PL03/IB/OT/06.

www.isp.org.pl

www.ksap.gov.pl

http://www.dsc.kprm.gov.pl/

http://mus.edu.pl

http://www.mazowieckie.pl/wai/pl/2/9107/Jezyk_urzedowy_bardziej_zrozumialy.html http://www.emetro.pl/emetro/1,85648,10611732,Wielokrotnie_zlozona_urzednicza_mowa_trawa.html

http://www.mazowieckie.pl/portal/pl/2/8698/Polska_Prezydencja_o_MUW_na_konferencji.html

http://thegovmonitor.com/world_news/britain/uk-breaking-down-racism-barriers-in-civil-service-21573.html,

http://eur-lex.europa.eu/Notice.do?mode

http:// www.leymann.se

http://www.newsweek.pl/artykuly/sekcje/polska/w-ministerstwach-szykanuja-pracownikow,51210,1,

http://www.gazetaprawna.pl/wiadomosci/artykuly/261548,byly_minister_skarbu_oskarzony_w_sprawie_prywatyzacji_ec_bialystok.html

http://www.halat.pl/ekologia01.html

www.prywatyzacja raporty NIK filetype:pdf

http://www.money.pl/archiwum/wiadomosci_agencyjne/iar/artykul/pracownicy;administracji;rzadowej;wykorzystywali;sluzbowe;karty;kredytowe;do;finansowania;prywatnych;wydatkow,241,0,346609.html

www.globalcorruptionreport.org

**Studies in Politics, Security and Society**

Edited by Stanisław Sulowski

Vol. 1 Robert Wiszniowski (ed.): Challenges to Representative Democracy. A European Perspective. 2015.

Vol. 2 Jarosław Szymanek: Theory of Political Representation. 2015.

Vol. 3 Alojzy Z. Nowak (ed.): Global Financial Turbulence and Euro Area. Polish Perspective. 2015.

Vol. 4 Jolanta Itrich-Drabarek: The Civil Service in Poland. Theory and Experience. 2015.

www.peterlang.com

www.ingramcontent.com/pod-product-compliance
Ingram Content Group UK Ltd.
Pitfield, Milton Keynes, MK11 3LW, UK
UKHW041824031026
15587UKWH00002B/555

9 783631 657430